issions of Love

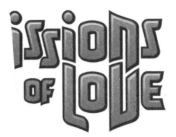

Volume 12

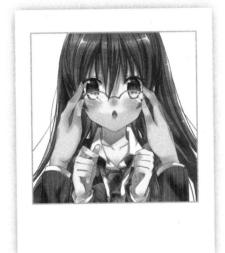

Ema Toyama

Missions of Love
Ema Toyama

Mission 45
Shigure's Brother
5

Mission 46
Twisted Affection
42

Mission 47
The Value of a Hairpin
79

Mission 48
Tactical Romance
115

Bonus Mission
~Backstage Theatre~
151

Character

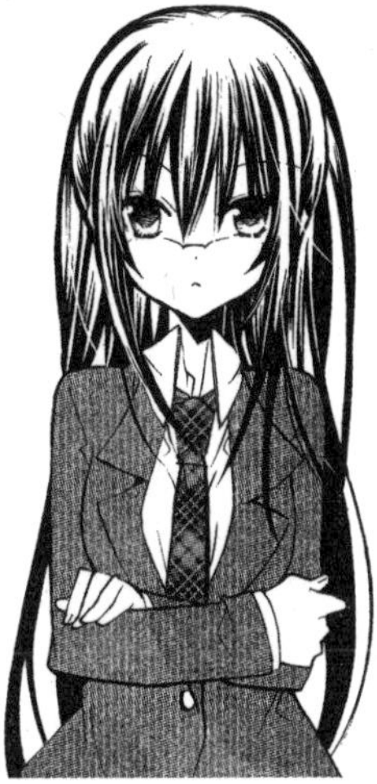

Shigure Kitami
The ever-popular, yet black-hearted, student body president. He made a game of charming all the girls and making them confess their love to him, then writing it all down in his student notebook, but Yukina discovered his secret!

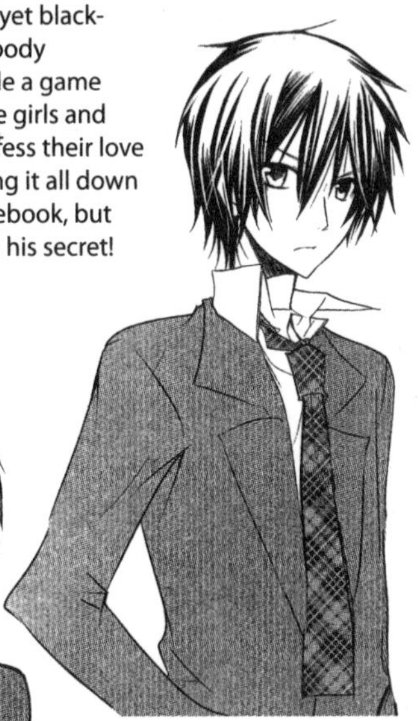

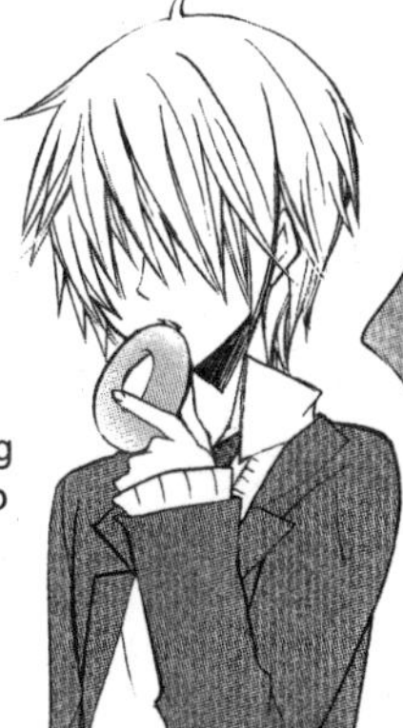

Yukina Himuro
A third-year junior high student who strikes terror into the hearts of all around her with her piercing gaze, feared as the "Absolute Zero Snow Woman." Only Akira knows that she is also the popular cell phone novelist Yupina.

Akira Shimotsuki
Yukina's cousin and fellow student. He loves to eat. He is always nearby watching over her, but he wants Yukina to see him as a man, so he changes his look!

XX me!

It is time for love.
Secret cellular phone novelist × The most popular boy in school.
Love mission of absolute servitude.

Story

The love missions began as research for a novel. In order to take her love to the next level, Yukina initiates a date mission, and chooses Akira to be her boyfriend. To resolve the remaining awkwardness between herself and Shigure, Yukina tries to tell him her honest feelings, but finds out she was actually talking to his younger brother Hisame!! Hisame appears to be plotting something…

Mami Mizuno
A childhood friend of Shigure's. A sickly girl. The teachers love her, and she's very popular with the boys. She's a beautiful young girl who always wears a smile, but deep down, her heart is black. She recently outgrew her long-held crush on Shigure.

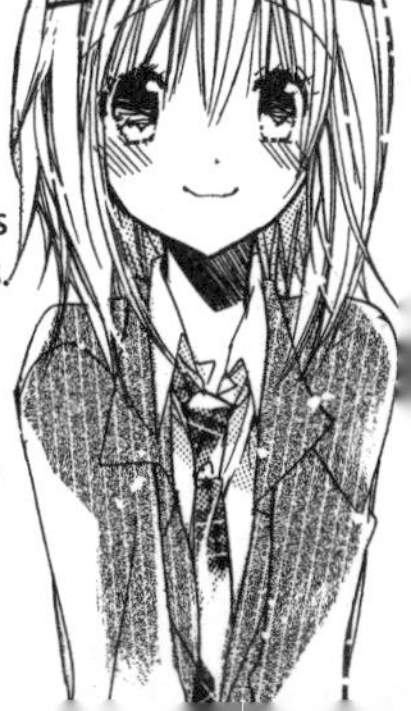

MISSIONS OF LOVE

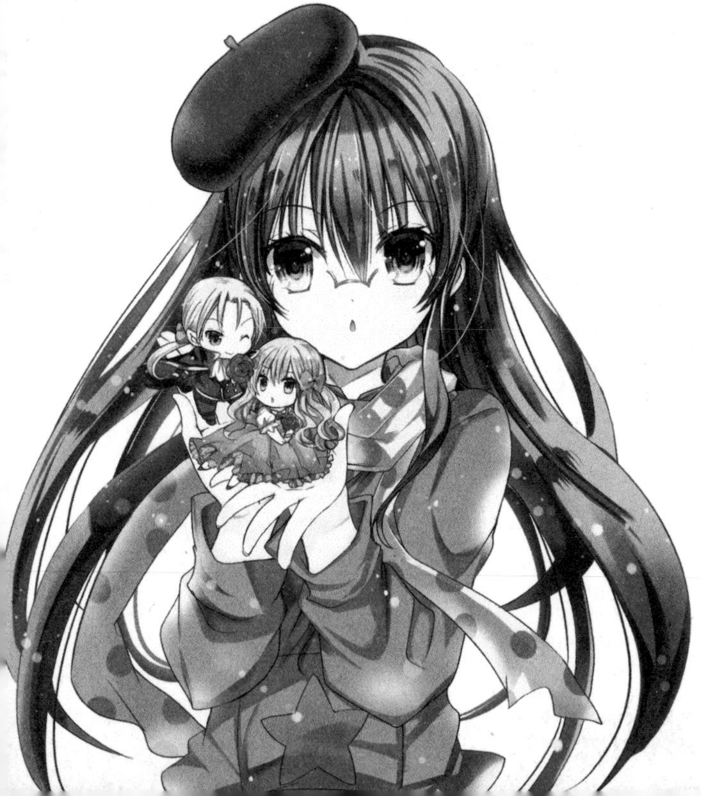

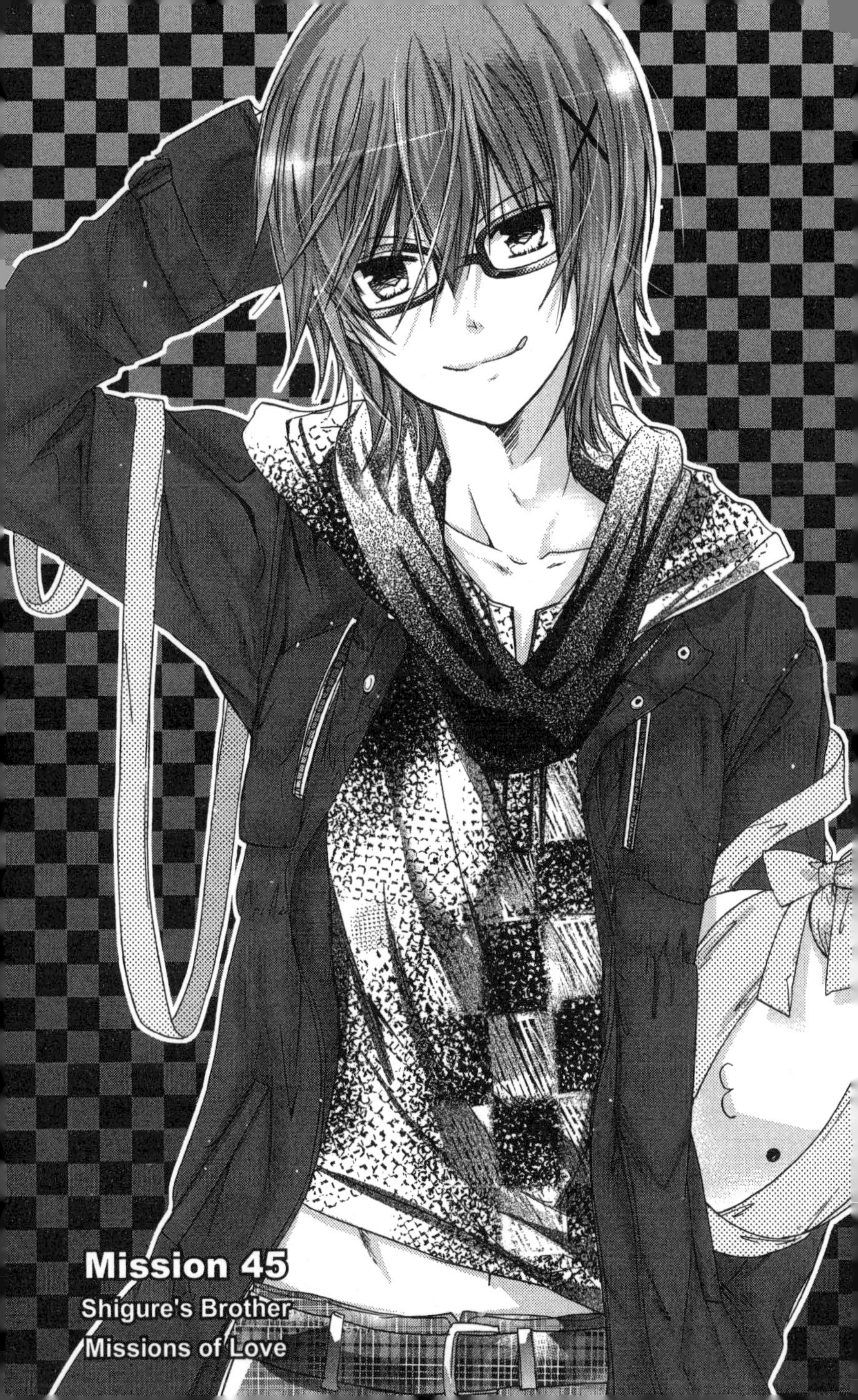

Mission 45

Shigure's Brother

Missions of Love

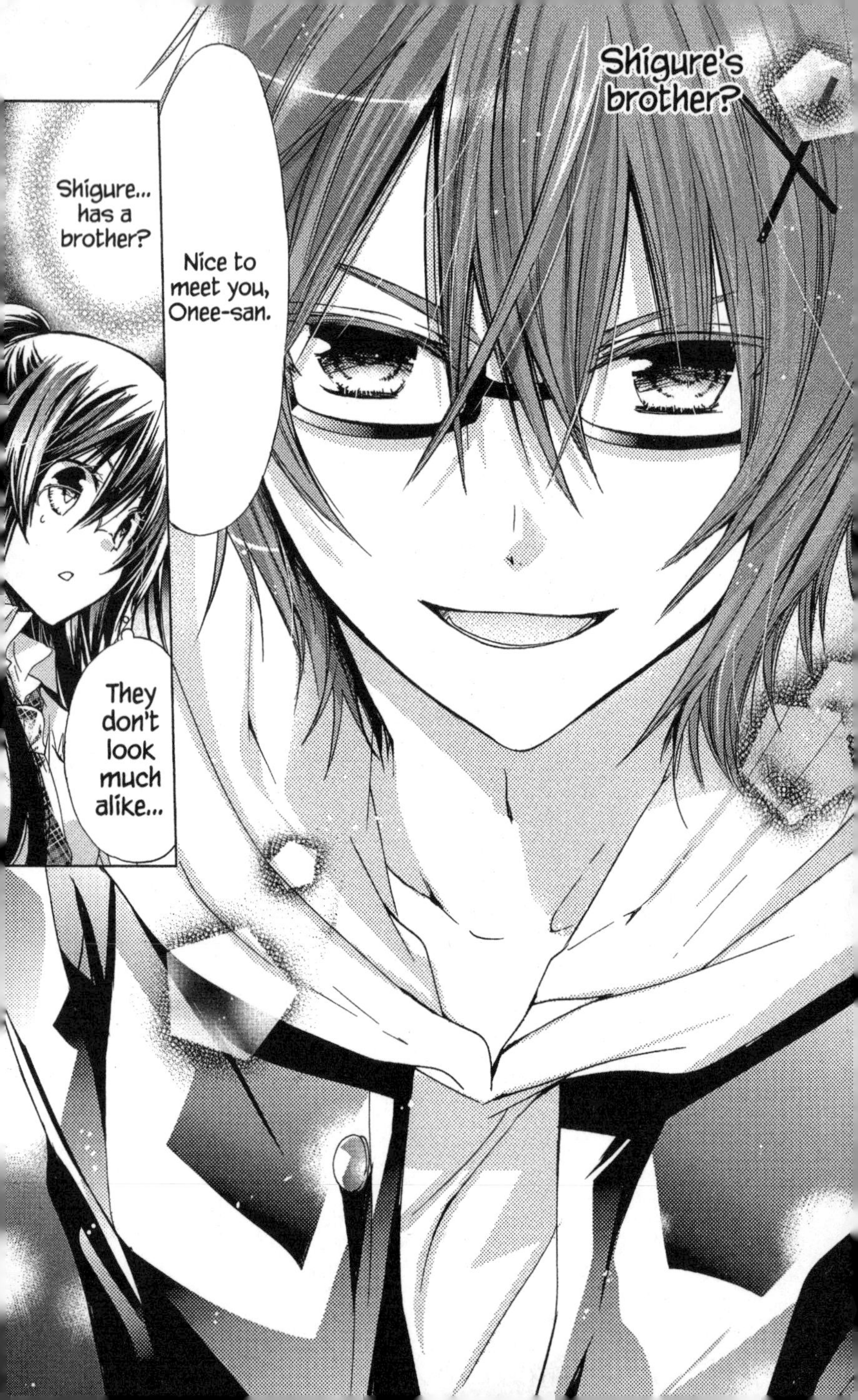
Shigure's brother?
Nice to meet you, Onee-san.
Shigure... has a brother?
They don't look much alike...

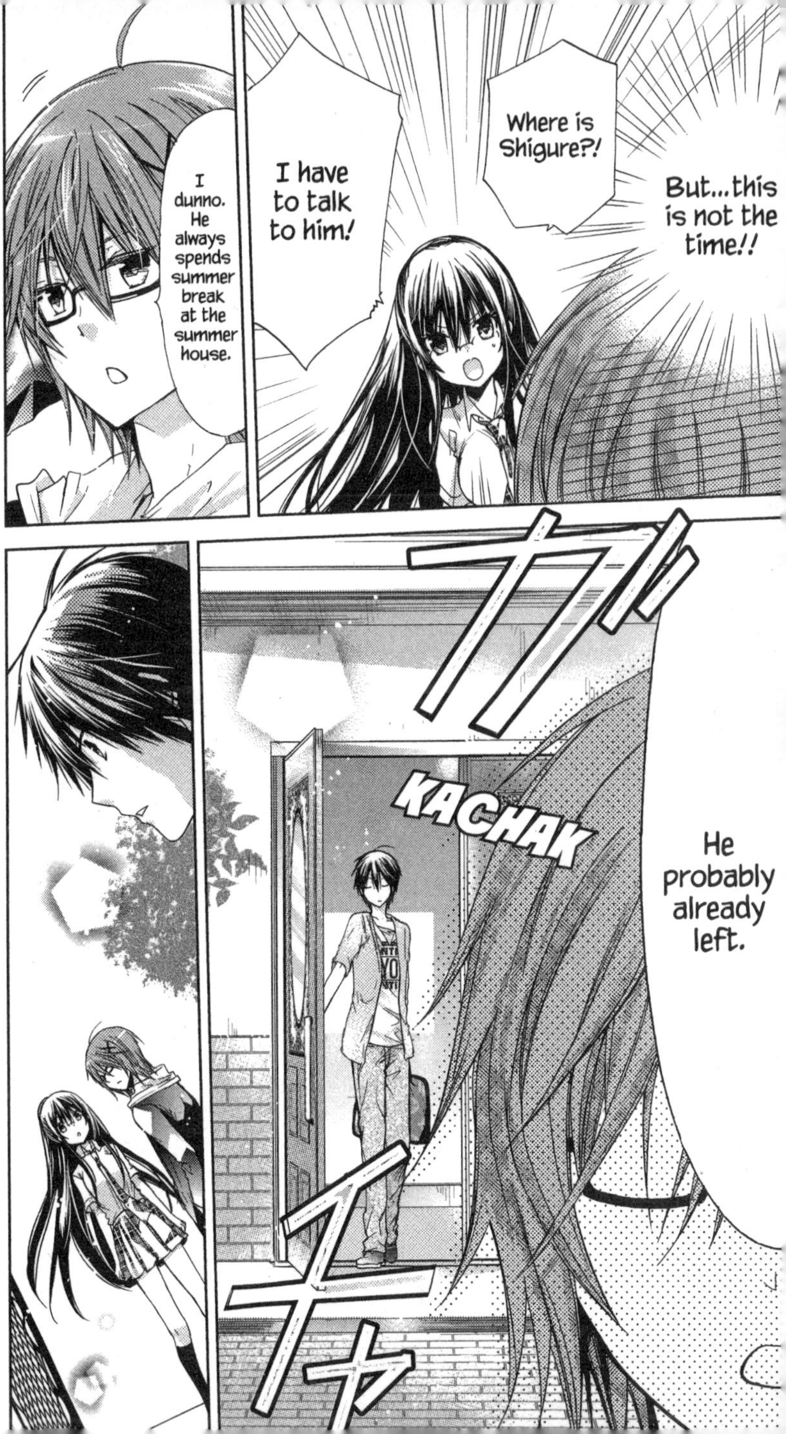
But...this is not the time!!
Where is Shigure?!
I have to talk to him!
I dunno. He always spends summer break at the summer house.
KACHAK
He probably already left.

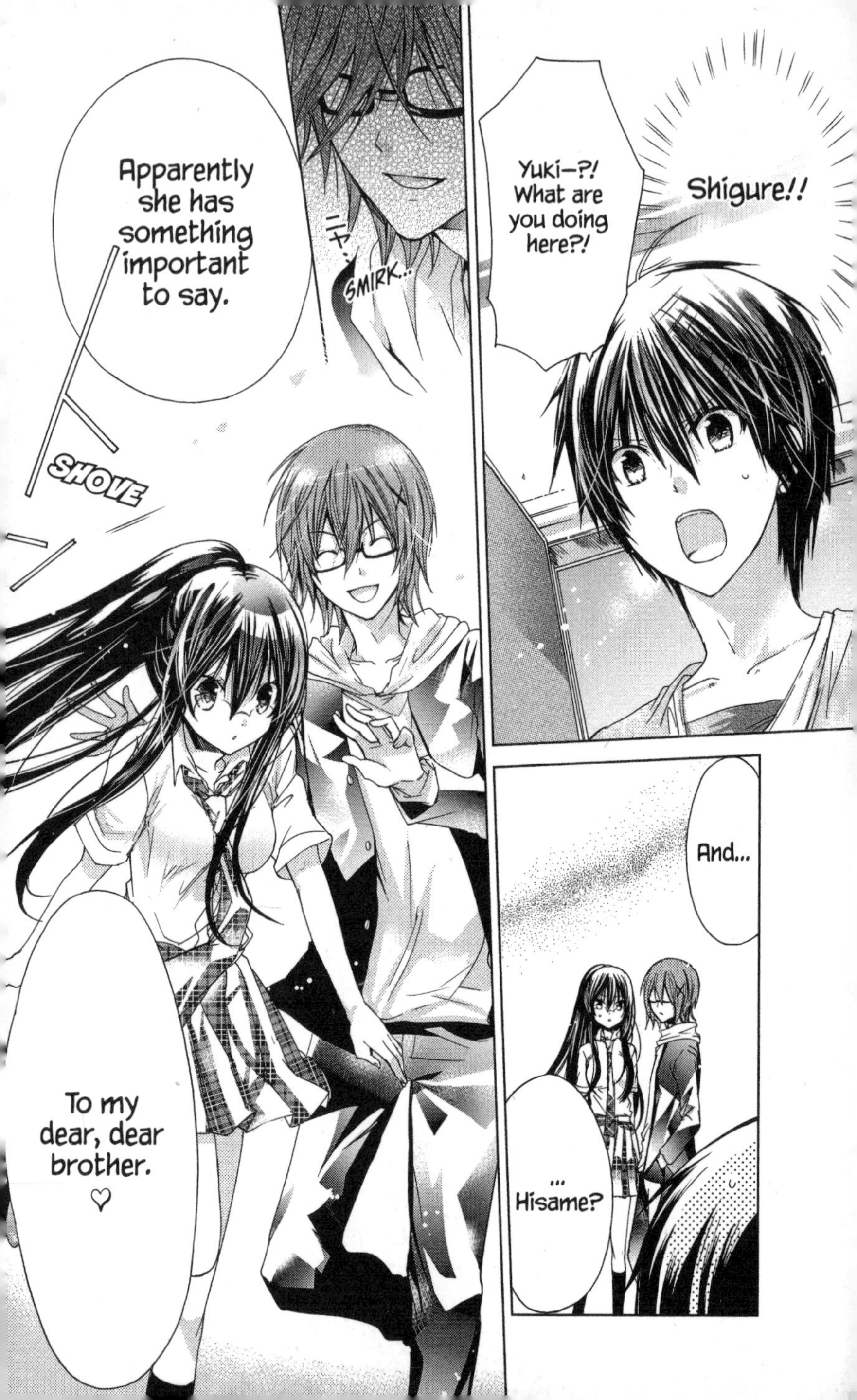
Shigure!!
Yuki–?! What are you doing here?!
And...
... Hisame?
Apparently she has something important to say.
ニヤ…
SMIRK...
SHOVE
To my dear, dear brother. ♡

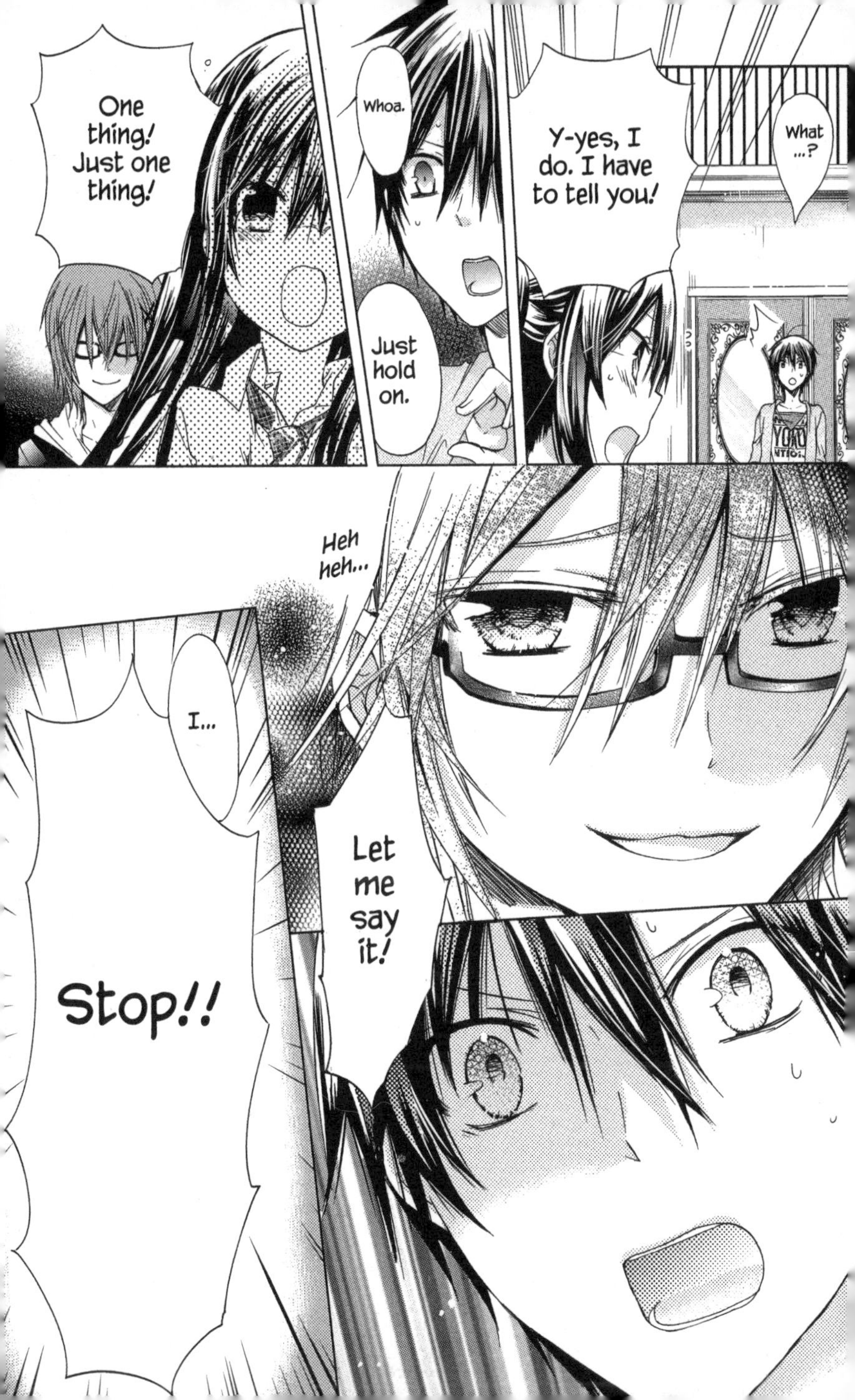
What ...?
Y-yes, I do. I have to tell you!
Whoa.
Just hold on.
One thing! Just one thing!
Heh heh...
Let me say it!
I...
Stop!!

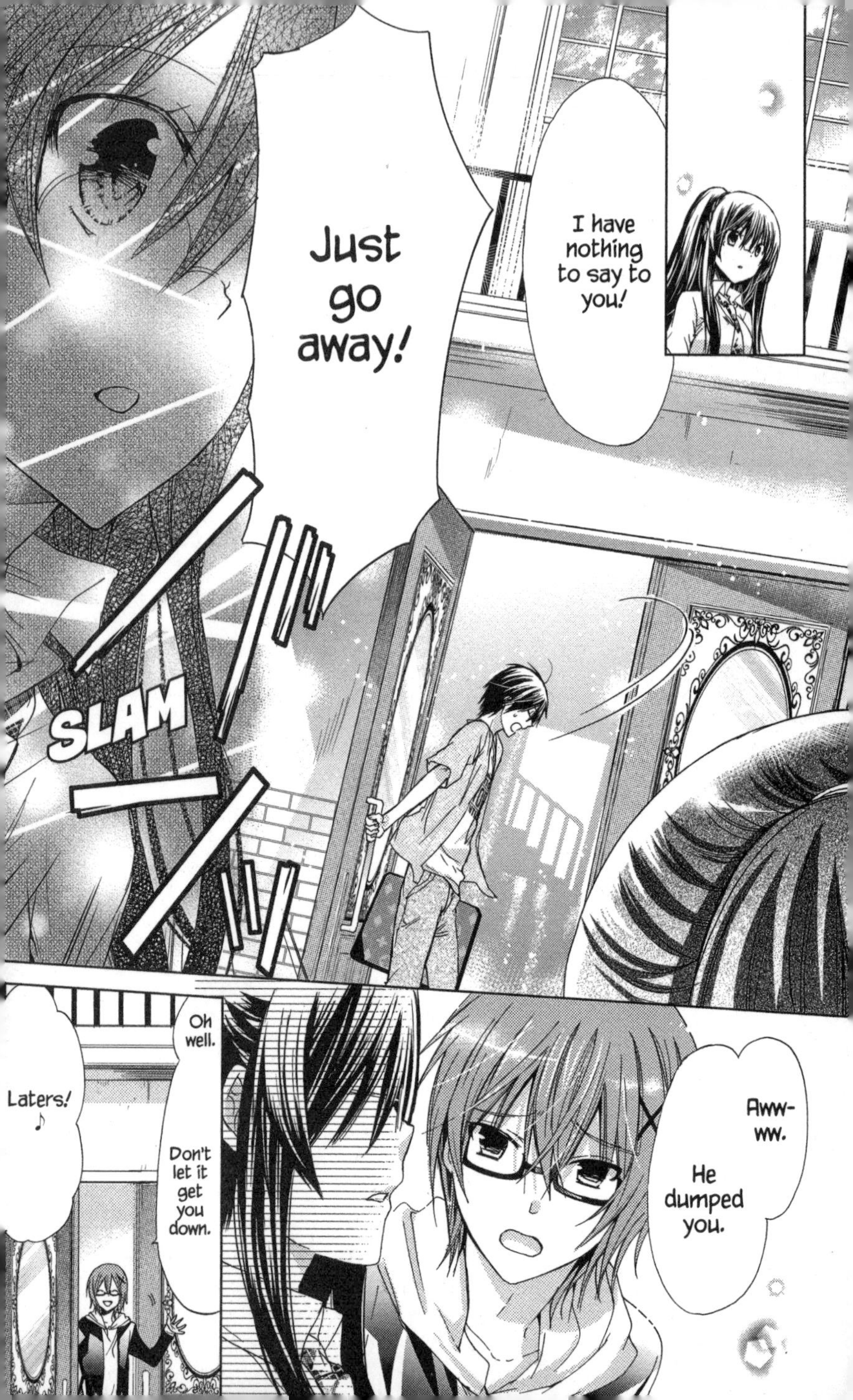
I have nothing to say to you!
Just go away!
SLAM
Aww-ww.
He dumped you.
Oh well.
Don't let it get you down.
Laters! ♪

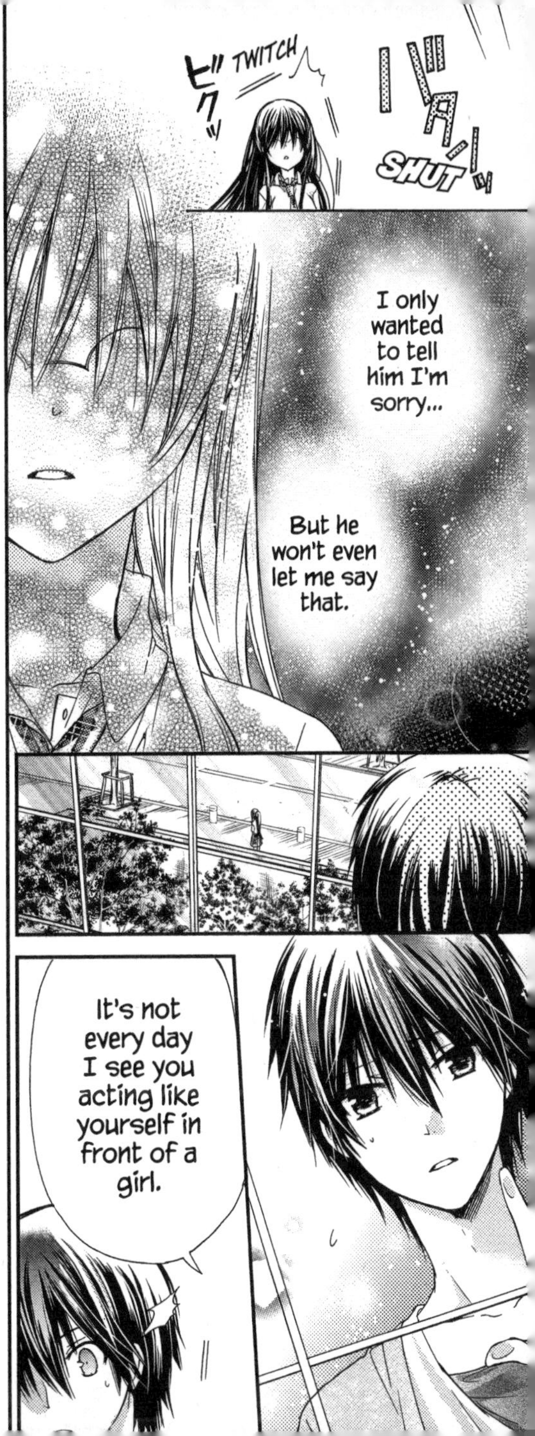
SHUT
TWITCH
I only wanted to tell him I'm sorry...
But he won't even let me say that.
It's not every day I see you acting like yourself in front of a girl.

At Last...!

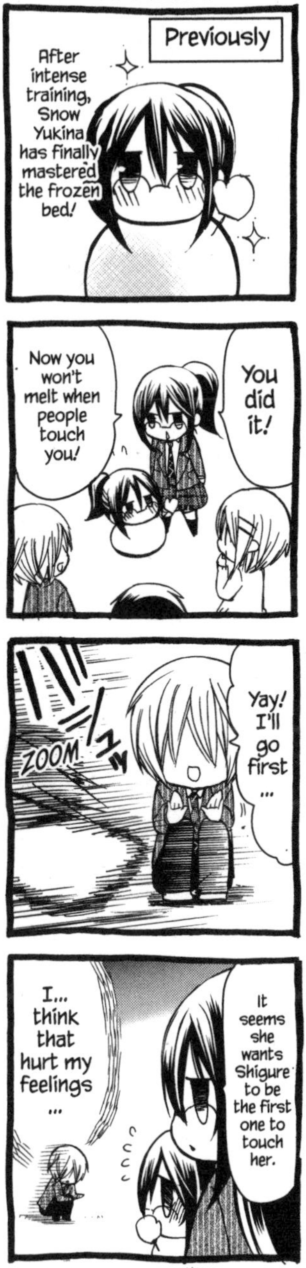
Previously
After intense training, Snow Yukina has finally mastered the frozen bed!
You did it!
Now you won't melt when people touch you!
ZOOM
Yay! I'll go first ...
It seems she wants Shigure to be the first one to touch her.
I... think that hurt my feelings ...

Hands with nowhere to go...

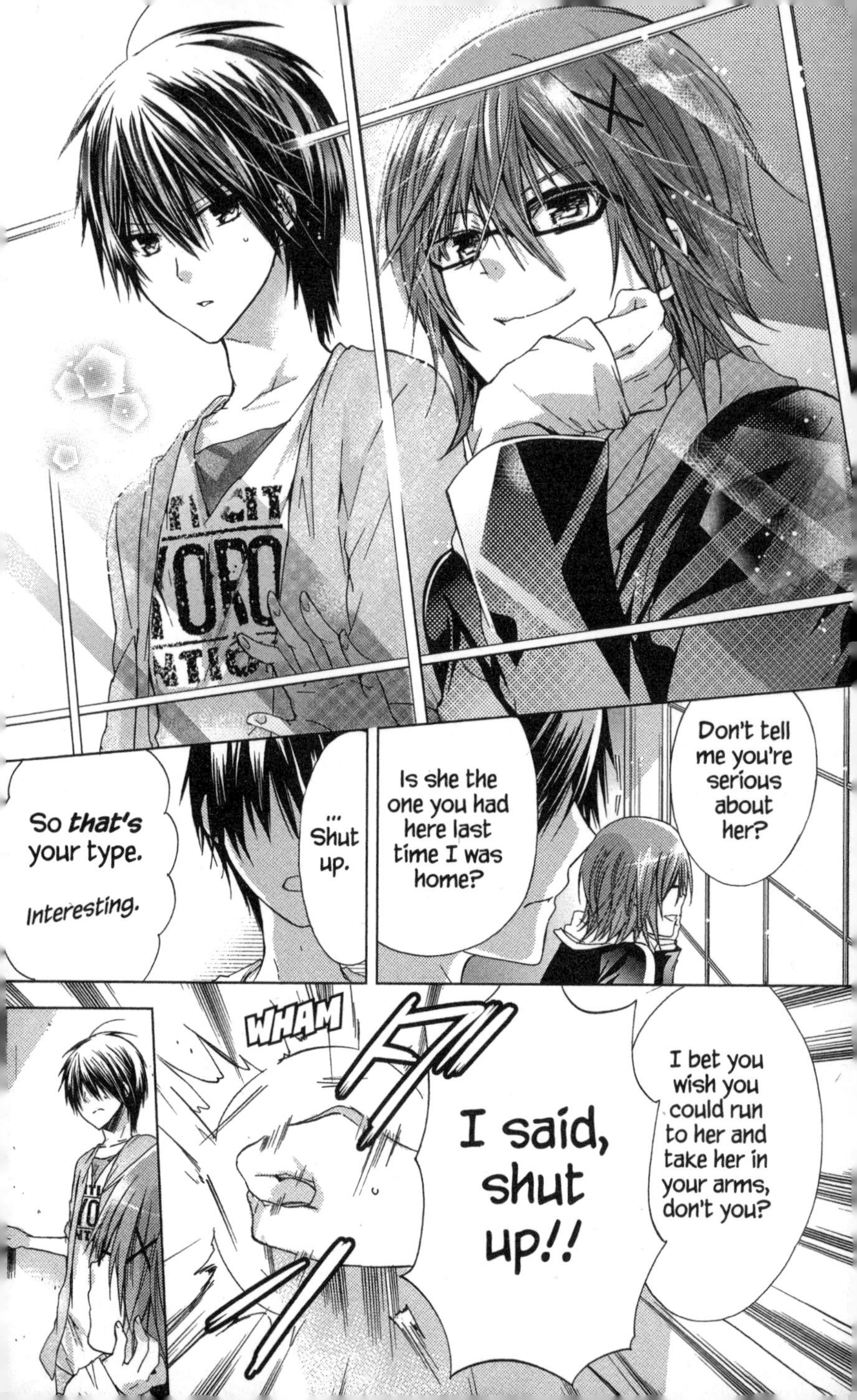
Don't tell me you're serious about her?
Is she the one you had here last time I was home?
... Shut up.
So *that's* your type.
Interesting.
I bet you wish you could run to her and take her in your arms, don't you?
I said, shut up!!
WHAM

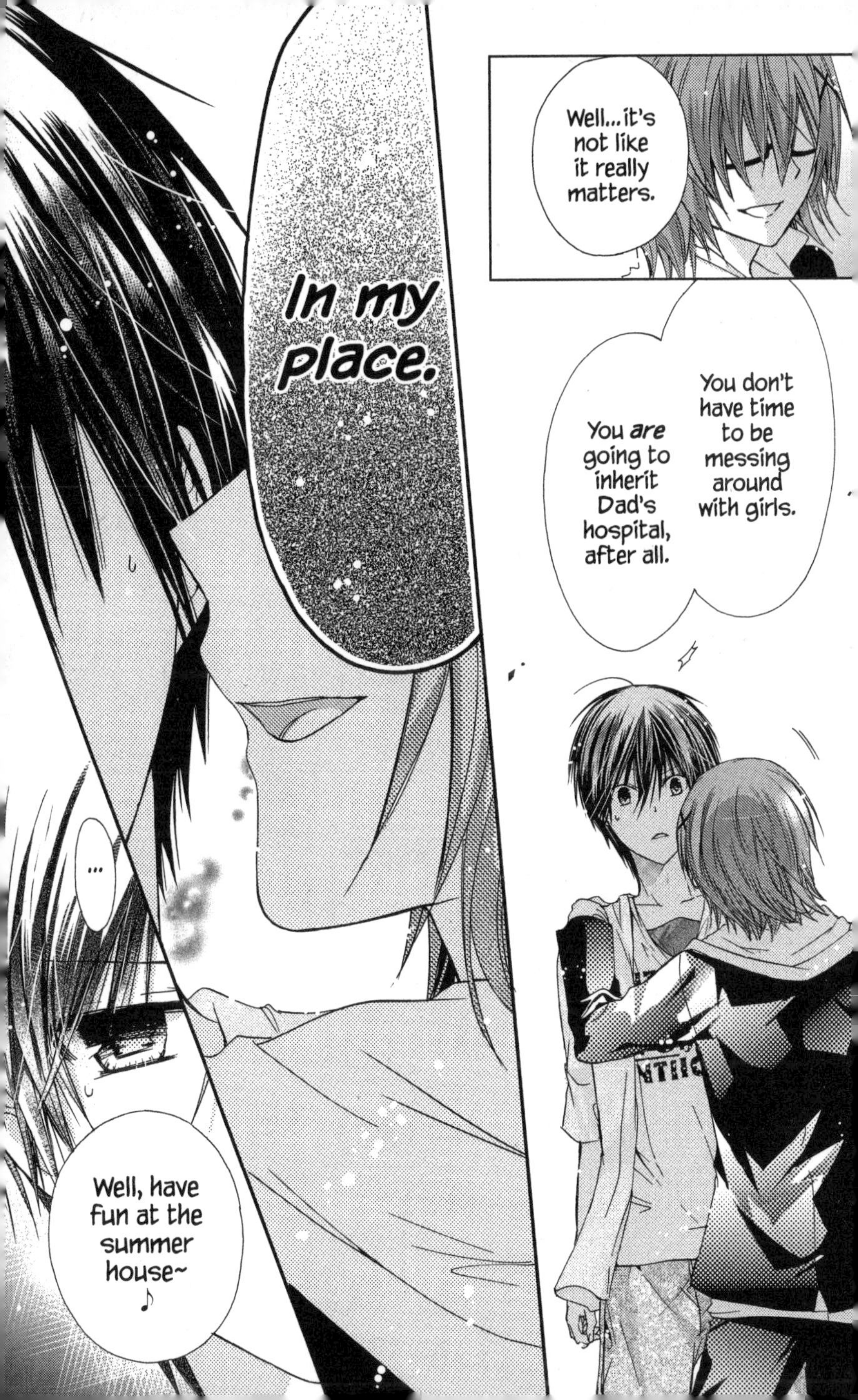
Well...it's not like it really matters.
You don't have time to be messing around with girls.
You *are* going to inherit Dad's hospital, after all.
In my place.
...
Well, have fun at the summer house~ ♪

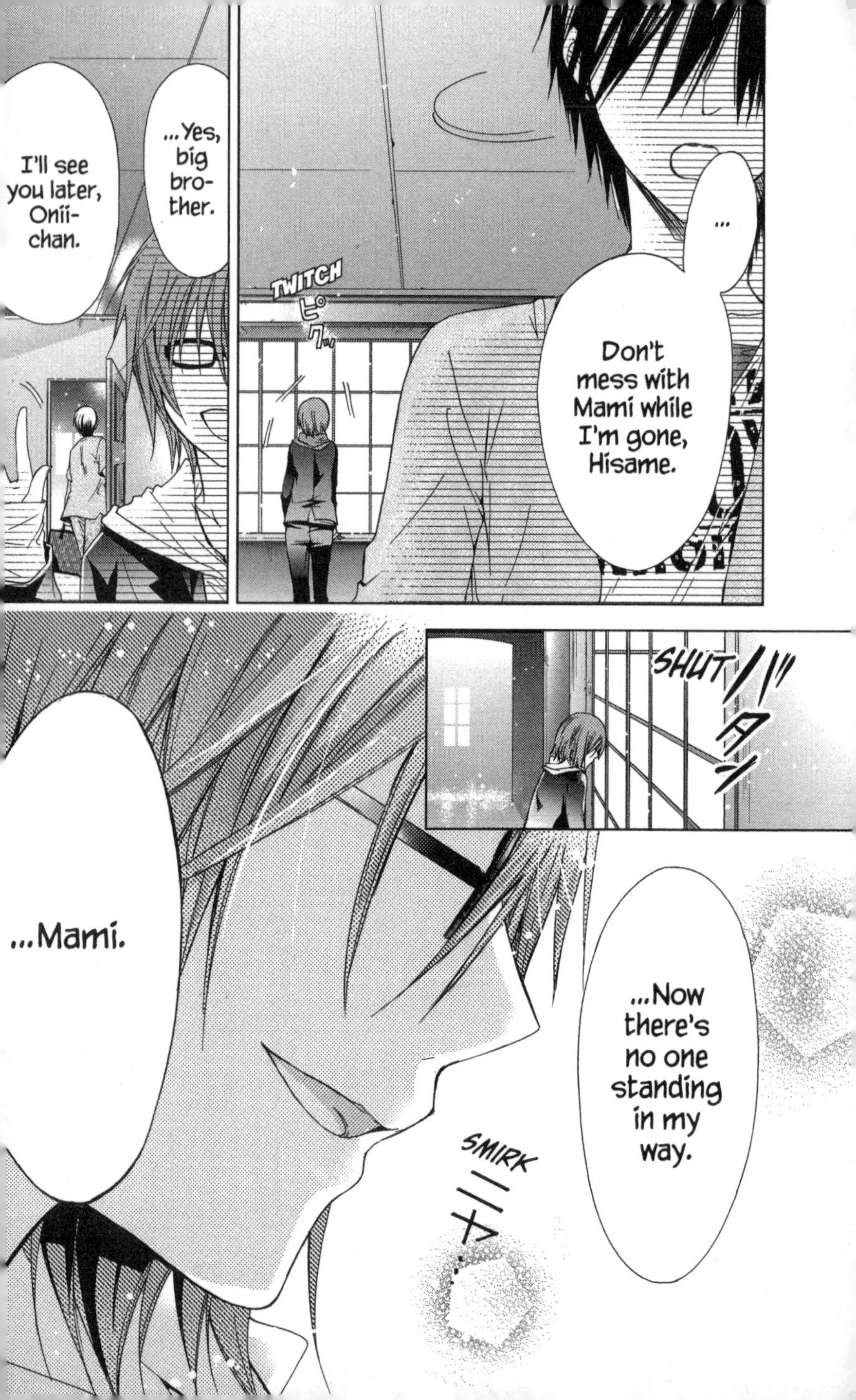
...
Don't mess with Mami while I'm gone, Hisame.
TWITCH
ピクッ
...Yes, big brother.
I'll see you later, Onii-chan.
SHUT
バタン
...Now there's no one standing in my way.
SMIRK
ニヤ…
...Mami.

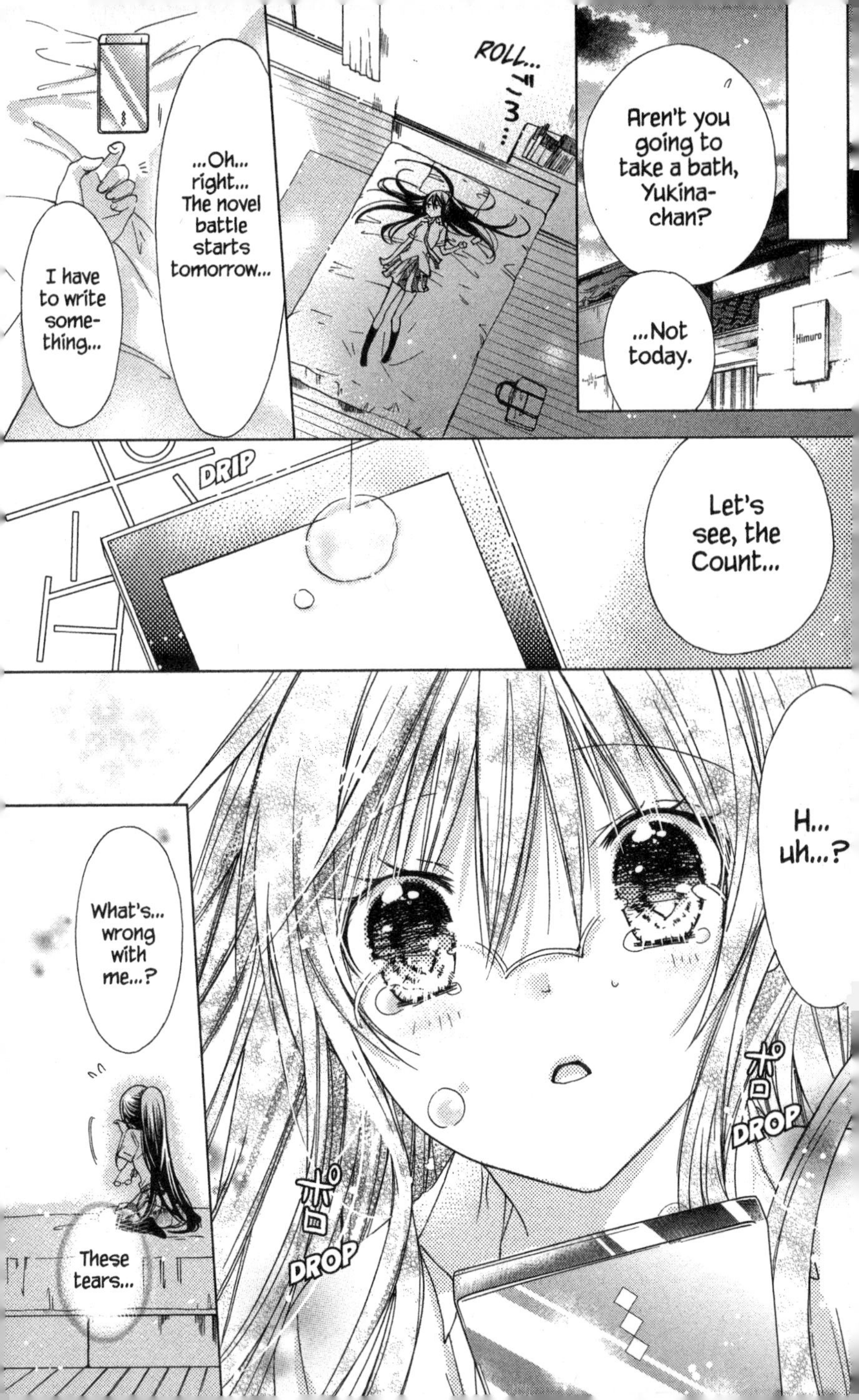

Himuro
Aren't you going to take a bath, Yukina-chan?
...Not today.
ROLL...
ゴロ...
...Oh... right... The novel battle starts tomorrow...
I have to write something...
Let's see, the Count...
DRIP
H... uh...?
ポロ
DROP
ポロ
DROP
What's... wrong with me...?
These tears...

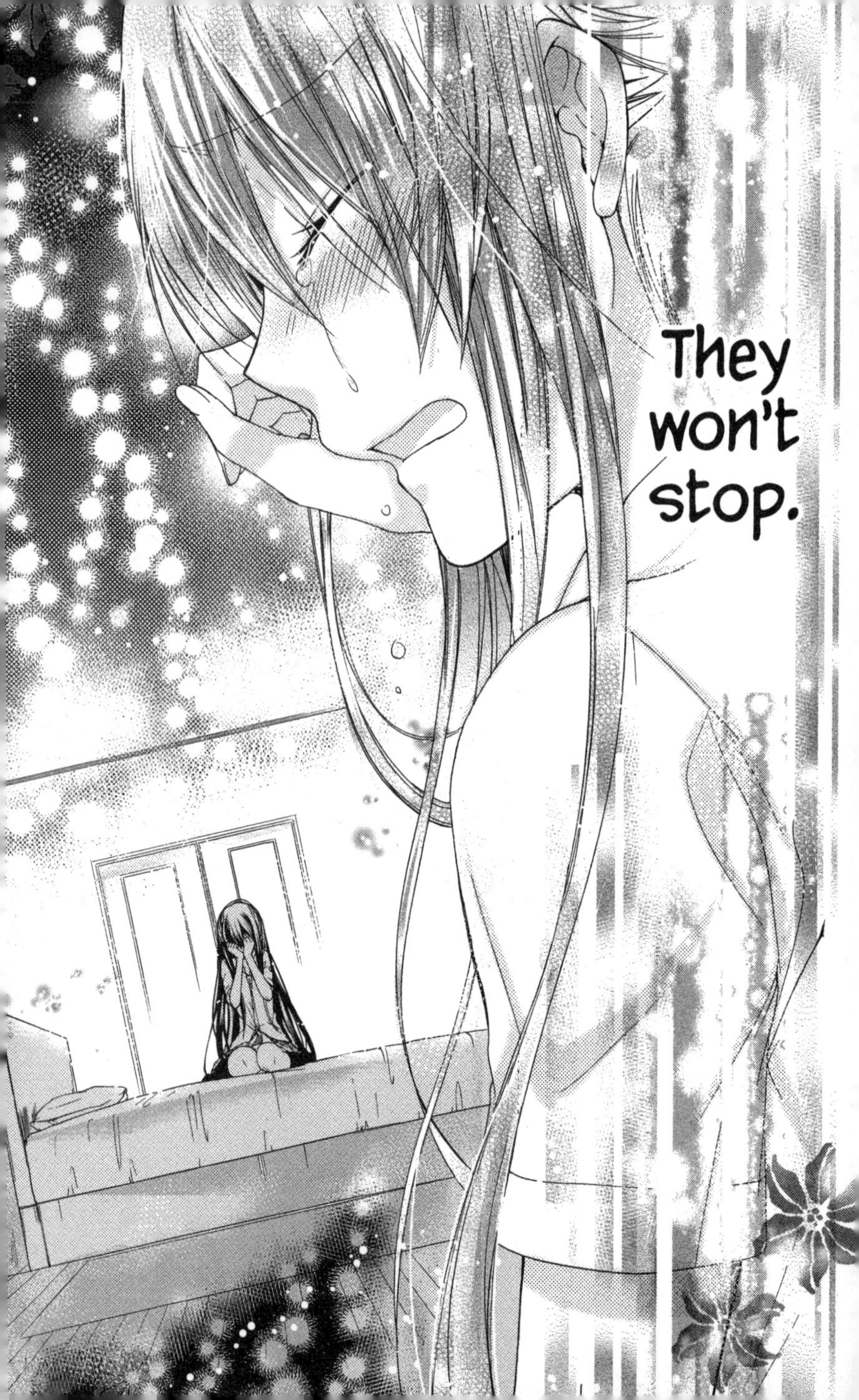
They won't stop.

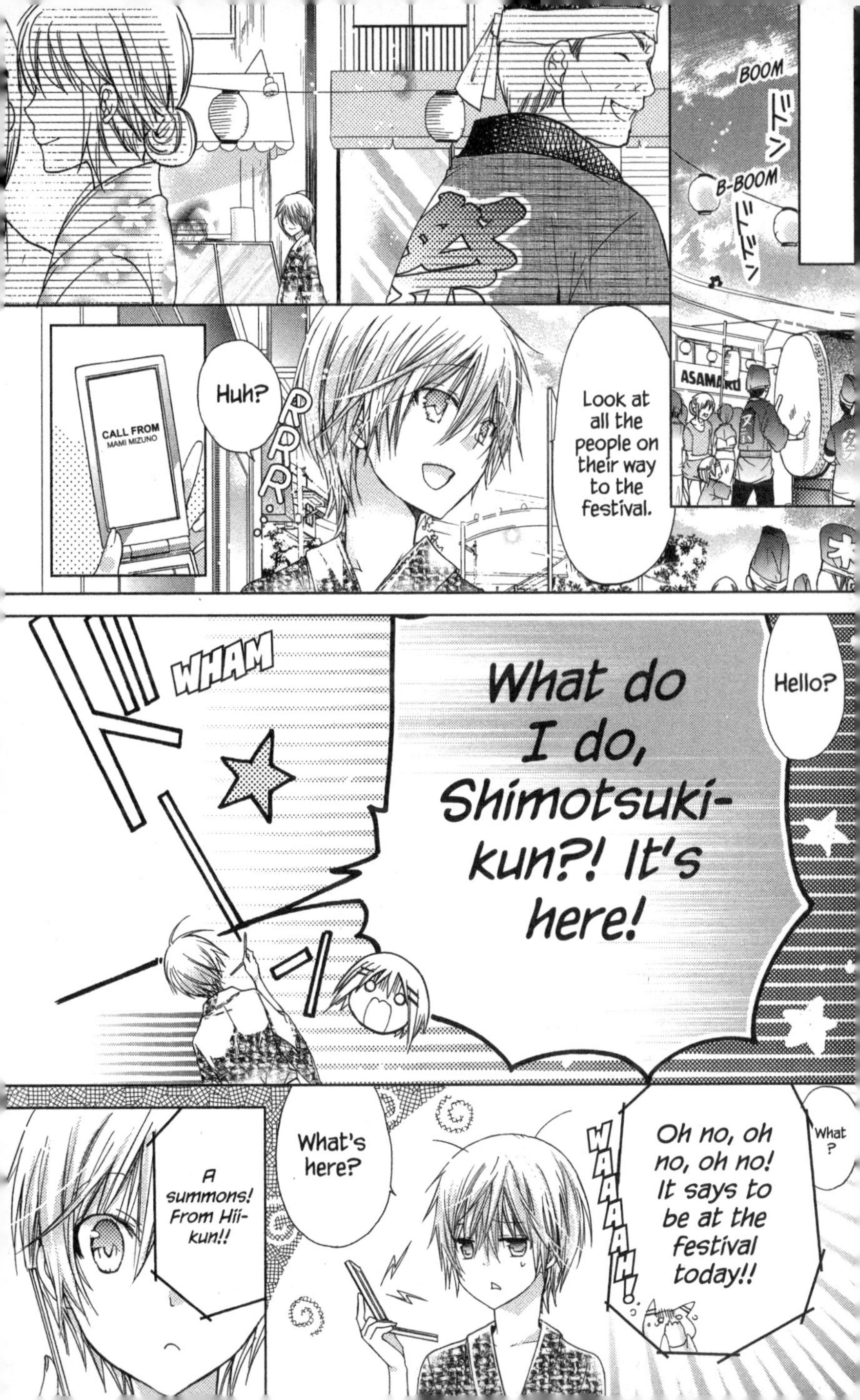
BOOM
B-BOOM
ASAMARU
Look at all the people on their way to the festival.
Huh?
RRRR
CALL FROM
MAMI MIZUNO
Hello?
What do I do, Shimotsuki-kun?! It's here!
WHAM
What?
Oh no, oh no, oh no! It says to be at the festival today!!
WAAAAAH!
What's here?
A summons! From Hii-kun!!

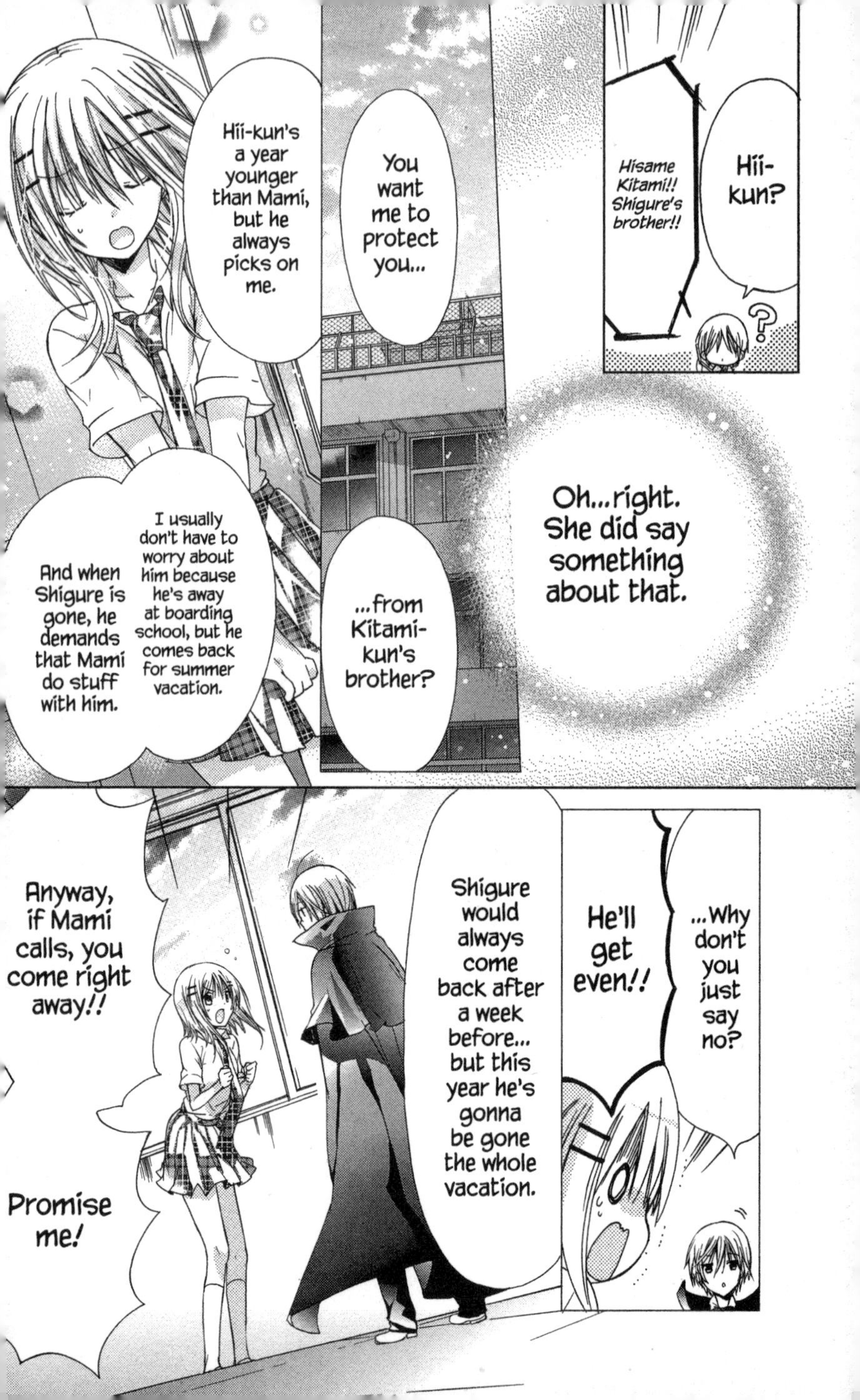
Hii-kun?
Hisame Kitami!! Shigure's brother!!
Oh...right. She did say something about that.
You want me to protect you...
...from Kitami-kun's brother?
Hii-kun's a year younger than Mami, but he always picks on me.
I usually don't have to worry about him because he's away at boarding school, but he comes back for summer vacation.
And when Shigure is gone, he demands that Mami do stuff with him.
...Why don't you just say no?
He'll get even!!
Shigure would always come back after a week before... but this year he's gonna be gone the whole vacation.
Anyway, if Mami calls, you come right away!!
Promise me!

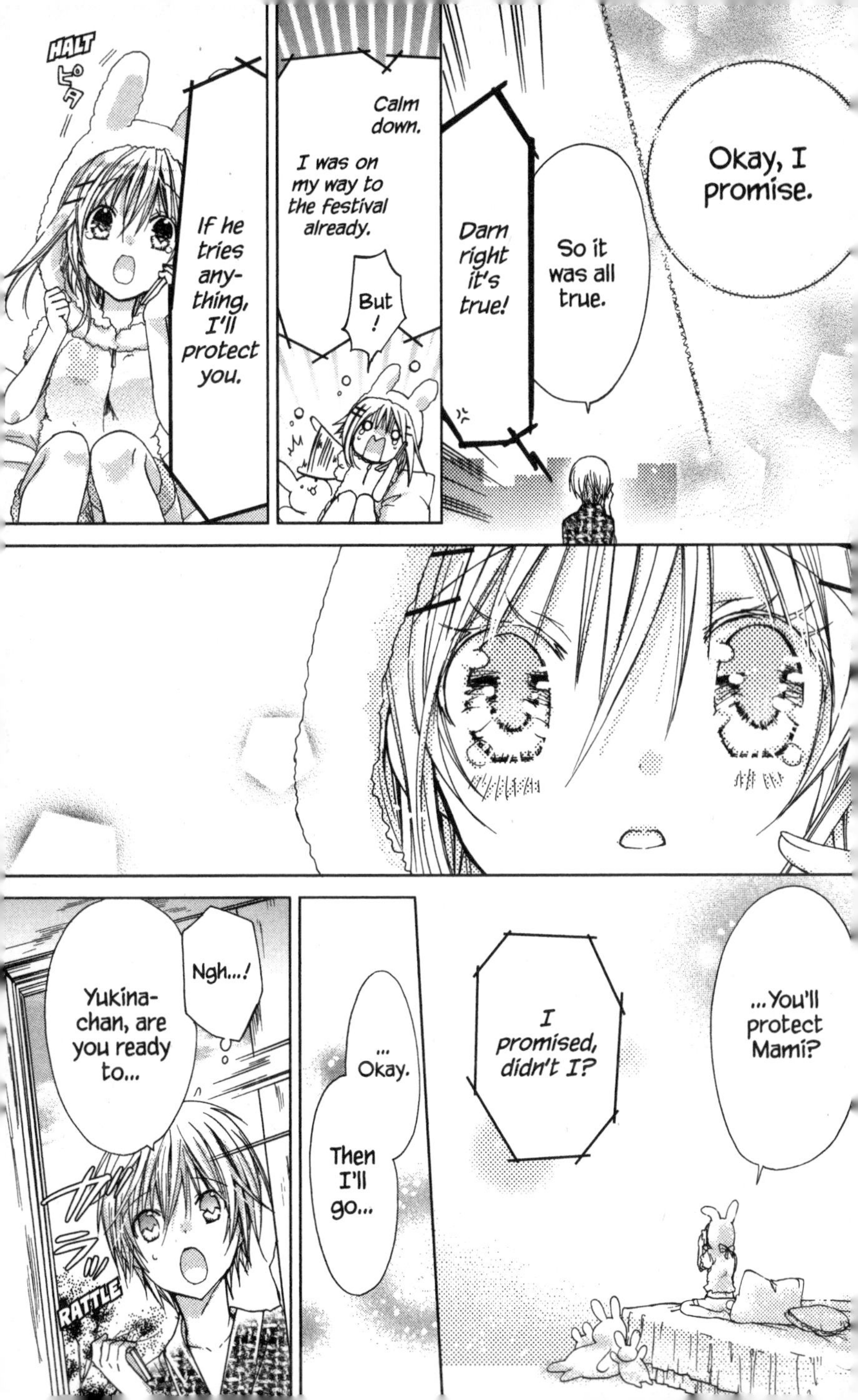

Okay, I promise.
So it was all true.
Darn right it's true!
Calm down.
I was on my way to the festival already.
But!
HALT
ピタ
If he tries any-thing, I'll protect you.
...You'll protect Mami?
I promised, didn't I?
... Okay.
Then I'll go...
Ngh...!
Yukina-chan, are you ready to...
ガラ
RATTLE

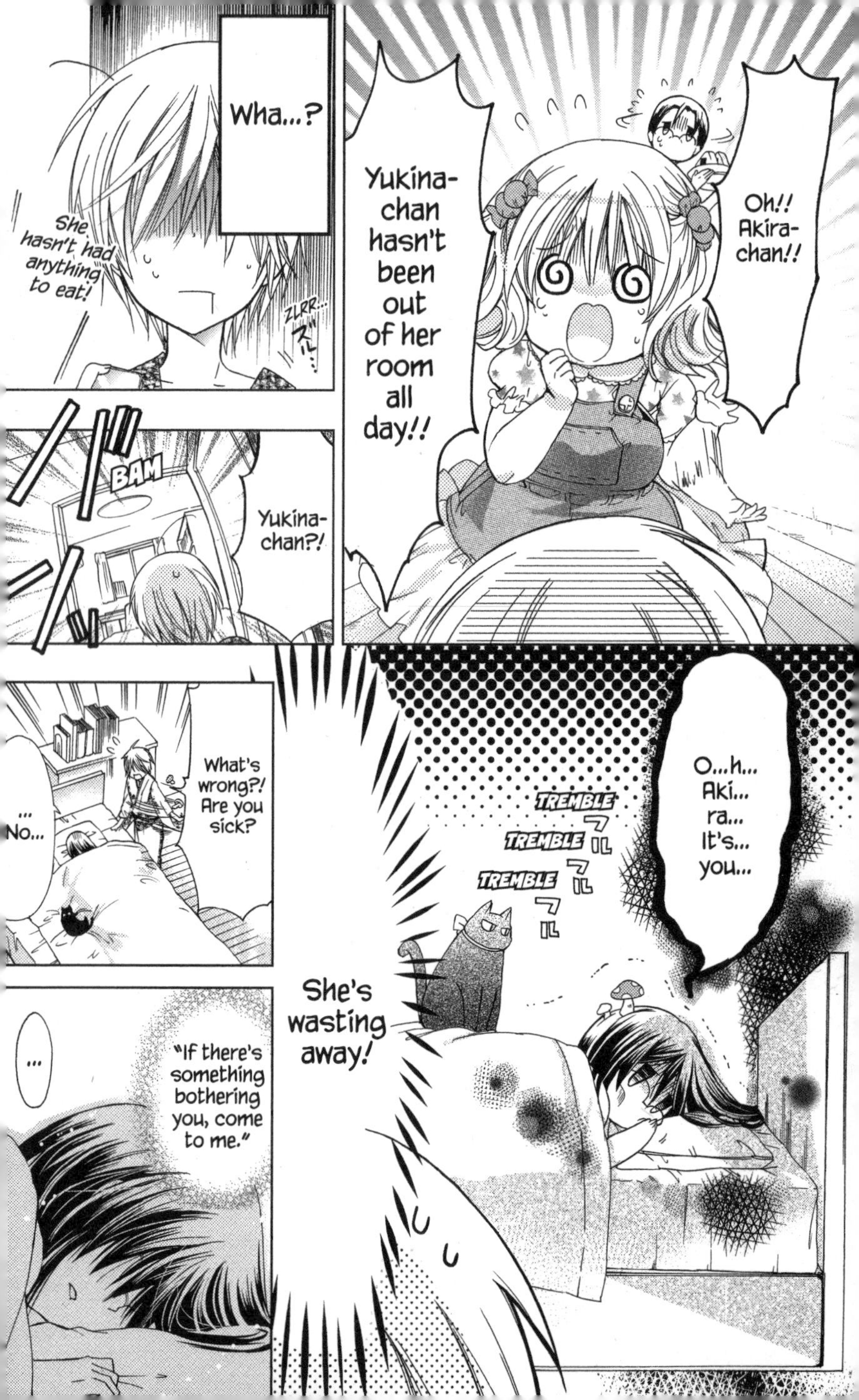
Oh!! Akira-chan!!
Yukina-chan hasn't been out of her room all day!!
Wha...?
She hasn't had anything to eat!
ZLRR...
ズル…
BAM
Yukina-chan?!
O...h... Aki... ra... It's... you...
TREMBLE
フル
TREMBLE
フル
TREMBLE
フル
She's wasting away!
What's wrong?! Are you sick?
... No...
"If there's something bothering you, come to me."
...

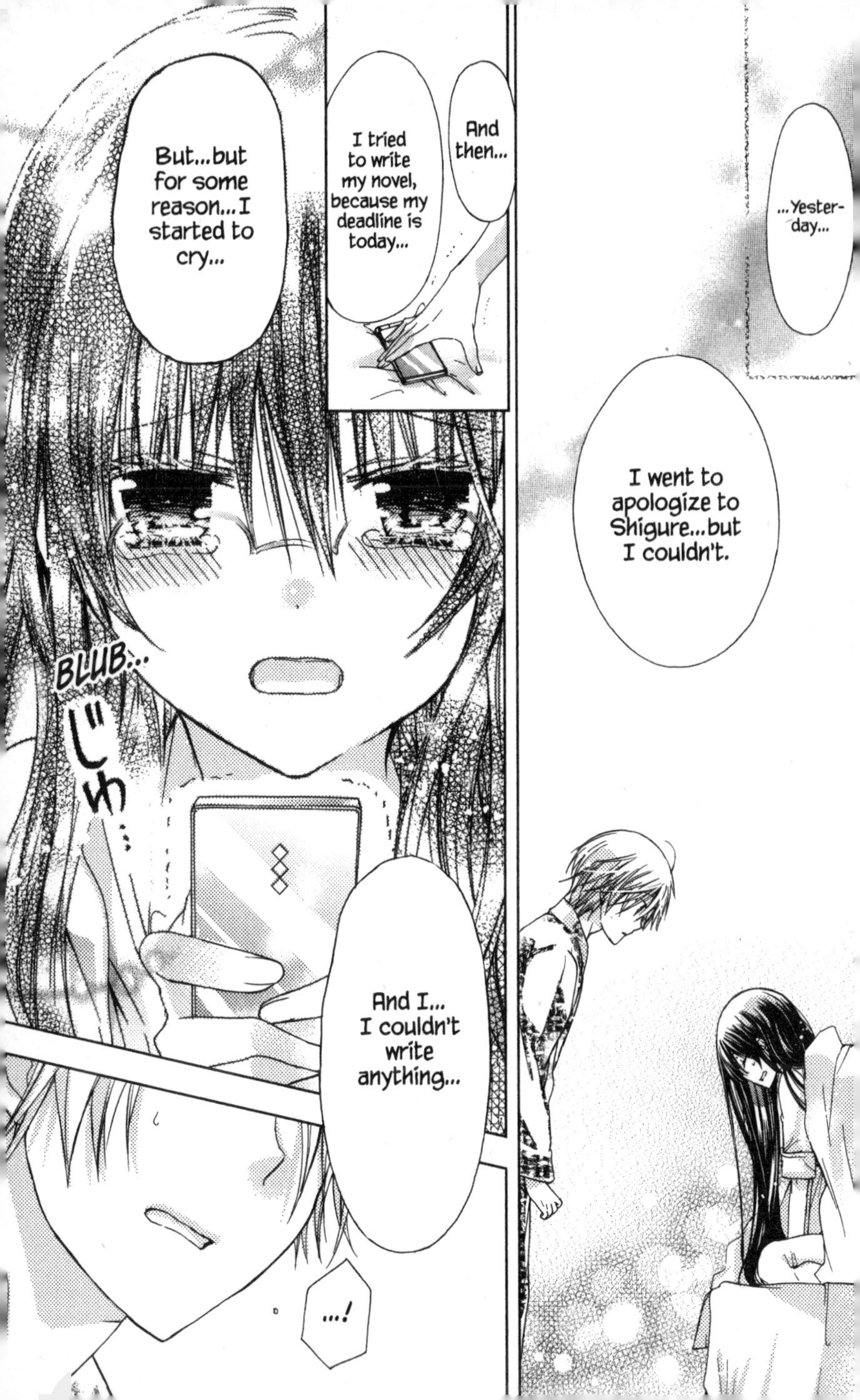
...Yester-day...
I went to apologize to Shigure...but I couldn't.
And then...
I tried to write my novel, because my deadline is today...
But...but for some reason...I started to cry...
BLUB...
じゅ...
And I... I couldn't write anything...
...!

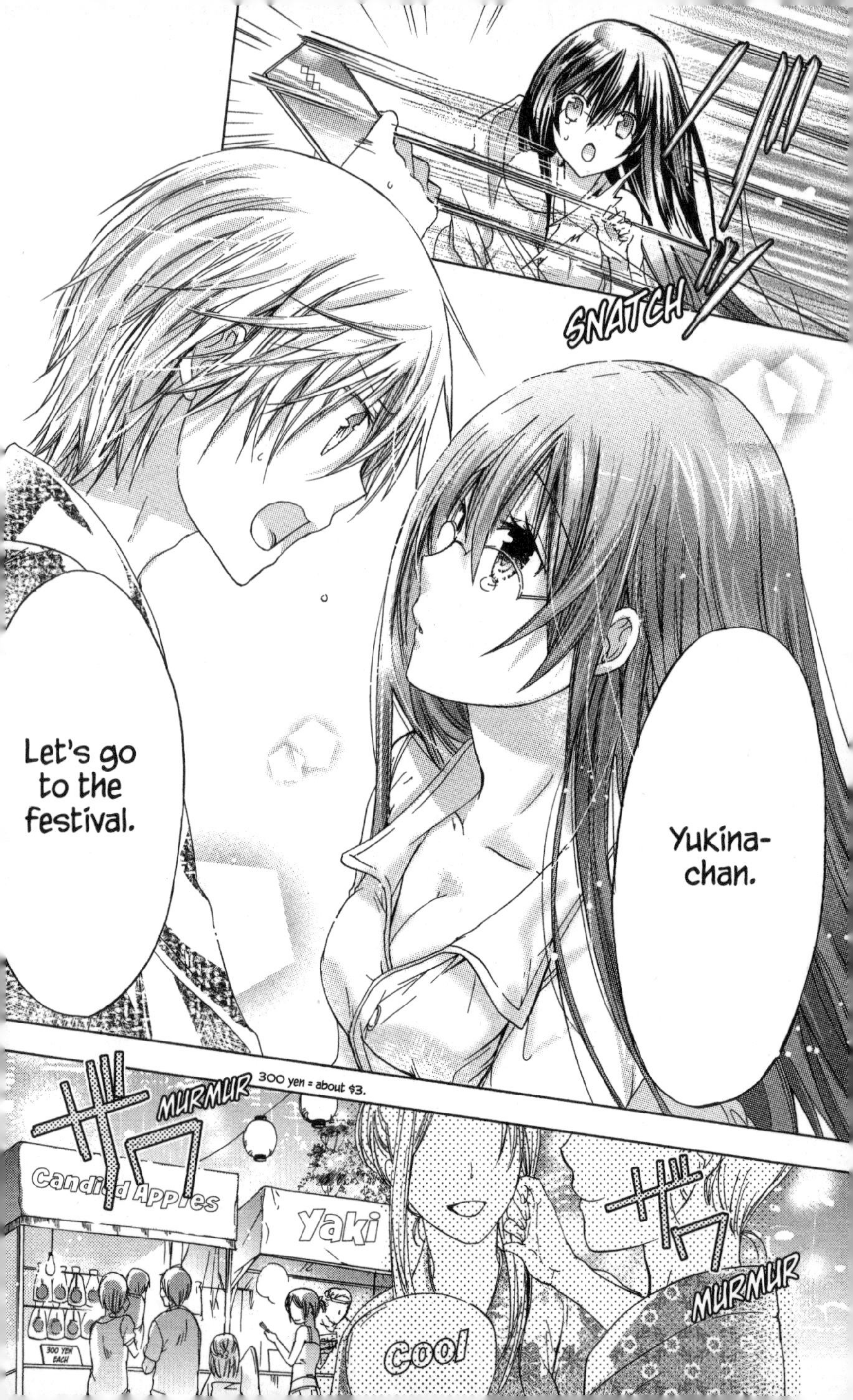
SNATCH
Yukina-chan.
Let's go to the festival.
MURMUR
Cool
MURMUR
300 yen = about $3.
Yaki
Candied Apples
300 YEN EACH

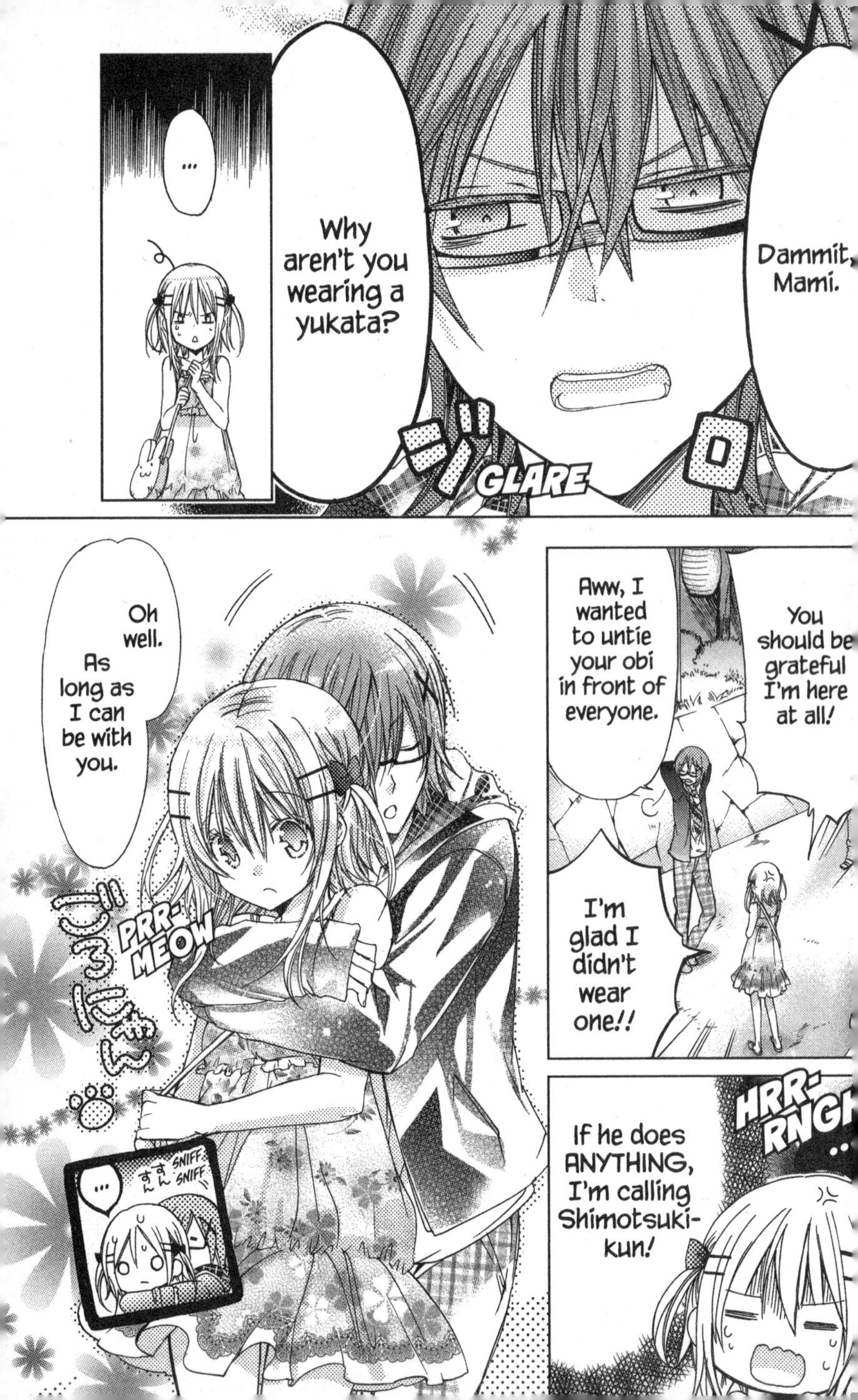
Dammit, Mami.
Why aren't you wearing a yukata?
GLARE
...
You should be grateful I'm here at all!
Aww, I wanted to untie your obi in front of everyone.
I'm glad I didn't wear one!!
HRR-RNGH...
If he does ANYTHING, I'm calling Shimotsuki-kun!
Oh well. As long as I can be with you.
PRR-MEOW
...
SNIFF SNIFF

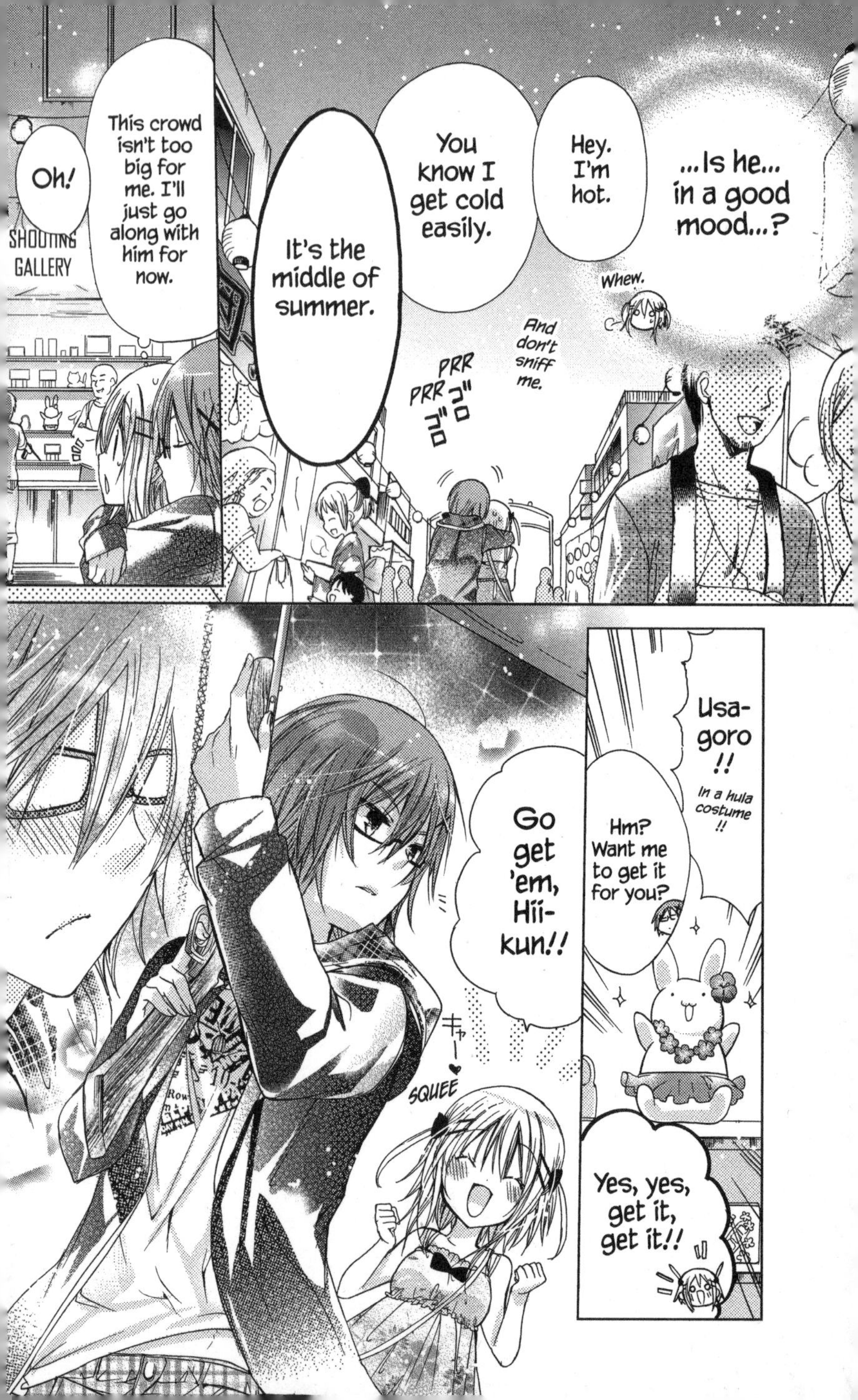
...Is he... in a good mood...?
Hey. I'm hot.
You know I get cold easily.
It's the middle of summer.
Whew.
And don't sniff me.
PRR PRR ゴロゴロ
This crowd isn't too big for me. I'll just go along with him for now.
Oh!
SHOOTING GALLERY
Usa-goro!!
In a hula costume!!
Hm? Want me to get it for you?
Yes, yes, get it, get it!!
Go get 'em, Hii-kun!!
キャー♥
SQUEE

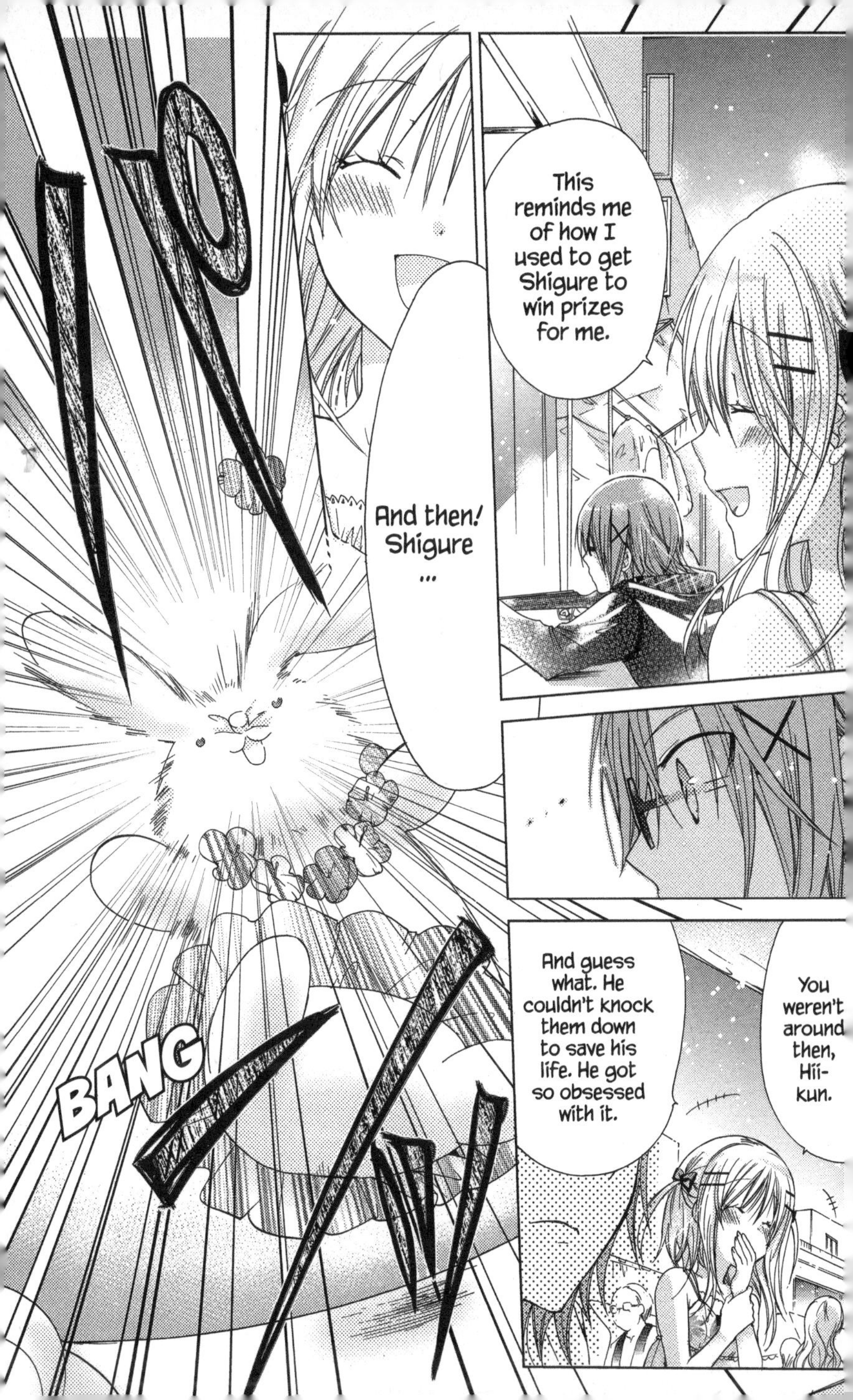
This reminds me of how I used to get Shigure to win prizes for me.
And then! Shigure ...
You weren't around then, Hii-kun.
And guess what. He couldn't knock them down to save his life. He got so obsessed with it.
BANG

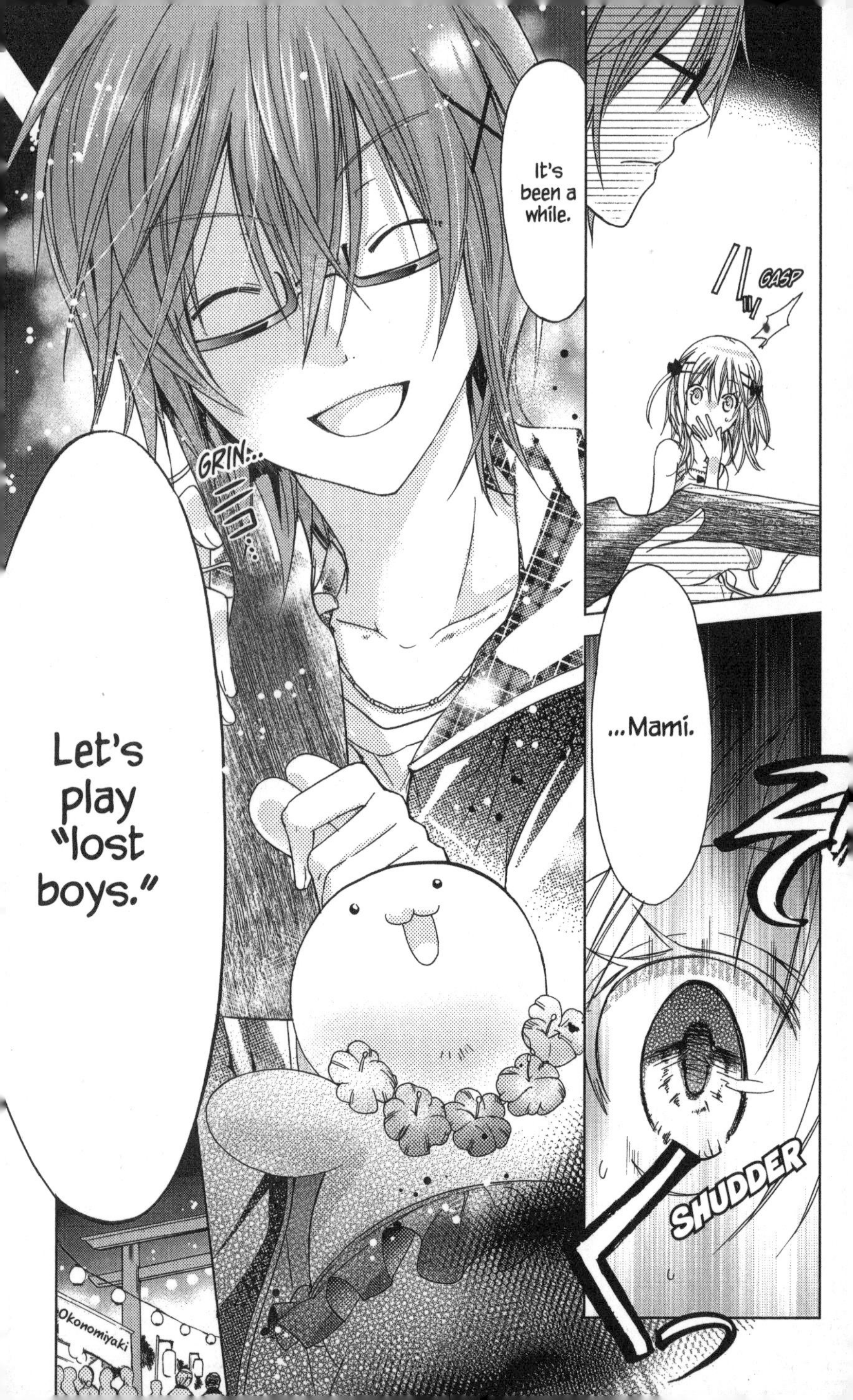
GASP
...Mami.
SHUDDER
It's been a while.
GRIN...
Let's play "lost boys."
Okonomiyaki

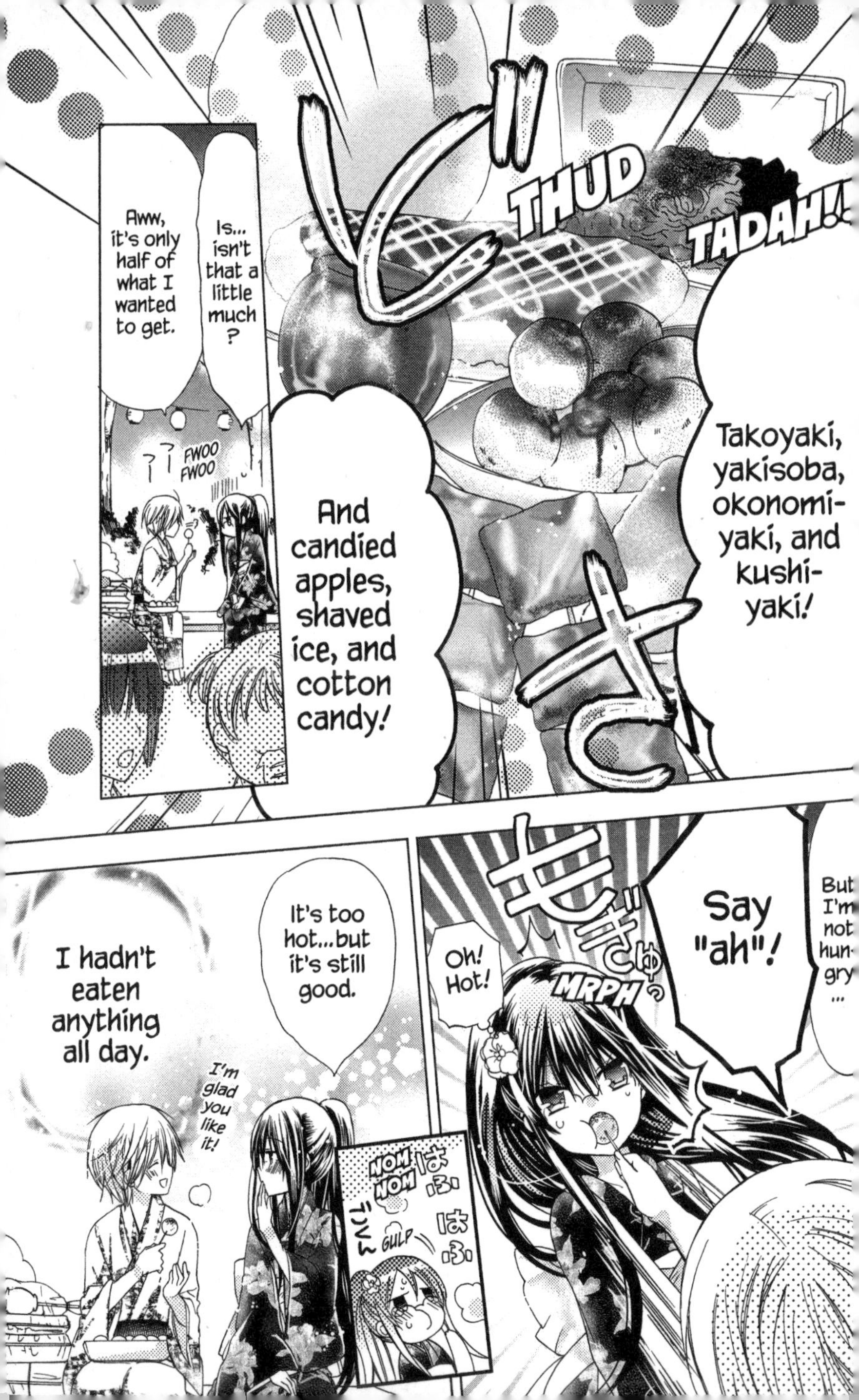
THUD
TADAH!!
Takoyaki, yakisoba, okonomi-yaki, and kushi-yaki!
And candied apples, shaved ice, and cotton candy!
Is... isn't that a little much?
Aww, it's only half of what I wanted to get.
FWOO FWOO
But I'm not hun-gry...
Say "ah"!
MRPH
Oh! Hot!
NOM NOM
GULP
It's too hot...but it's still good.
I'm glad you like it!
I hadn't eaten anything all day.

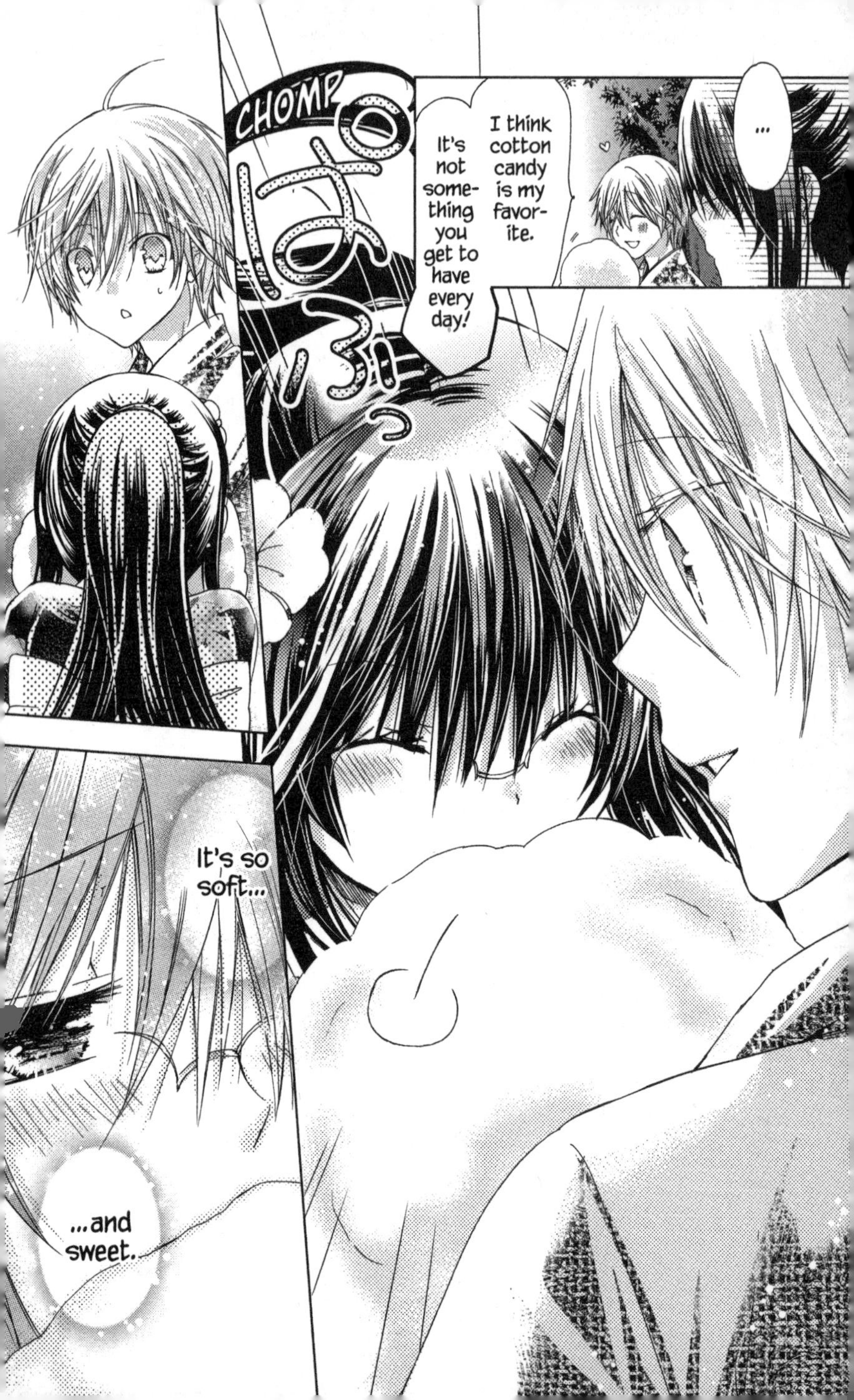
...
I think cotton candy is my favor-ite. It's not some-thing you get to have every day!
CHOMP
It's so soft...
...and sweet.

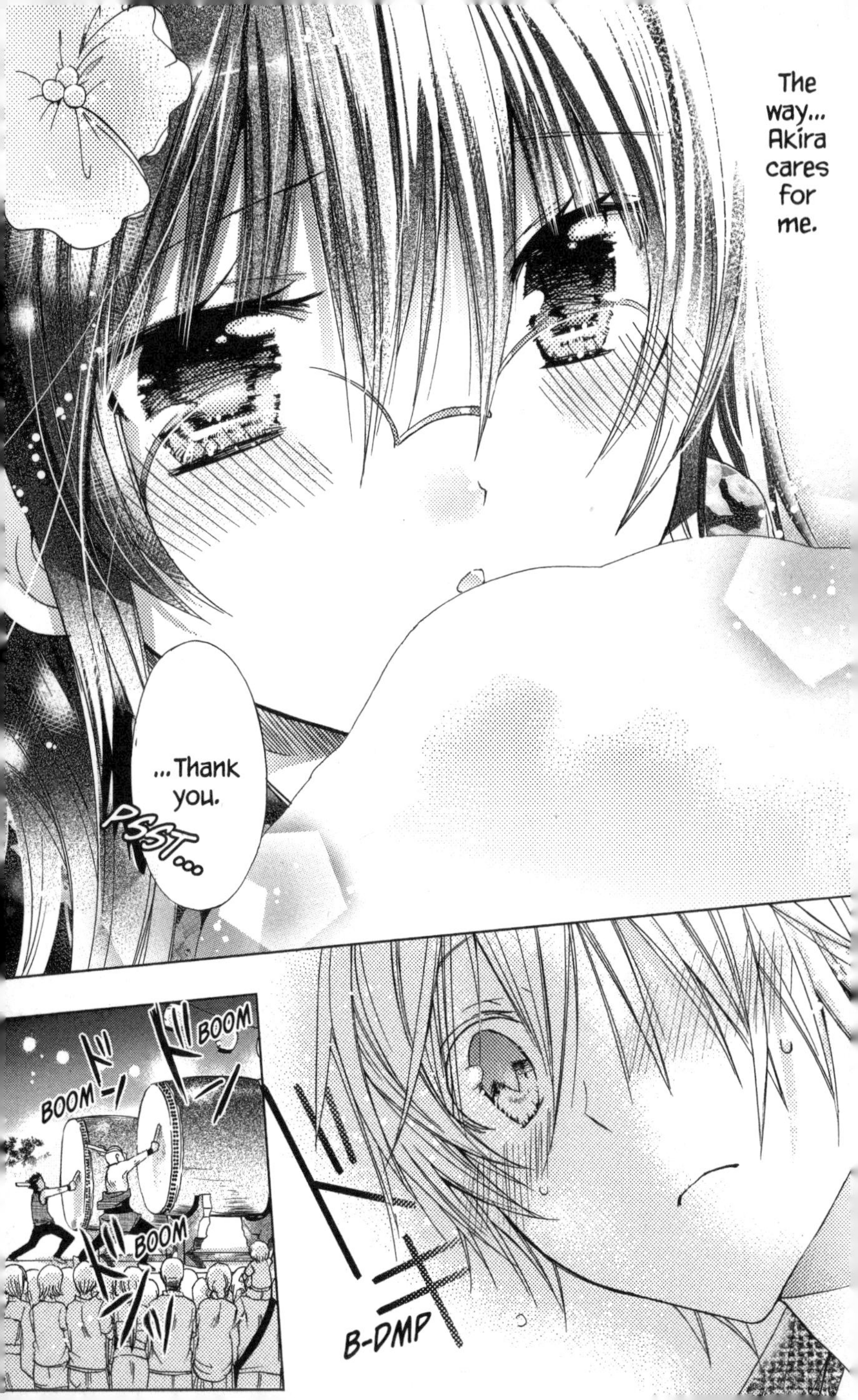

The way... Akira cares for me.
...Thank you.
PSST...
B-DMP
BOOM
BOOM
BOOM

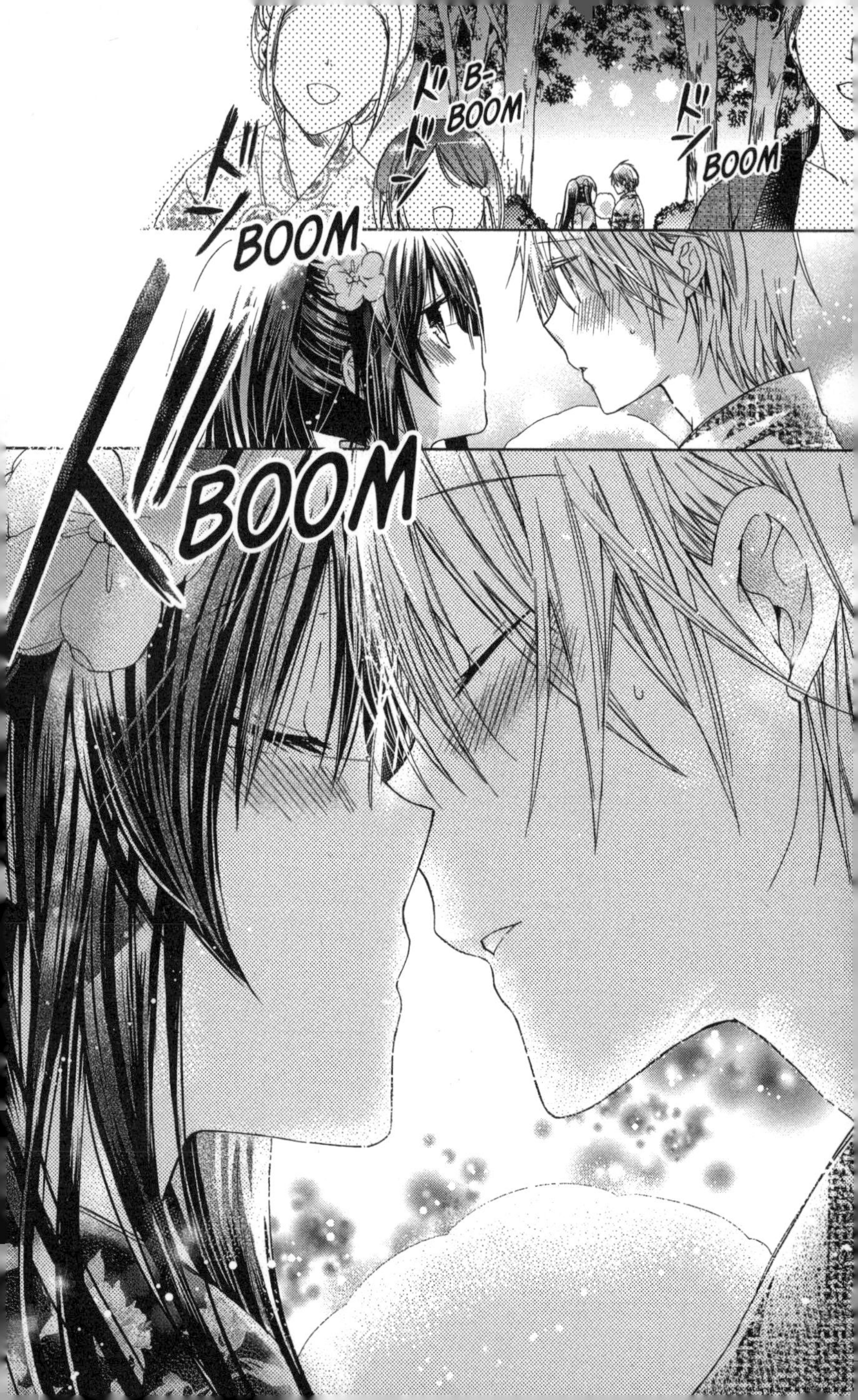
BOOM
B-BOOM
BOOM
BOOM

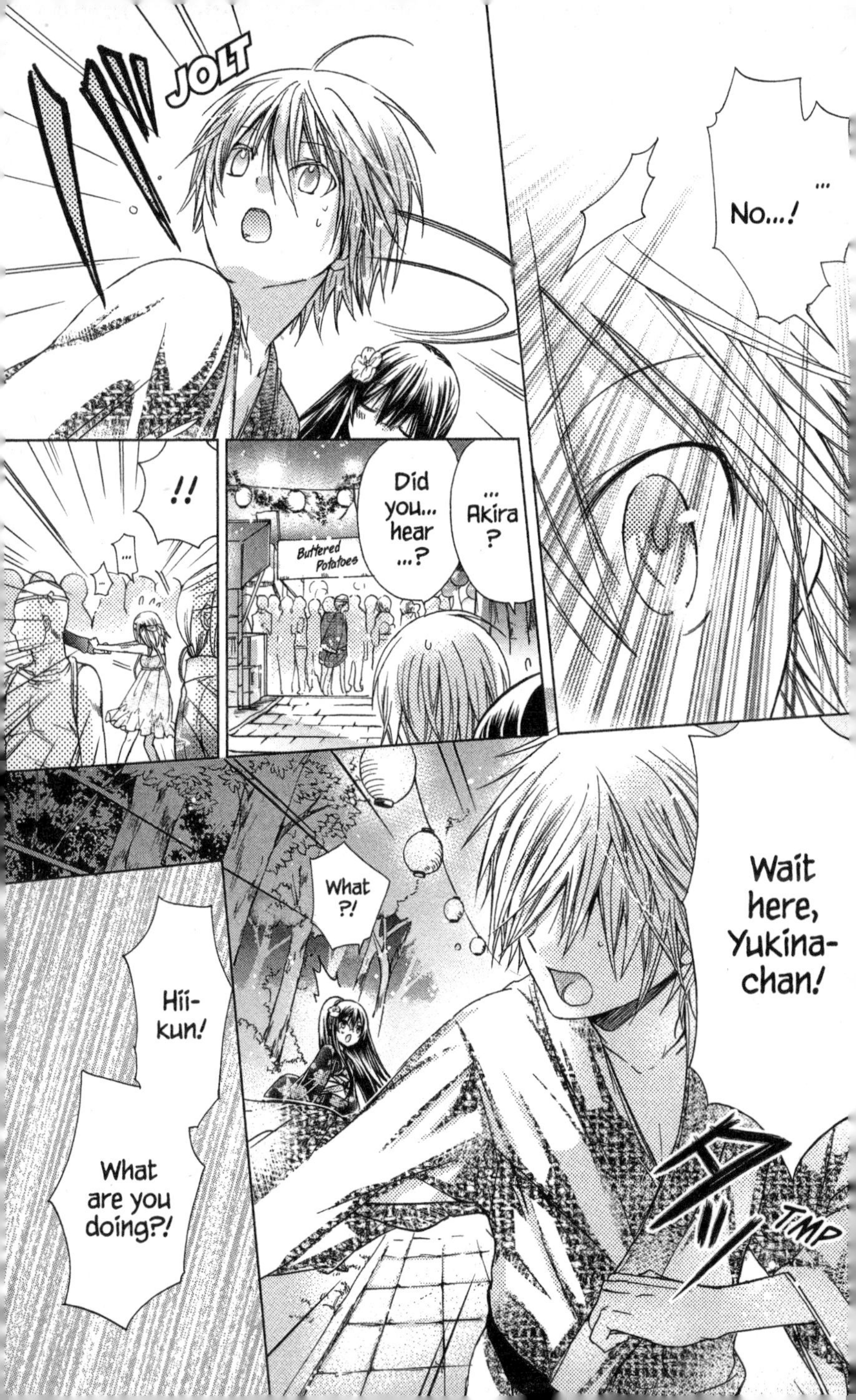
...
No...!
JOLT
... Akira?
Did you... hear...?
!!
...
...
Wait here, Yukina-chan!
TMP
What?!
Hii-kun!
What are you doing?!

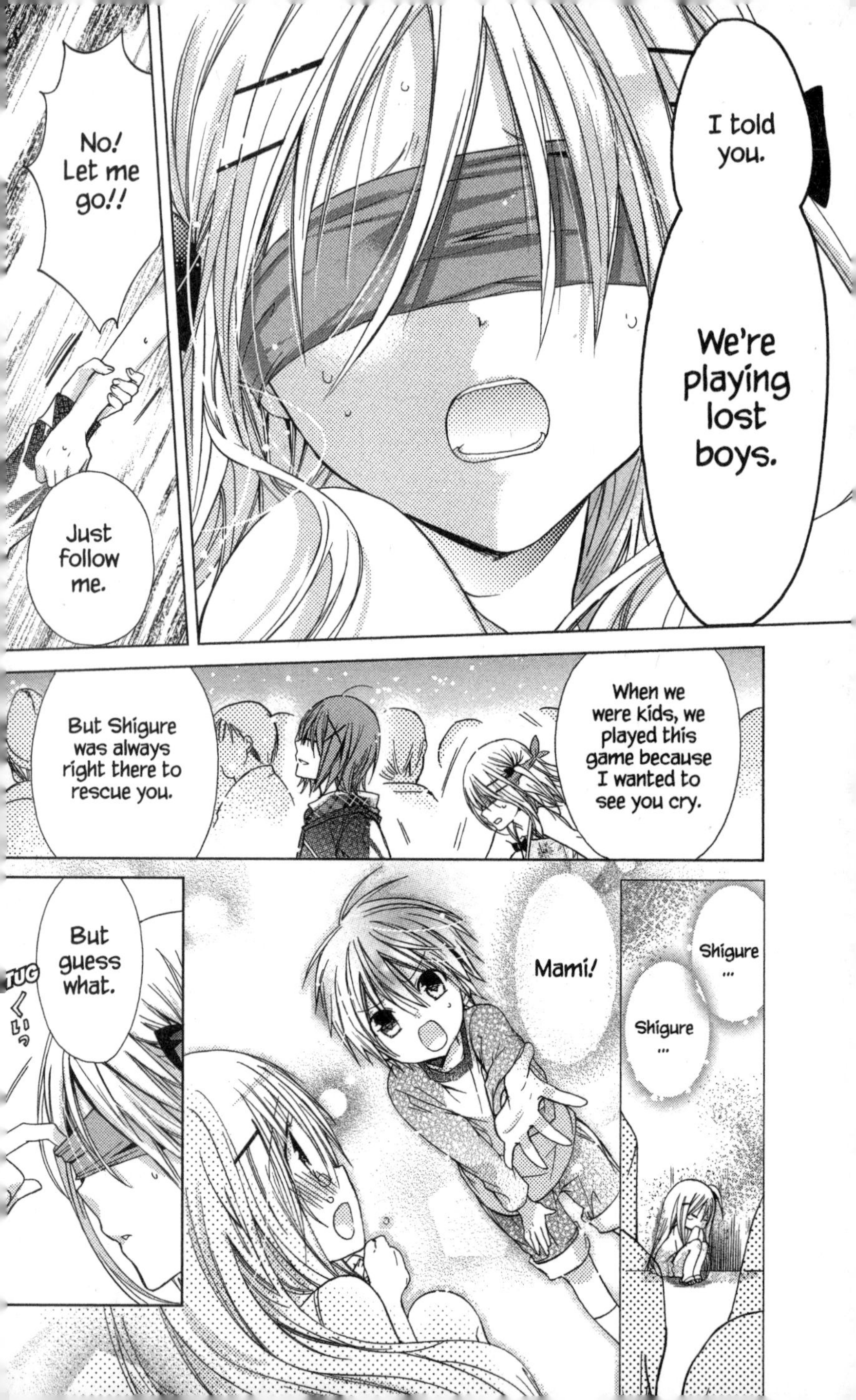

I told you.
We're playing lost boys.
No! Let me go!!
Just follow me.
When we were kids, we played this game because I wanted to see you cry.
But Shigure was always right there to rescue you.
Shigure ...
Shigure ...
Mami!
But guess what.
TUG

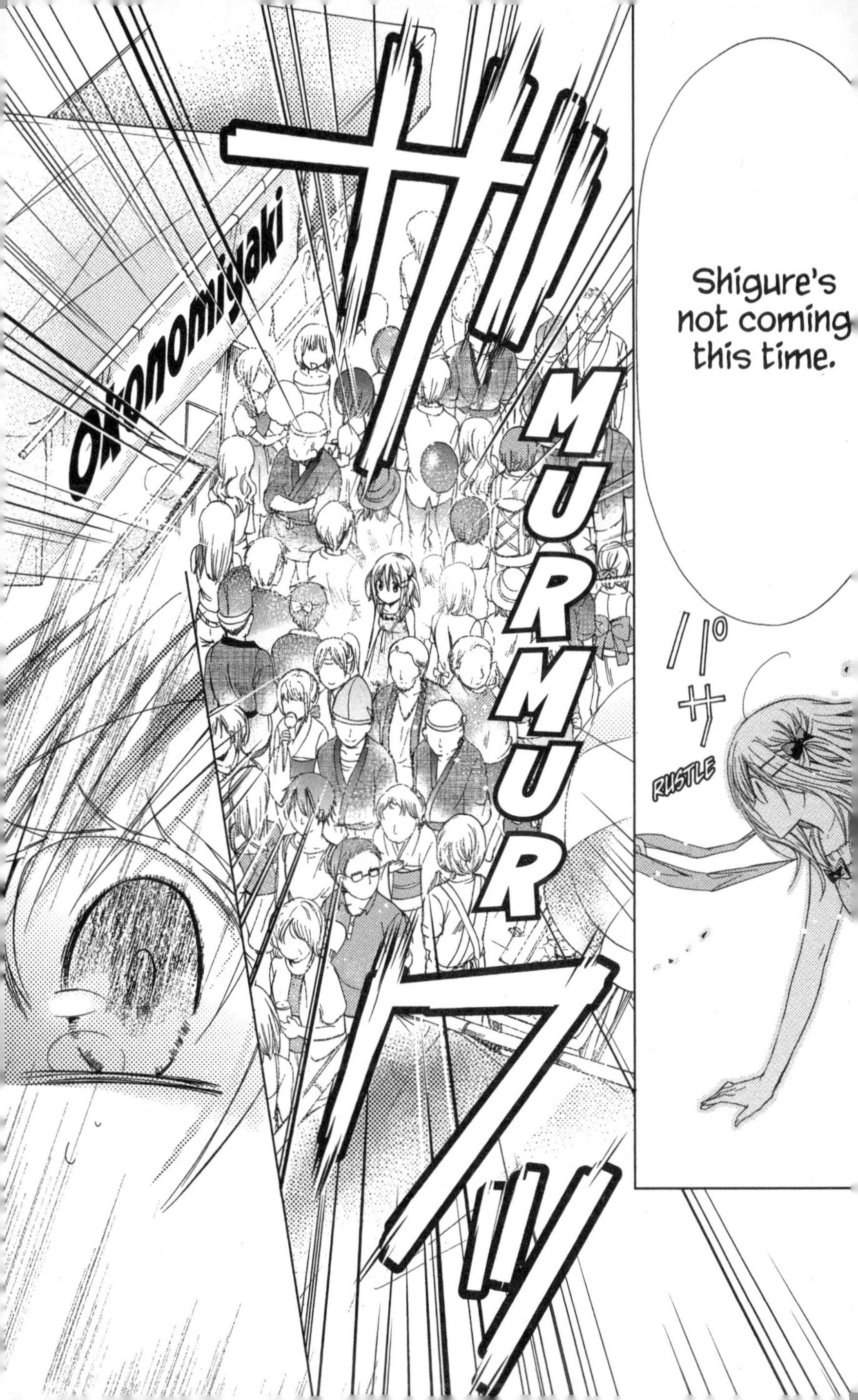
Shigure's not coming this time.
パサ
RUSTLE
Okonomiyaki
MURMUR

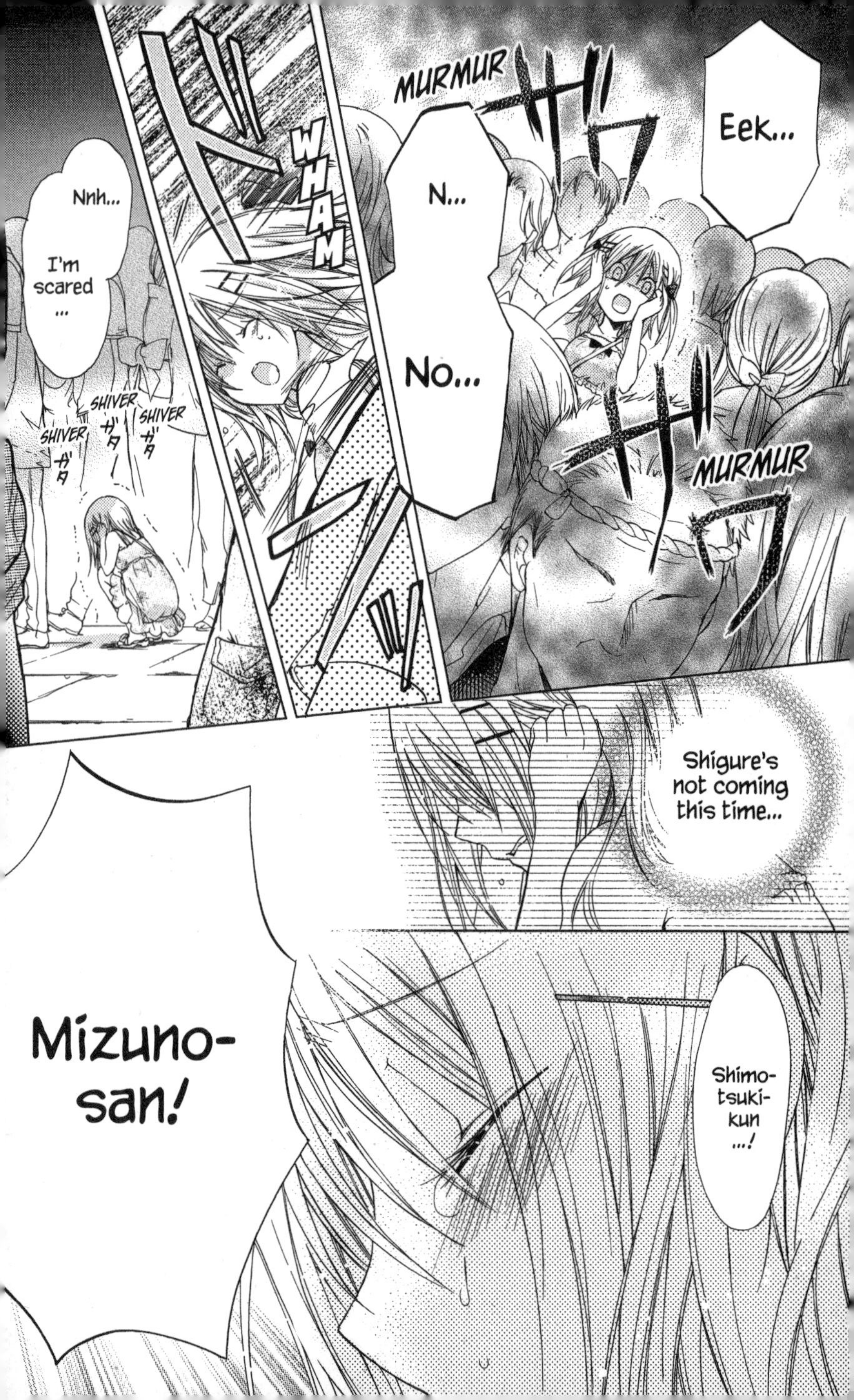
Eek...
MURMUR
N...
No...
MURMUR
WHAM
Nnh...
I'm scared ...
SHIVER
SHIVER
SHIVER
Shigure's not coming this time...
Shimo-tsuki-kun ...!
Mizuno-san!

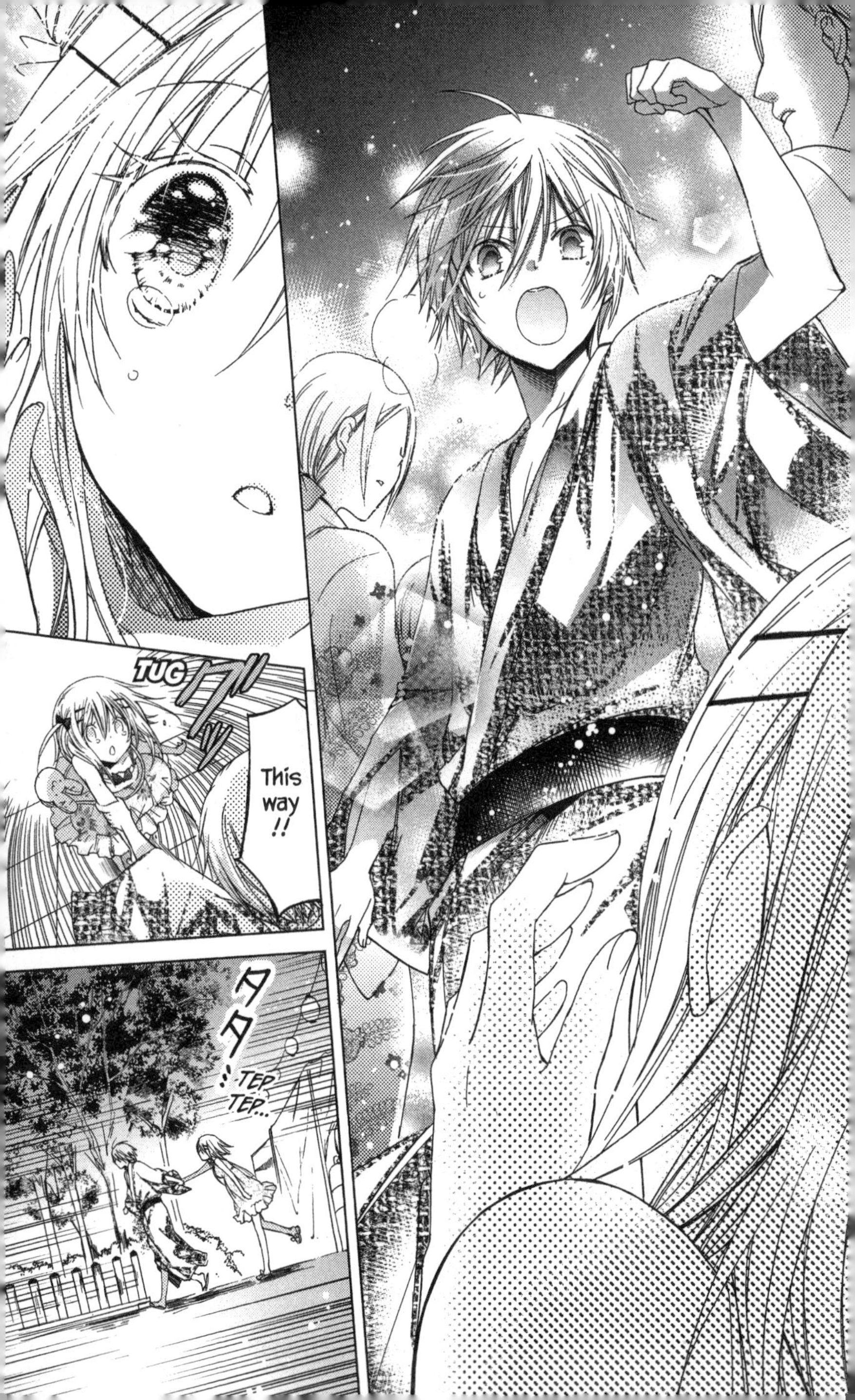
TUG
This way !!
TEP TEP...

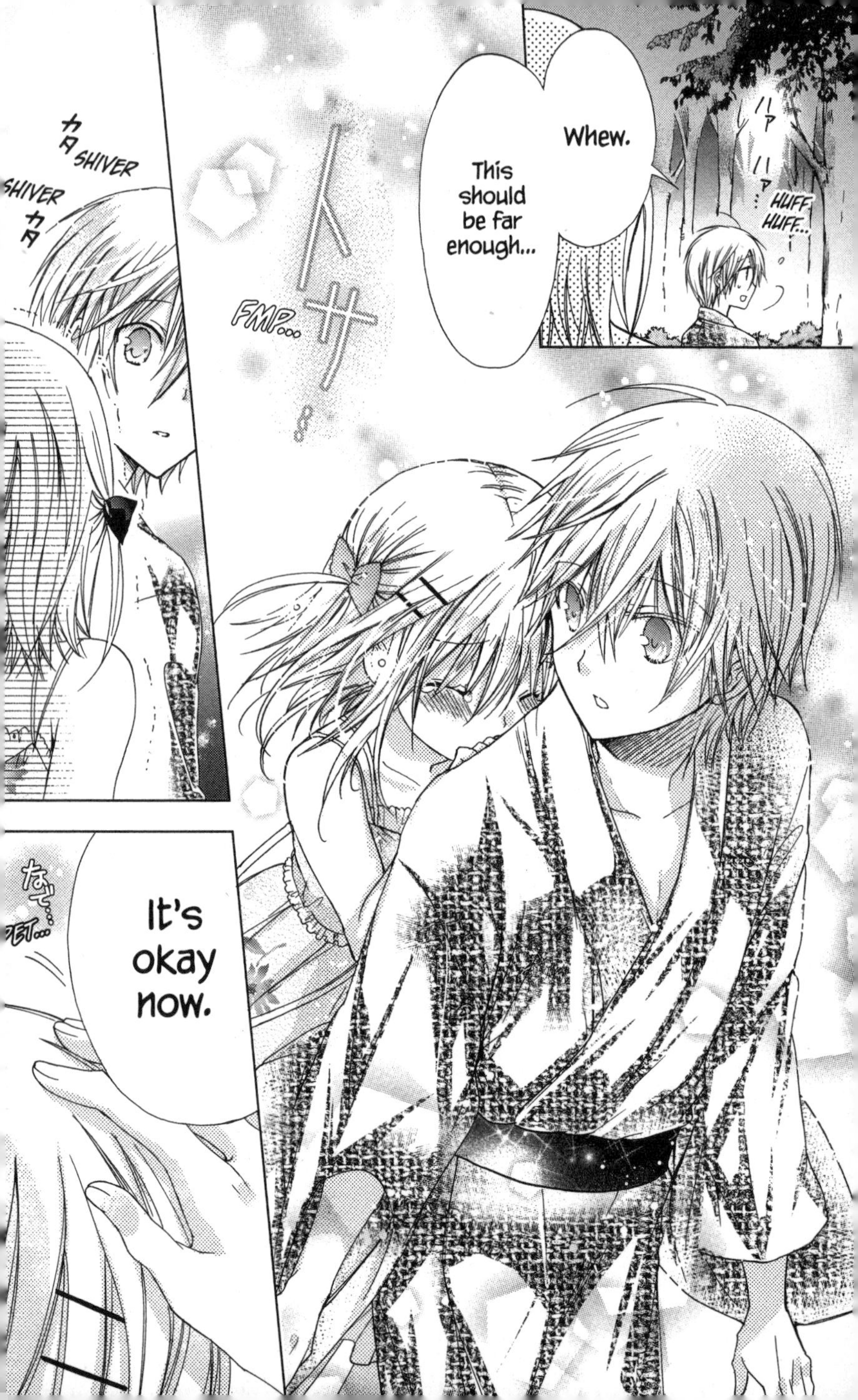

ハァ ハァ…
HUFF HUFF...
Whew.
This should be far enough...
FMP...
カタ SHIVER
SHIVER カタ
It's okay now.
なで…
PET...

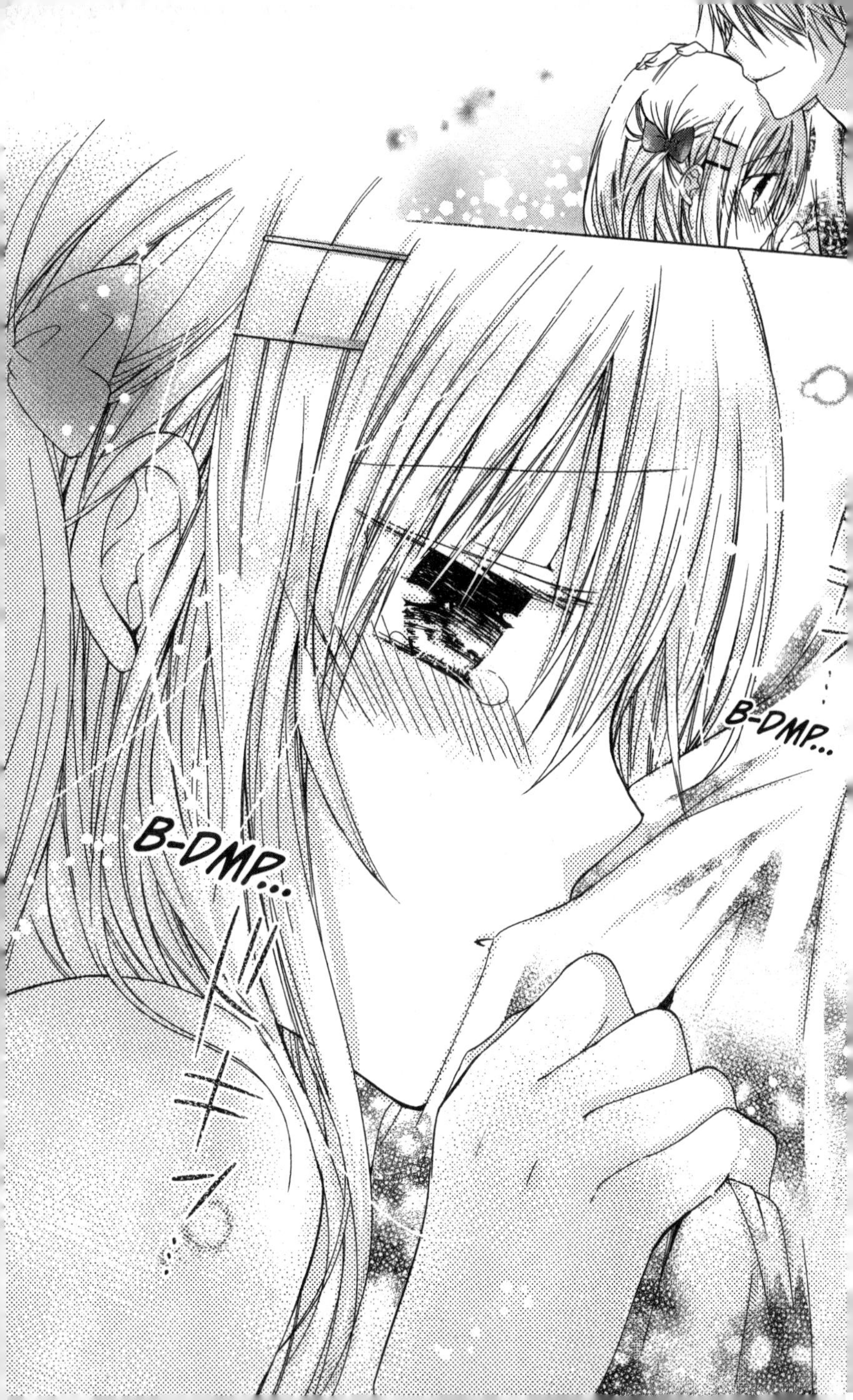
B-DMP...
B-DMP...

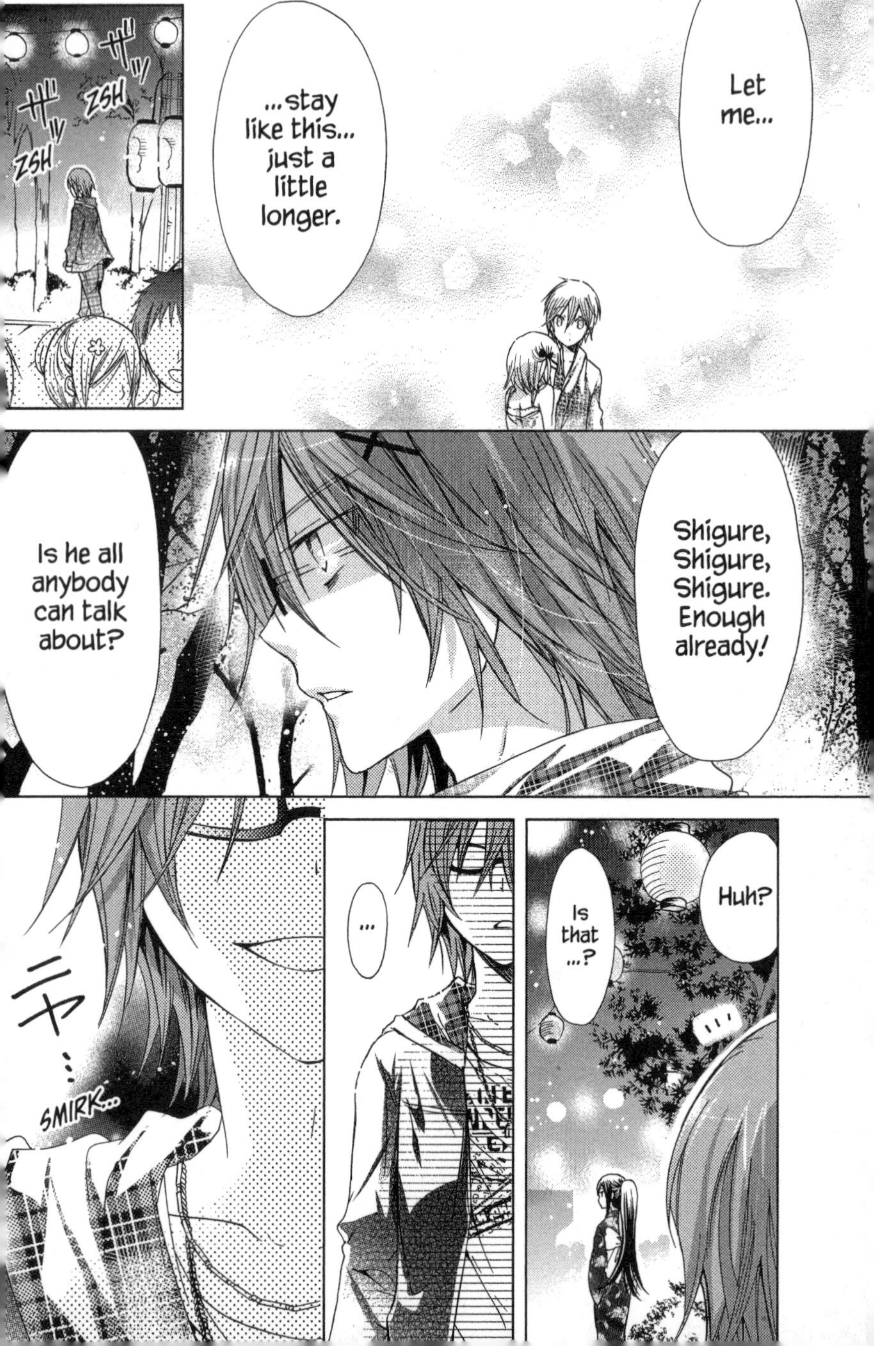

Let me...
...stay like this... just a little longer.
ZSH
ZSH
Shigure, Shigure, Shigure. Enough already!
Is he all anybody can talk about?
Huh?
Is that ...?
...
SMIRK...

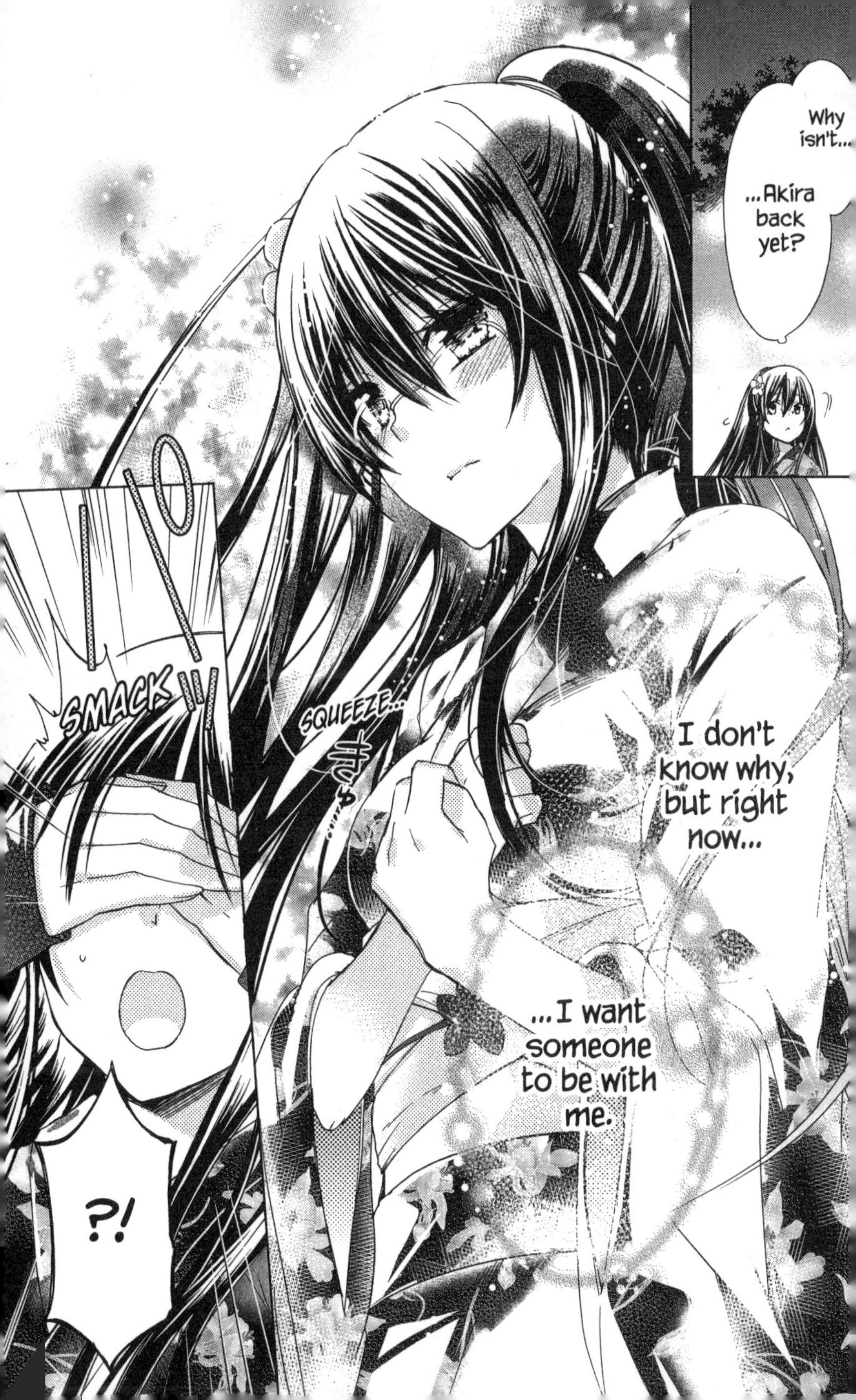
Why isn't...
...Akira back yet?
I don't know why, but right now...
...I want someone to be with me.
SQUEEZE...
SMACK!!!
?!

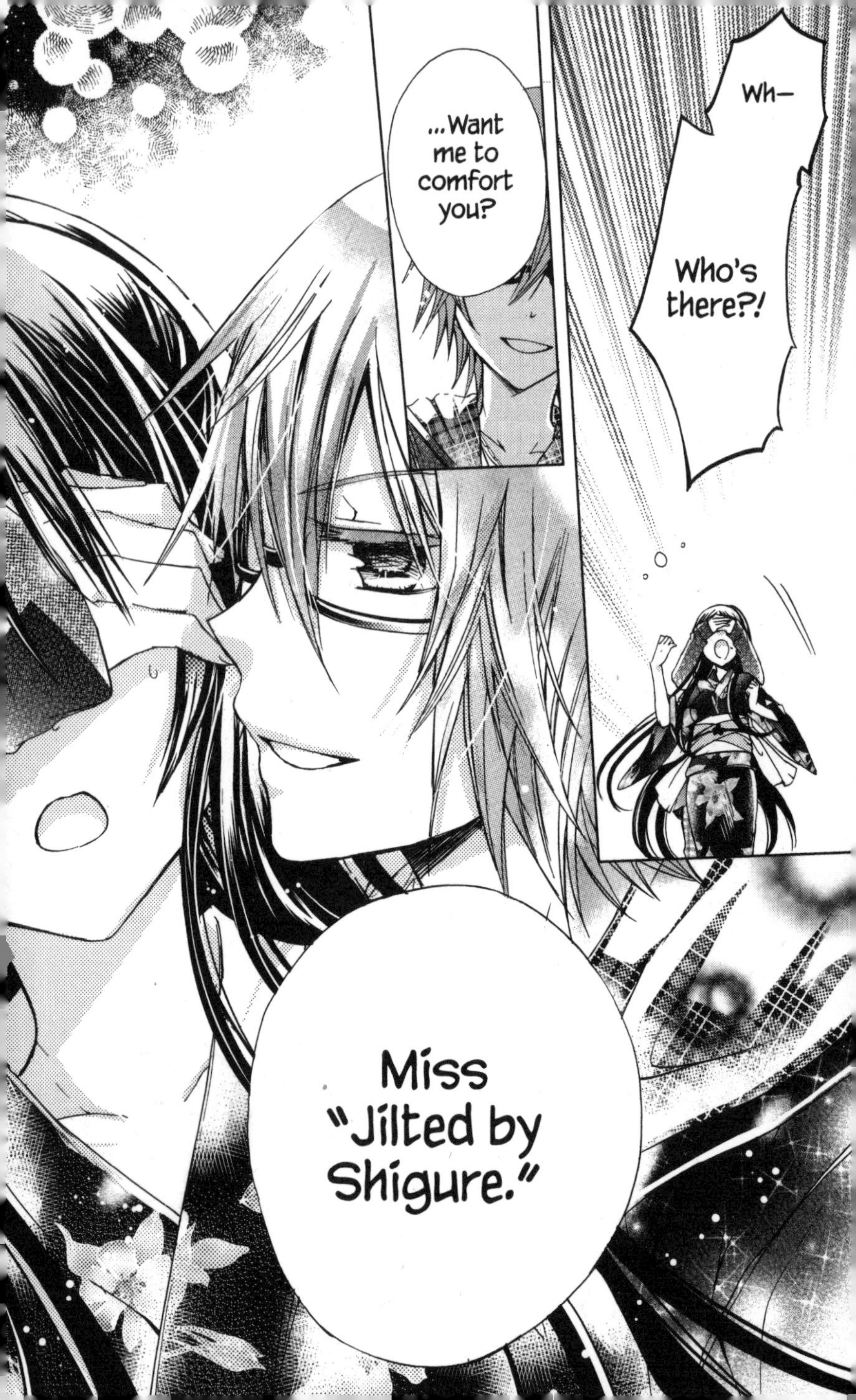
Wh— Who's there?!
...Want me to comfort you?
Miss "Jilted by Shigure."

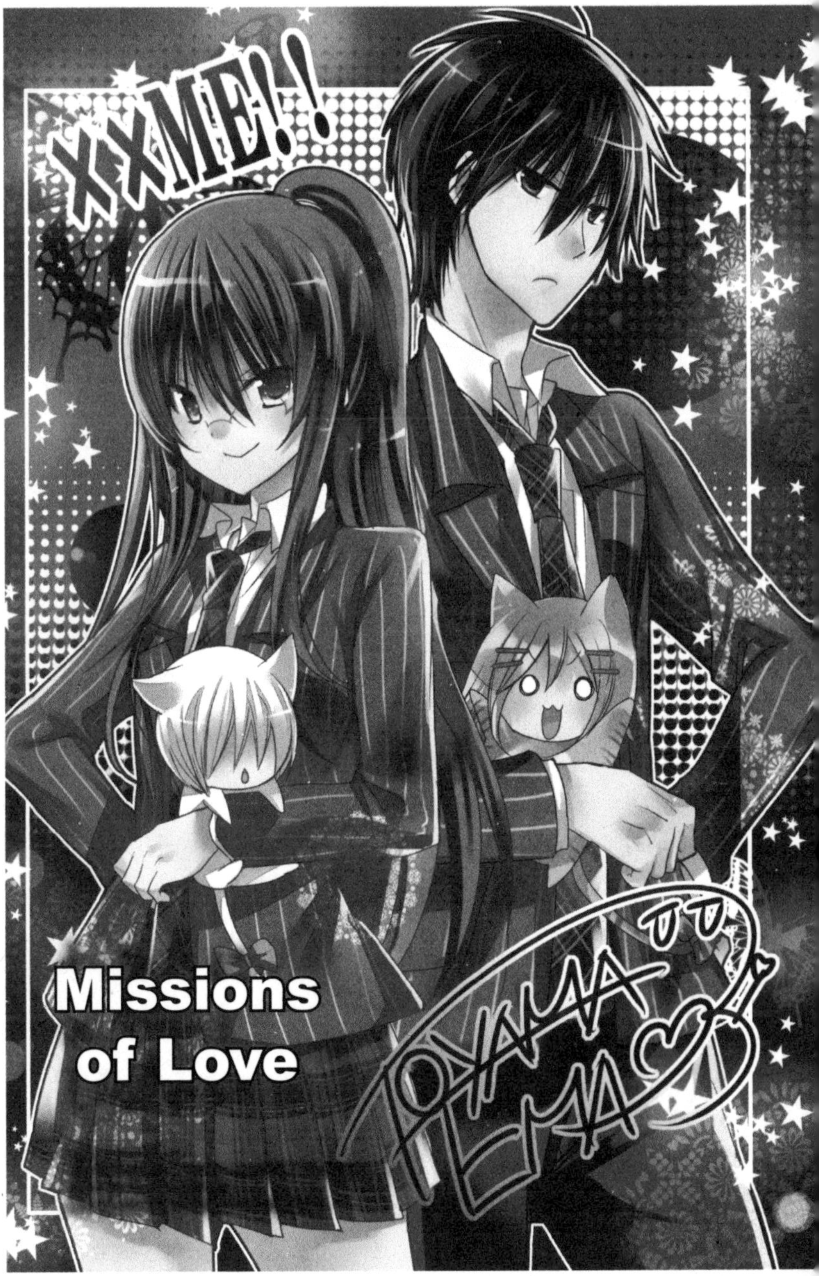
XXME!!
Missions of Love
TOYAMA EMA

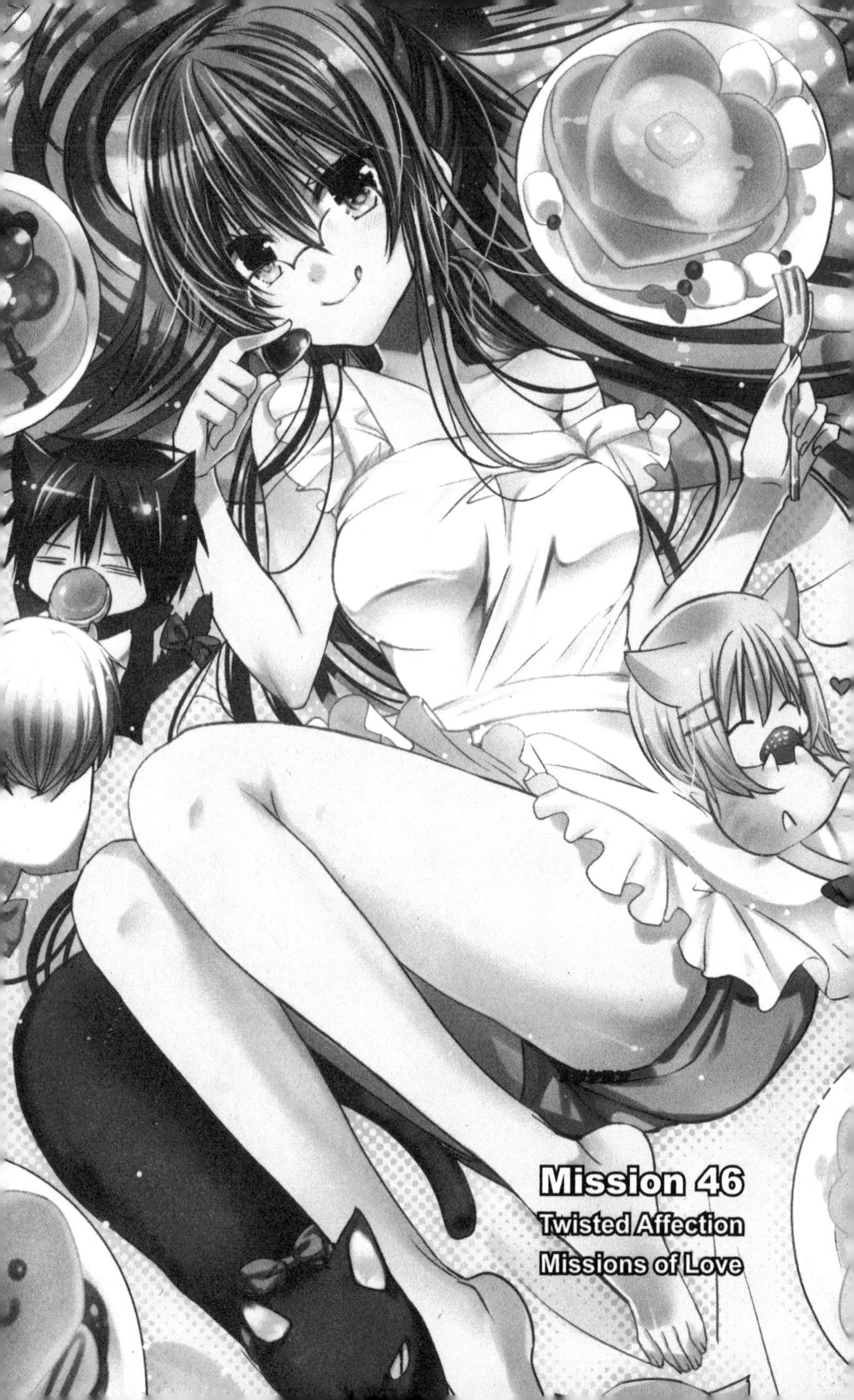
Mission 46
Twisted Affection
Missions of Love

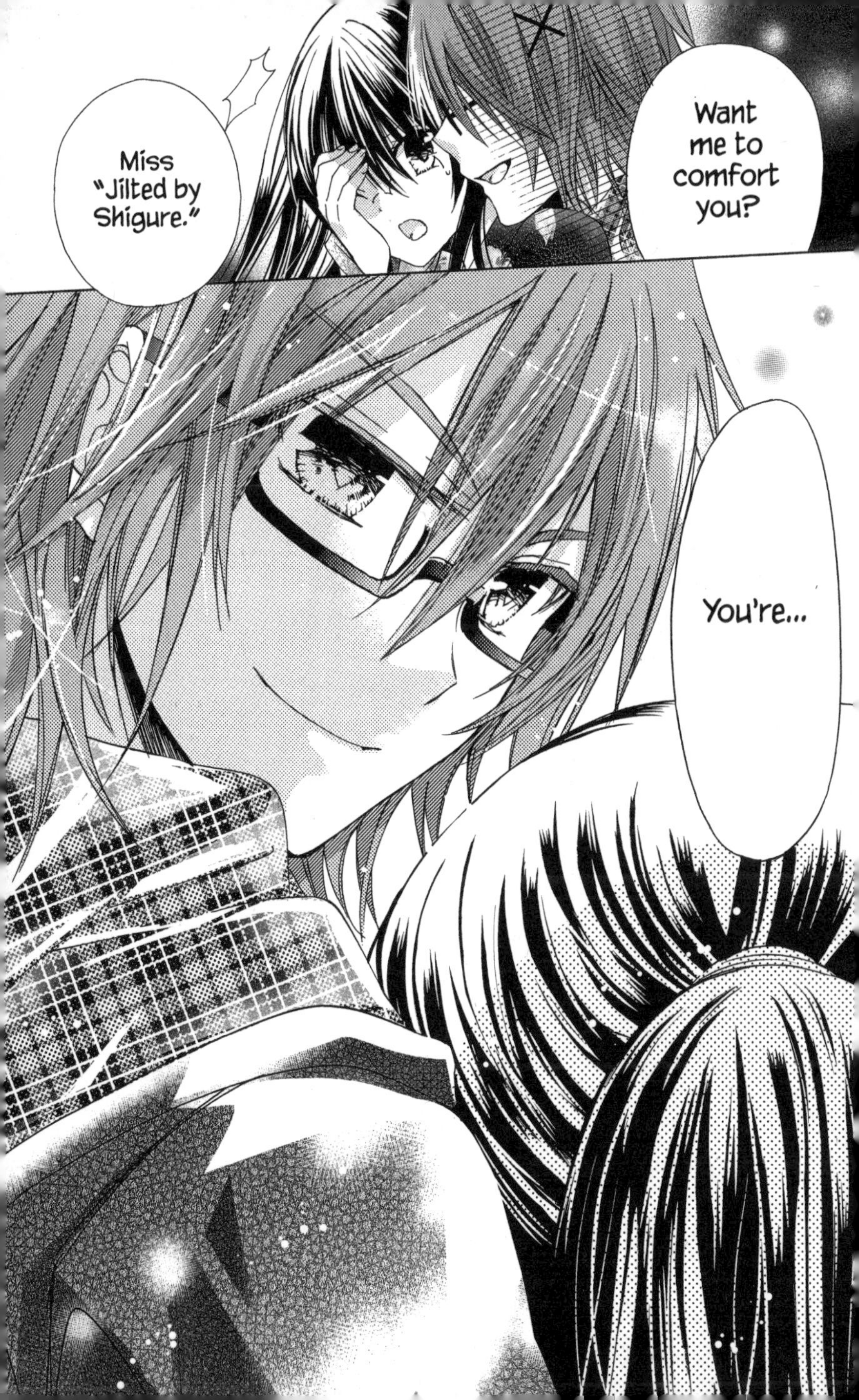
Want me to comfort you?
Miss "Jilted by Shigure."
You're...

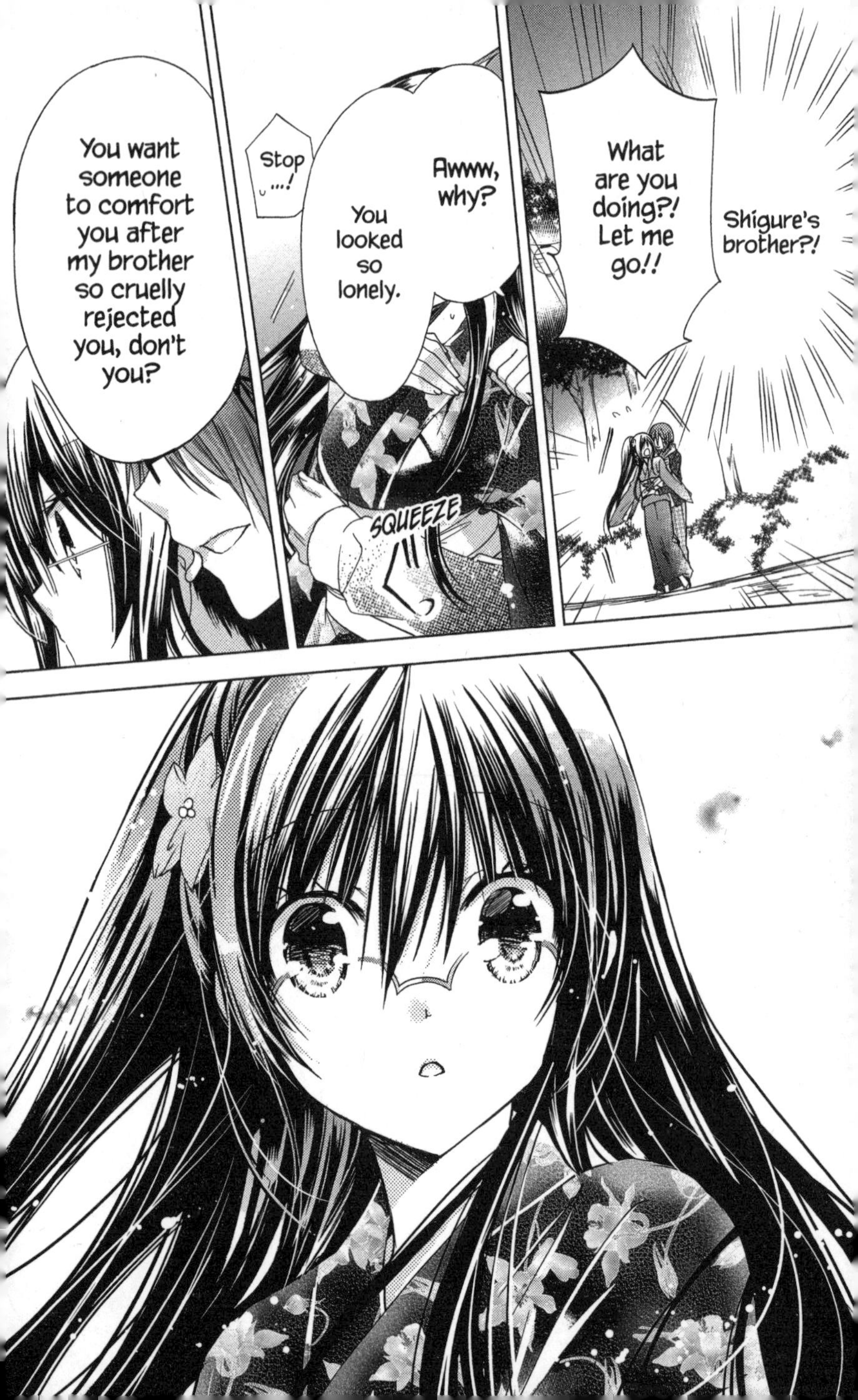
Shigure's brother?!
What are you doing?! Let me go!!
Stop...!
Awww, why?
You looked so lonely.
SQUEEZE
You want someone to comfort you after my brother so cruelly rejected you, don't you?

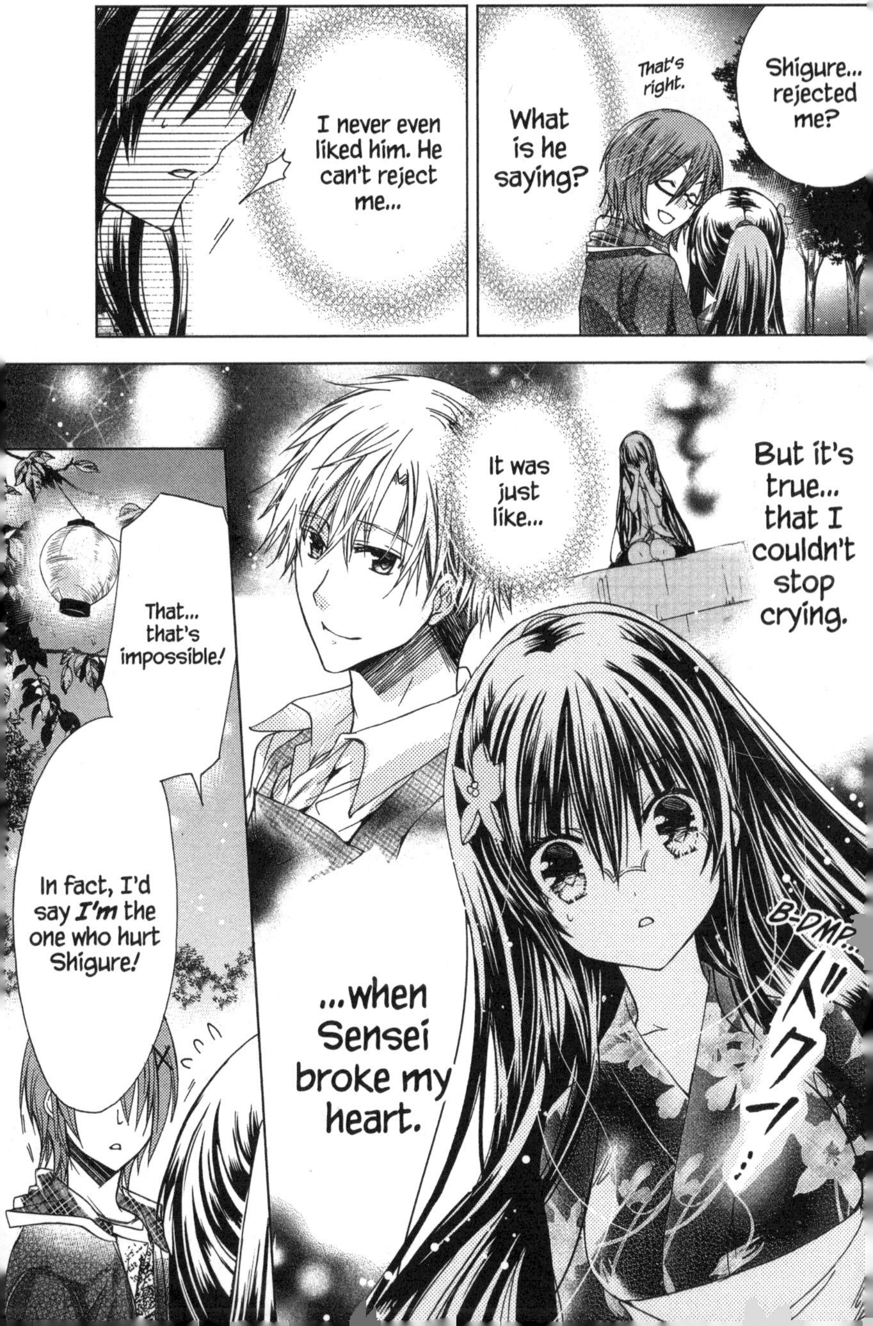
Shigure... rejected me?
That's right.
What is he saying?
I never even liked him. He can't reject me...
But it's true... that I couldn't stop crying.
It was just like...
B-DMP...
...when Sensei broke my heart.
That... that's impossible!
In fact, I'd say *I'm* the one who hurt Shigure!

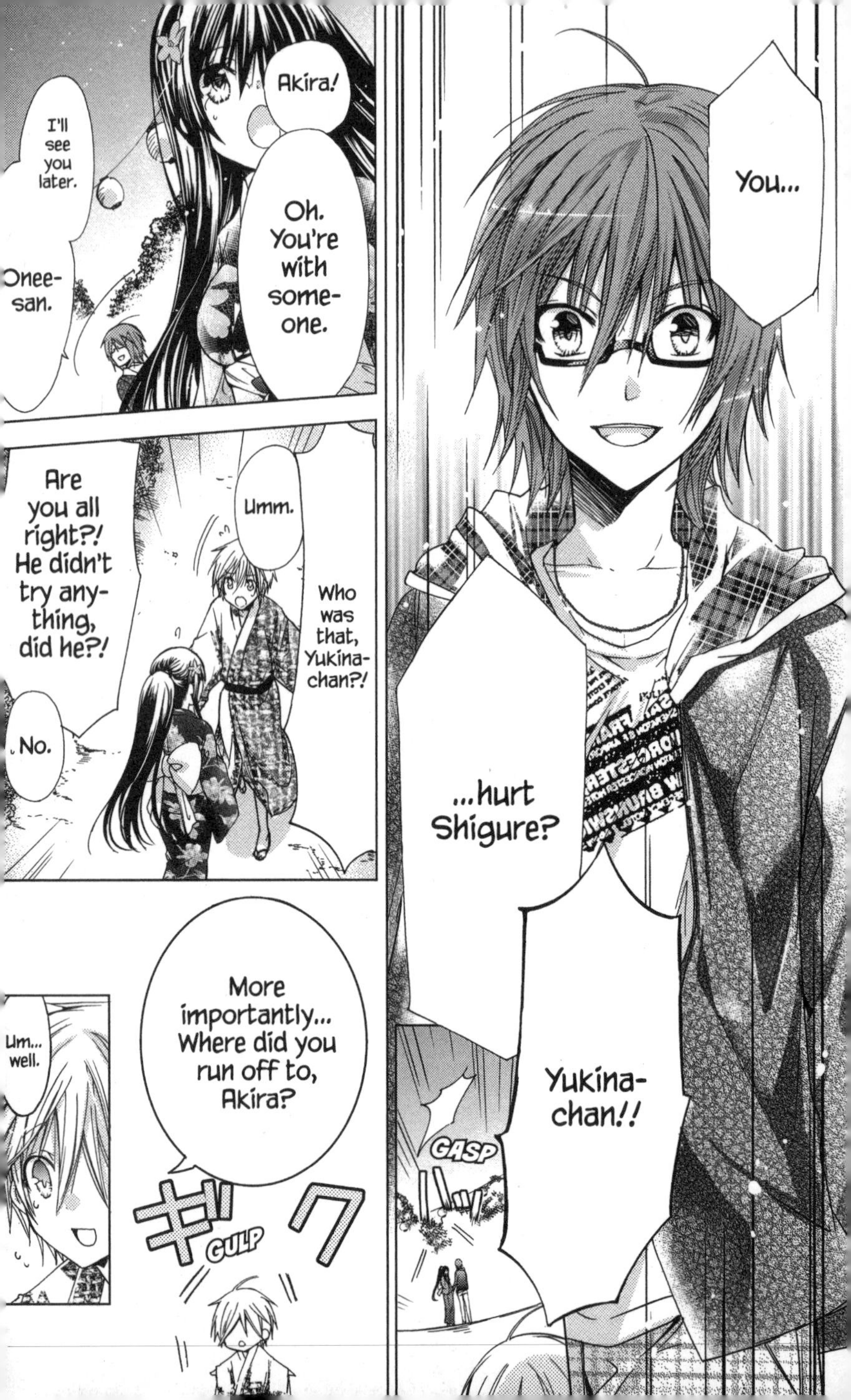
You...
...hurt Shigure?
Yukina-chan!!
GASP
Akira!
Oh. You're with someone.
I'll see you later.
Onee-san.
Umm.
Who was that, Yukina-chan?!
Are you all right?! He didn't try anything, did he?!
No.
More importantly... Where did you run off to, Akira?
GULP
Um... well.

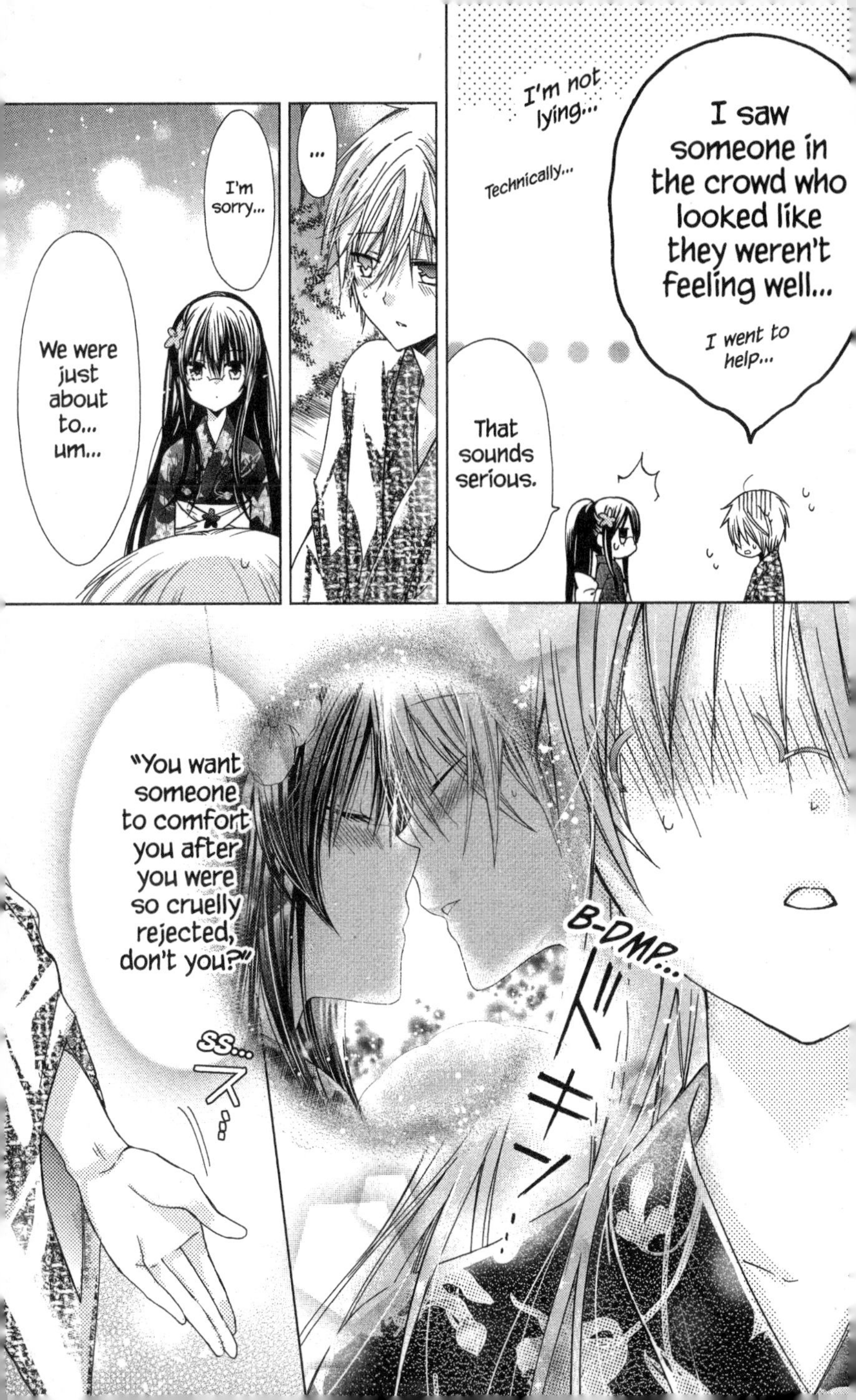
I saw someone in the crowd who looked like they weren't feeling well...
I went to help...
I'm not lying...
Technically...
That sounds serious.
...
I'm sorry...
We were just about to... um...
B-DMP...
"You want someone to comfort you after you were so cruelly rejected, don't you?"
SS...

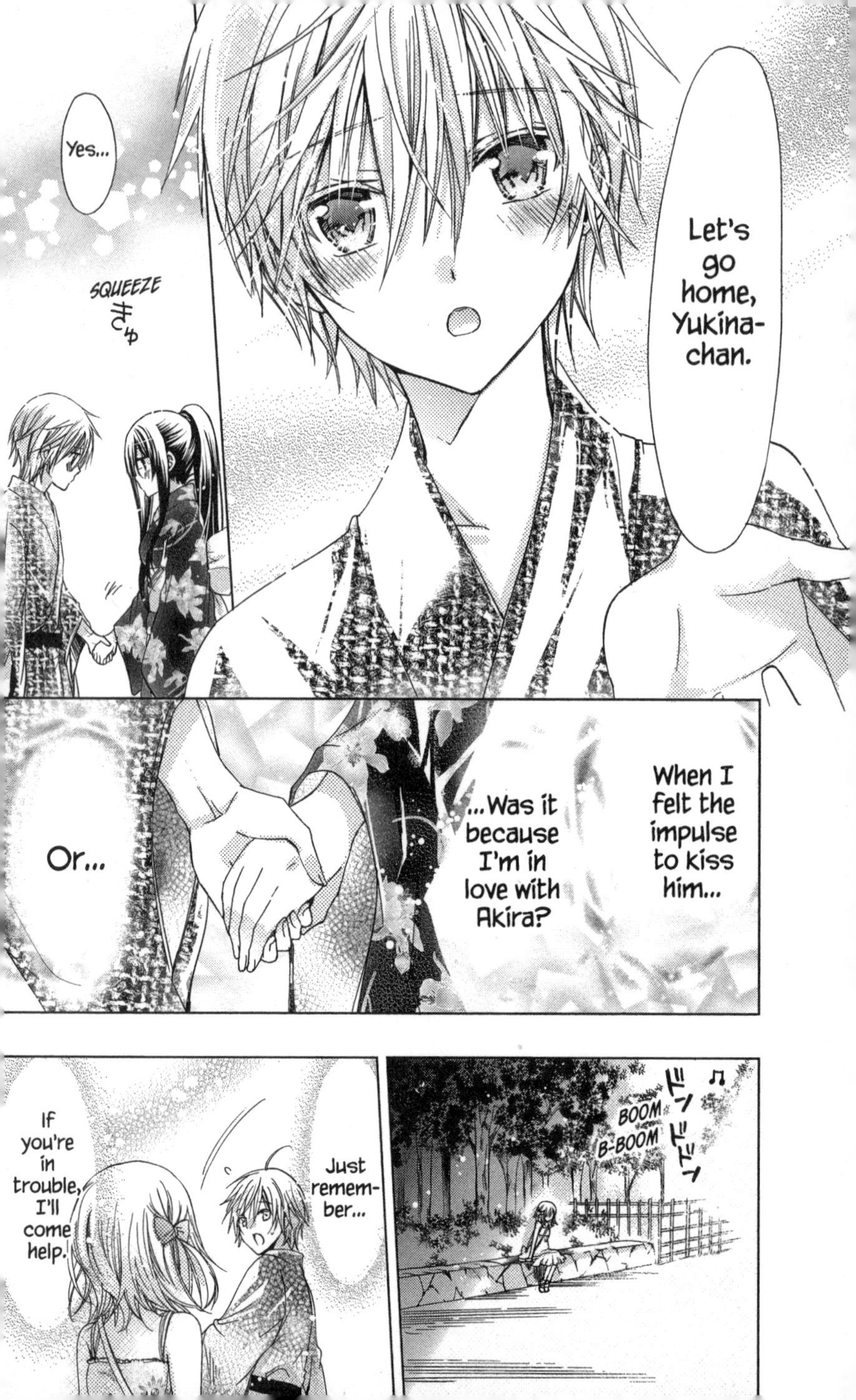
Let's go home, Yukina-chan.
Yes...
SQUEEZE
きゅ
When I felt the impulse to kiss him...
...Was it because I'm in love with Akira?
Or...
ドンドドンッ
BOOM B-BOOM
♫
Just remember...
If you're in trouble, I'll come help!

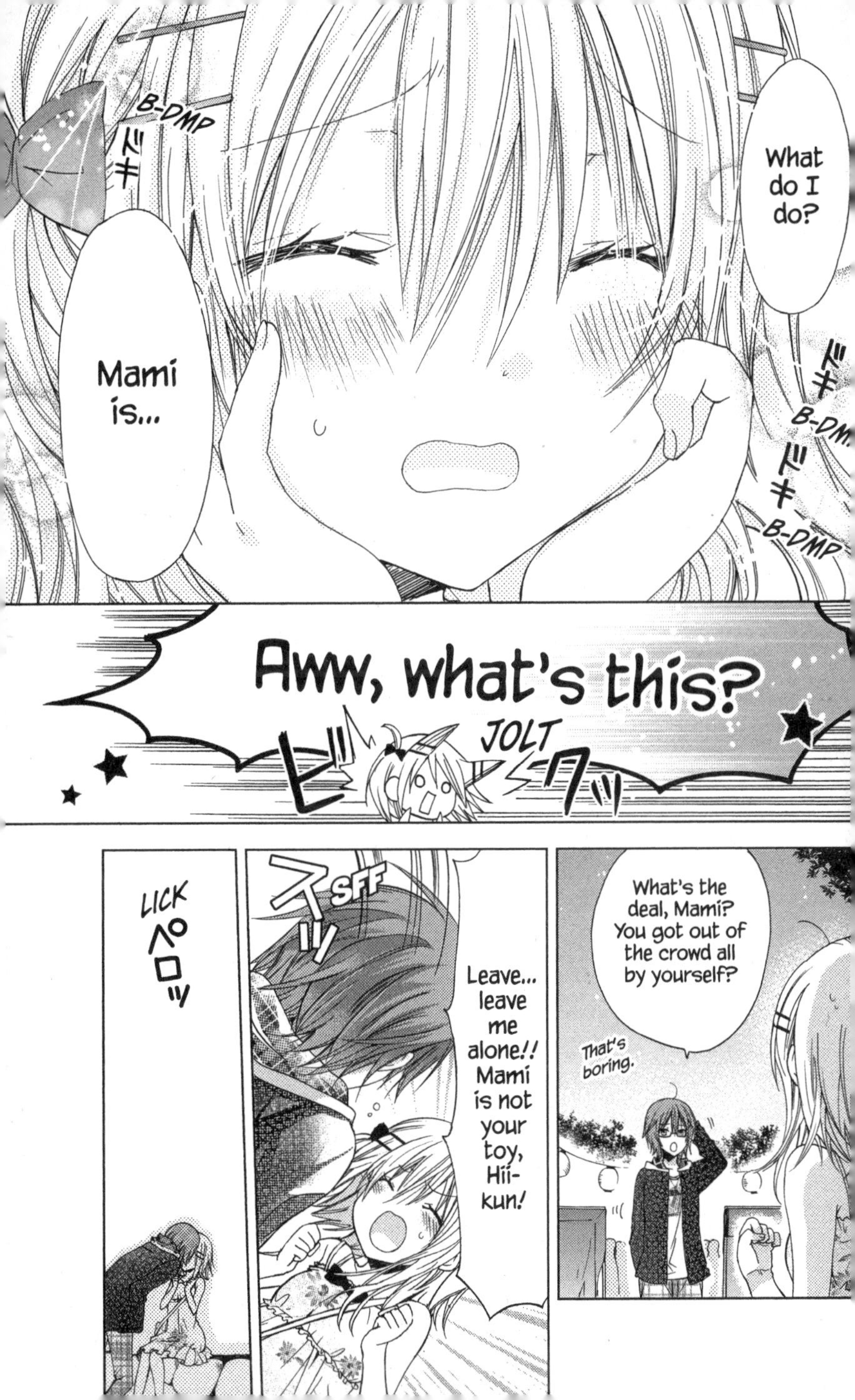
What do I do?
ドキ B-DMP
ドキ B-DMP
B-DMP ドキ
Mami is...
Aww, what's this?
JOLT ビクッ
What's the deal, Mami? You got out of the crowd all by yourself?
That's boring.
SFF スッ
Leave... leave me alone!! Mami is not your toy, Hii-kun!
LICK ペロッ

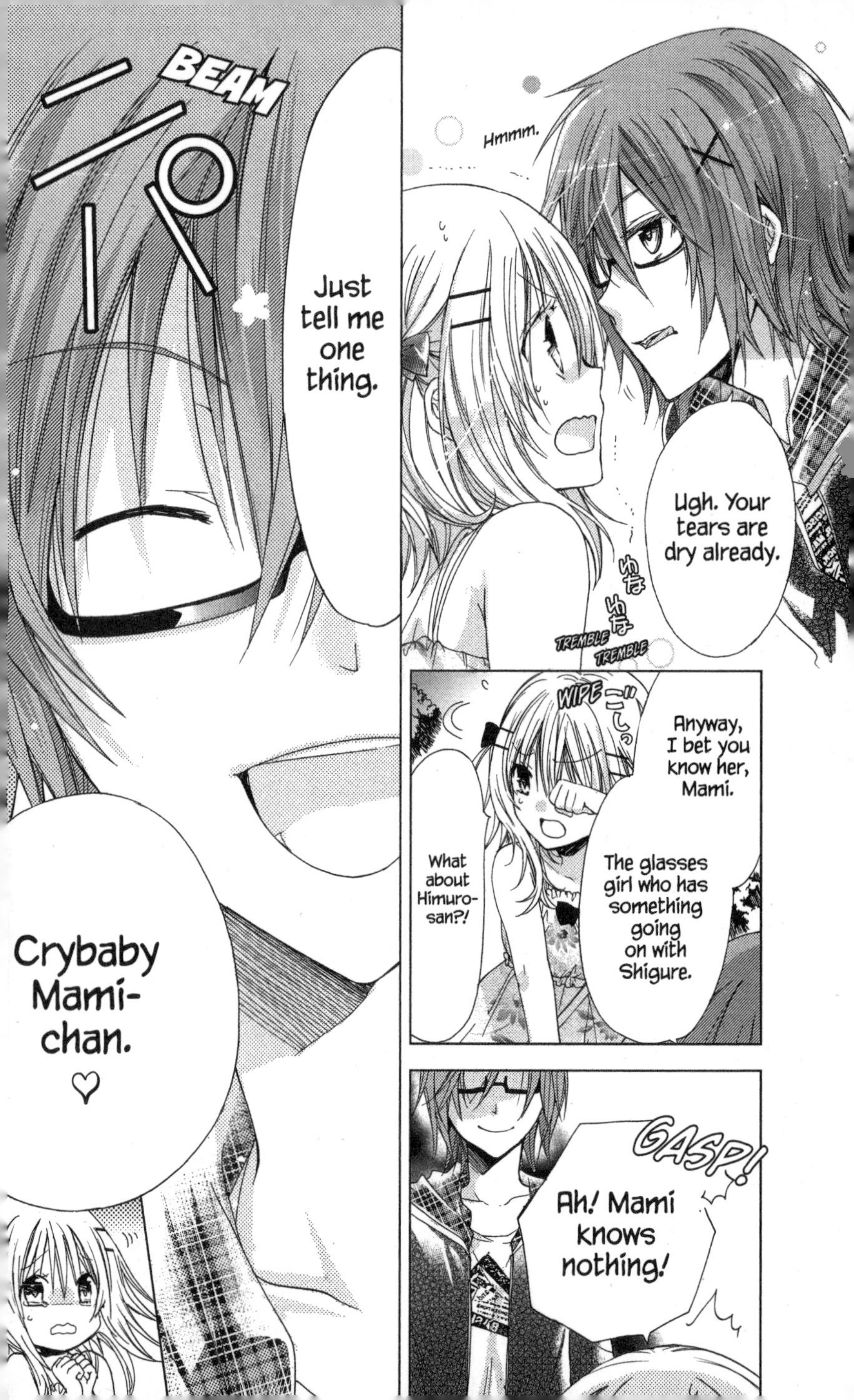
Hmmm.
Ugh. Your tears are dry already.
TREMBLE TREMBLE
WIPE
ごしっ
Anyway, I bet you know her, Mami.
The glasses girl who has something going on with Shigure.
What about Himuro-san?!
GASP!
Ah! Mami knows nothing!
BEAM
Just tell me one thing.
Crybaby Mami-chan. ♡

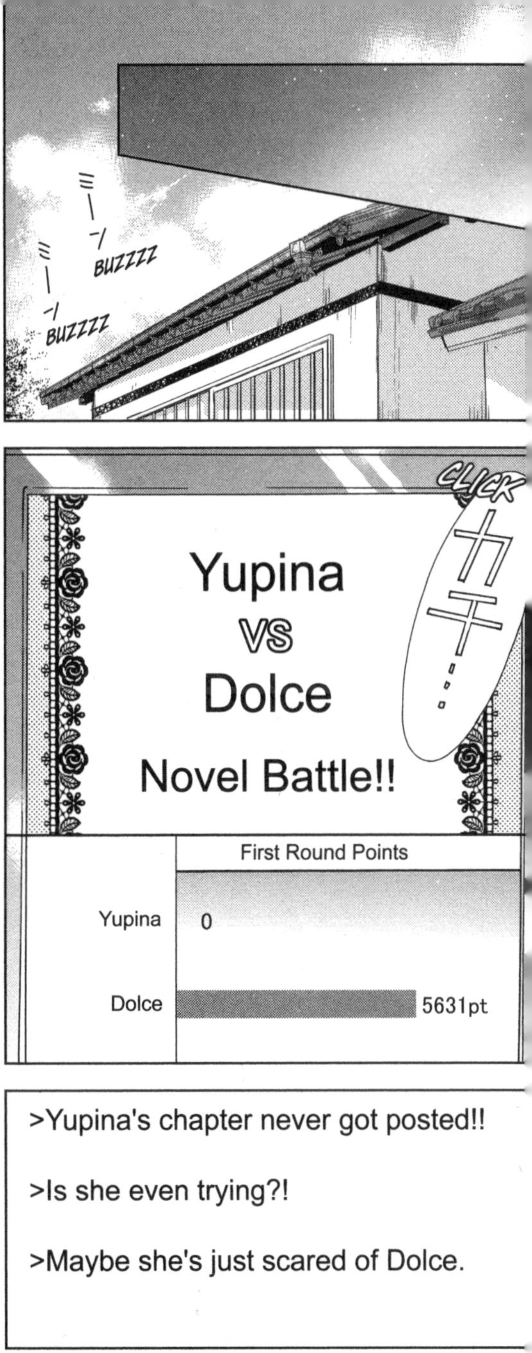
BUZZZZ
BUZZZZ
CLICK
カチ…
Yupina VS Dolce Novel Battle!!
First Round Points
Yupina 0
Dolce 5631pt
>Yupina's chapter never got posted!!
>Is she even trying?!
>Maybe she's just scared of Dolce.

Pet Pet ♡ Snow Yukina

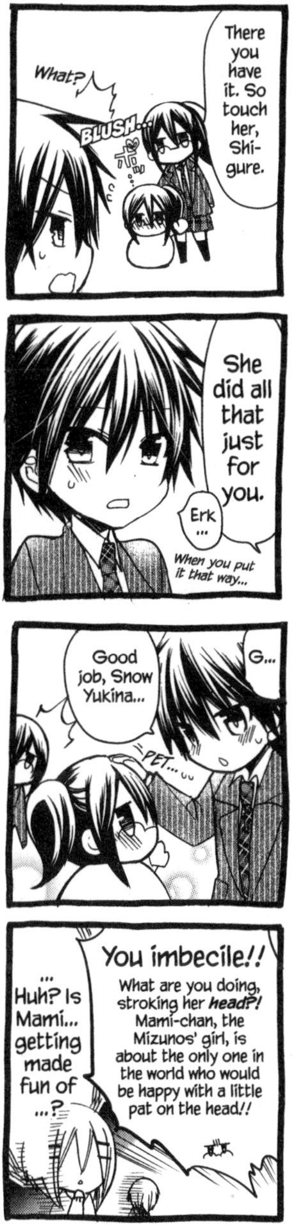
There you have it. So touch her, Shigure.
What?
BLUSH...
She did all that just for you.
Erk...
When you put it that way...
G...
Good job, Snow Yukina...
PET...
You imbecile!!
What are you doing, stroking her head?! Mami-chan, the Mizunos' girl, is about the only one in the world who would be happy with a little pat on the head!!
... Huh? Is Mami... getting made fun of ...?

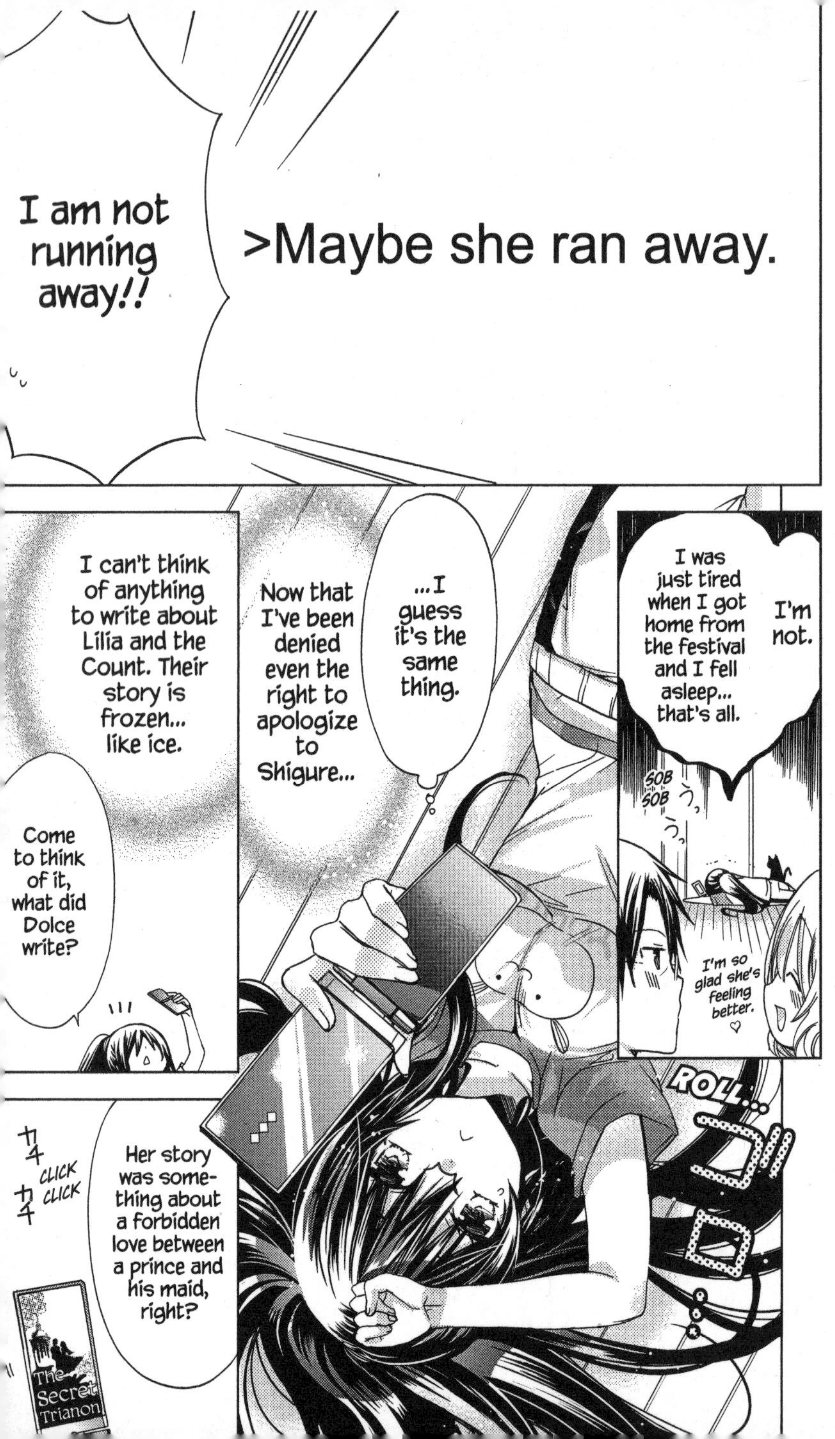

>Maybe she ran away.
I am not running away!!
I'm not.
I was just tired when I got home from the festival and I fell asleep... that's all.
SOB SOB
I'm so glad she's feeling better. ♡
...I guess it's the same thing.
Now that I've been denied even the right to apologize to Shigure...
I can't think of anything to write about Lilia and the Count. Their story is frozen... like ice.
Come to think of it, what did Dolce write?
ROLL...
CLICK CLICK
Her story was something about a forbidden love between a prince and his maid, right?
The Secret Trianon

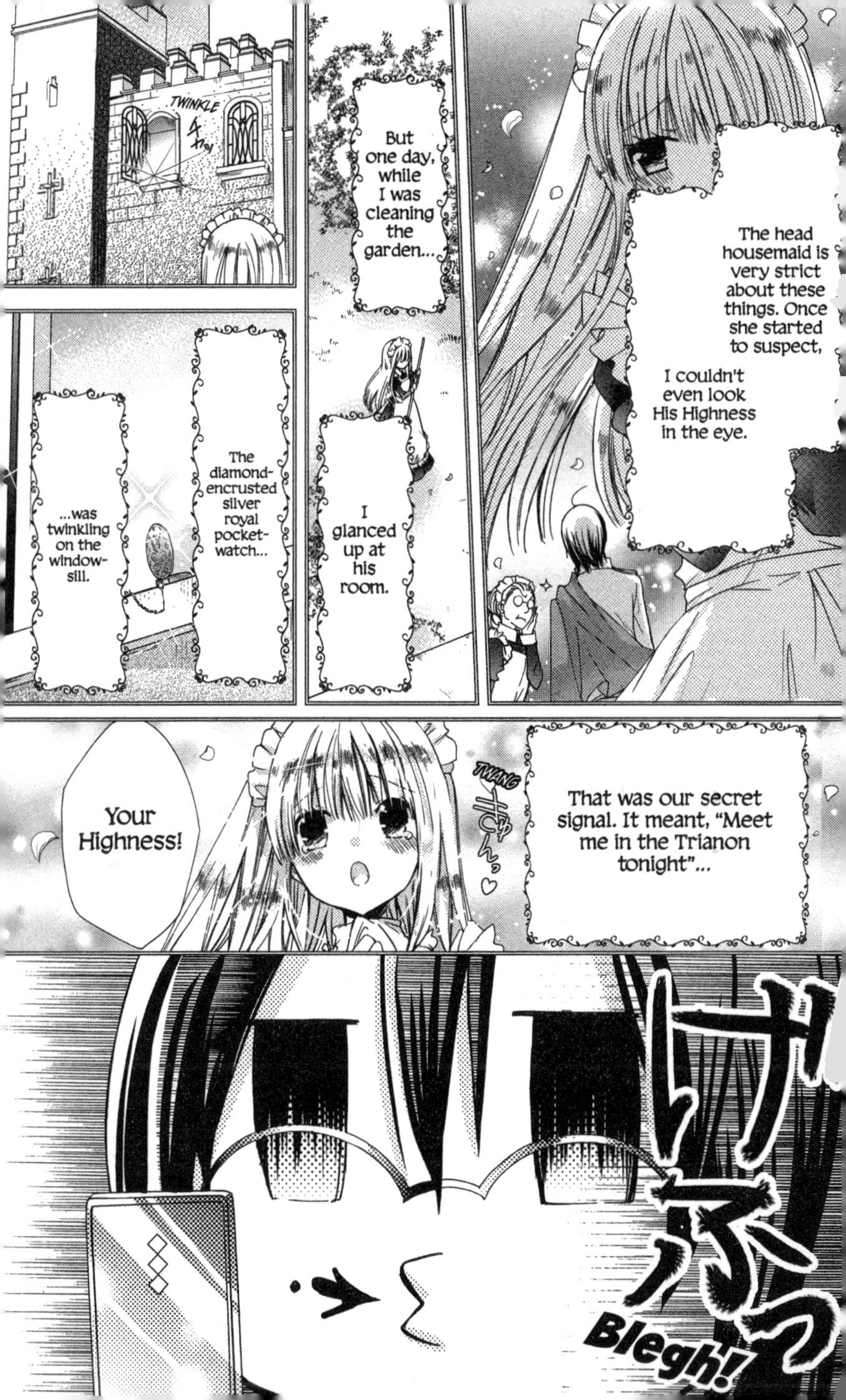
The head housemaid is very strict about these things. Once she started to suspect,
I couldn't even look His Highness in the eye.
But one day, while I was cleaning the garden...
I glanced up at his room.
TWINKLE
The diamond-encrusted silver royal pocket-watch...
...was twinkling on the window-sill.
That was our secret signal. It meant, “Meet me in the Trianon tonight”...
TWANG
Your Highness!
Blegh!

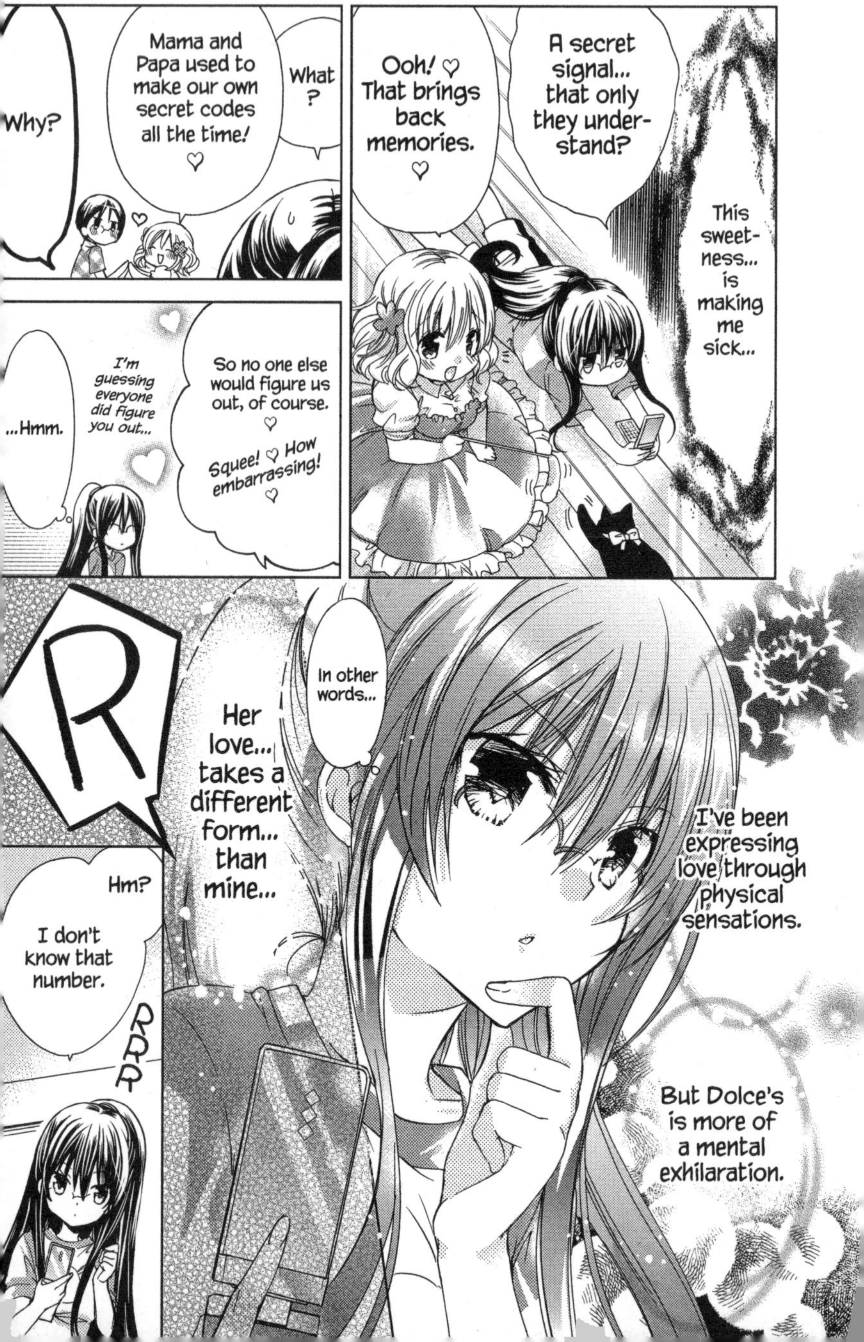
A secret signal... that only they under-stand?
Ooh! ♡ That brings back memories. ♡
This sweet-ness... is making me sick...
What?
Mama and Papa used to make our own secret codes all the time! ♡
Why?
So no one else would figure us out, of course. ♡
Squee! ♡ How embarrassing! ♡
I'm guessing everyone did figure you out...
...Hmm.
I've been expressing love through physical sensations.
But Dolce's is more of a mental exhilaration.
In other words...
Her love... takes a different form... than mine...
R
Hm?
I don't know that number.
RRR

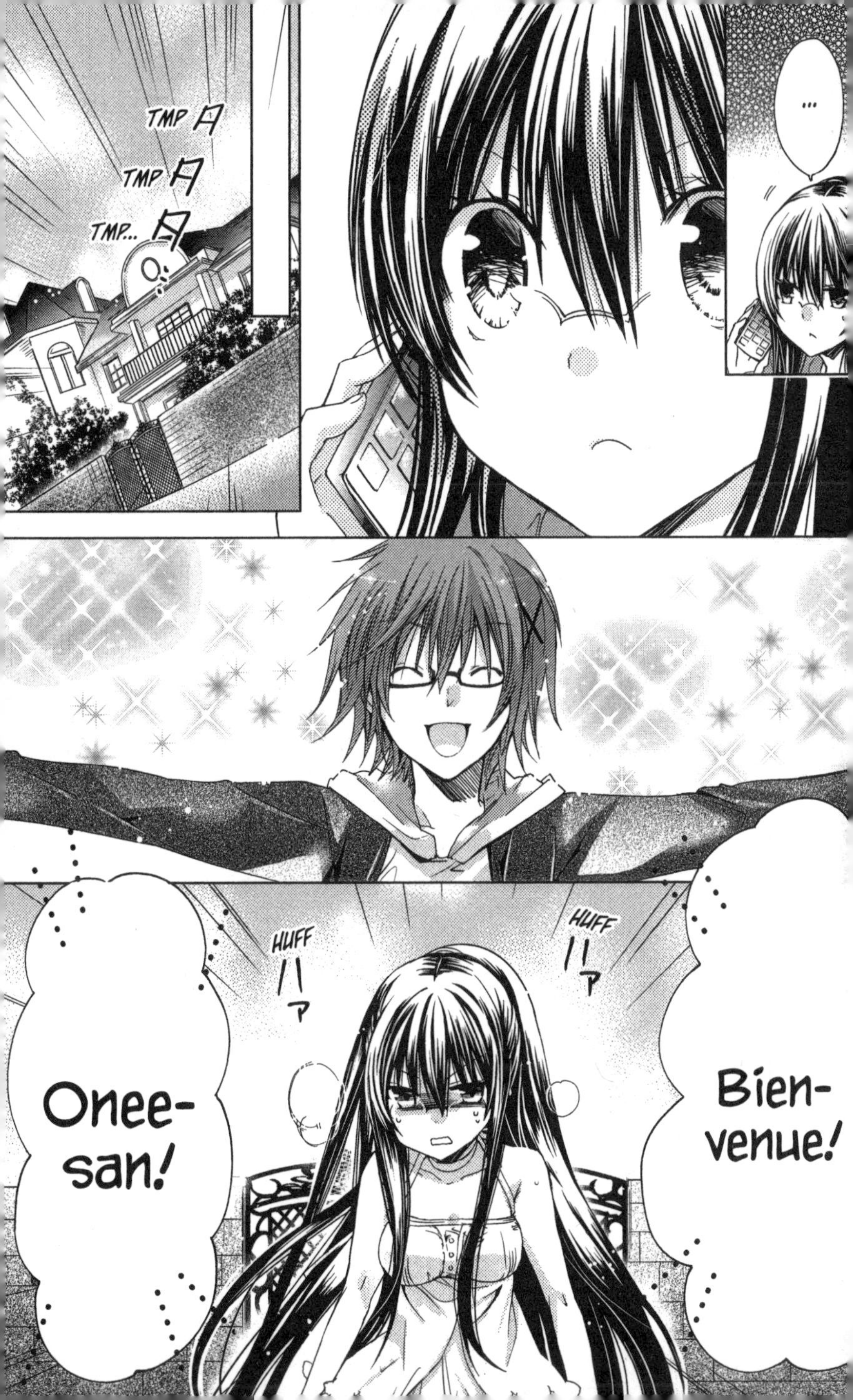
...
TMP
TMP
TMP...
Bien-venue!
HUFF ハア
HUFF ハア
Onee-san!

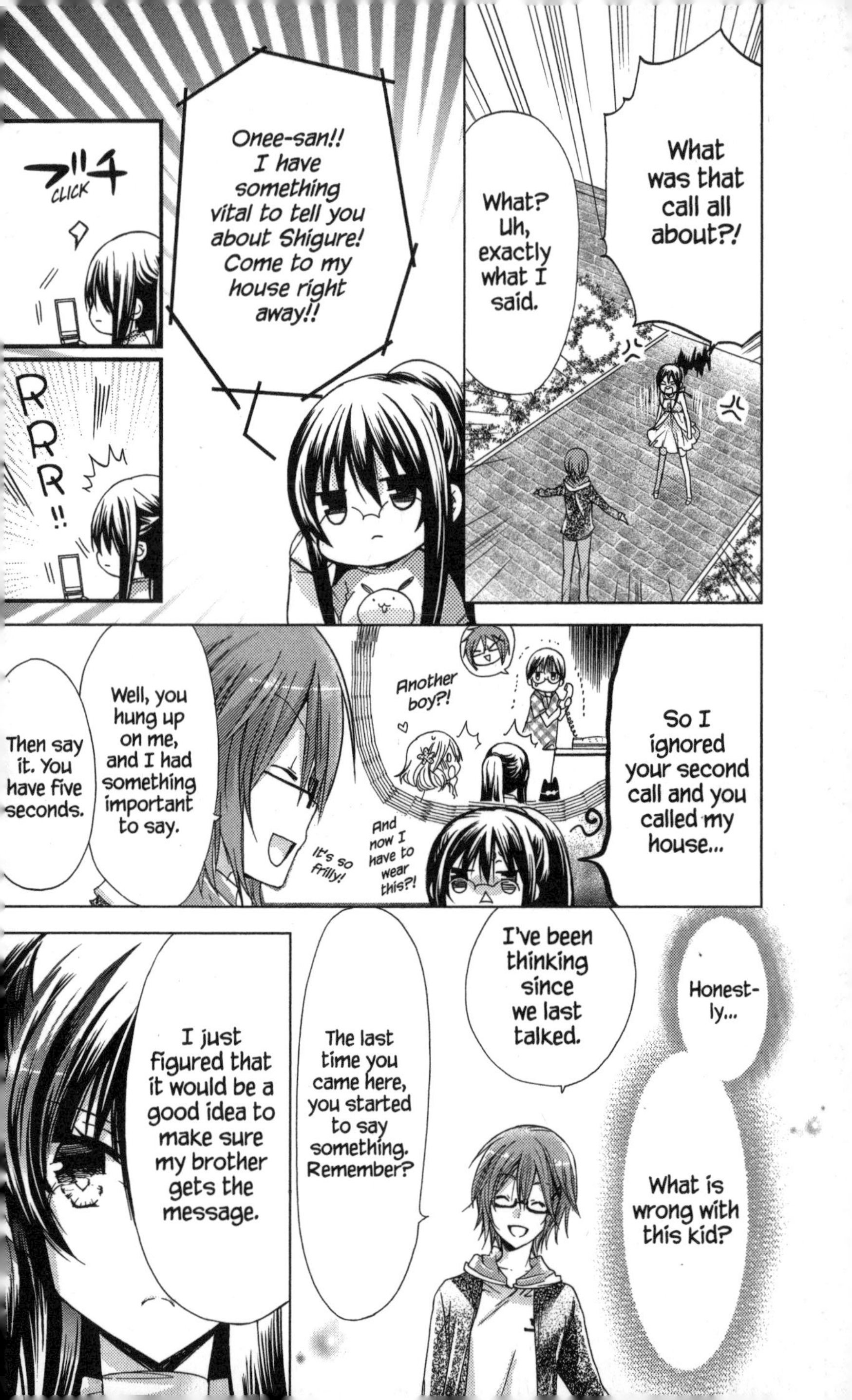
What was that call all about?!
What? Uh, exactly what I said.
Onee-san!! I have something vital to tell you about Shigure! Come to my house right away!!
CLICK
RRR!!
So I ignored your second call and you called my house...
Another boy?!
And now I have to wear this?!
It's so frilly!
Well, you hung up on me, and I had something important to say.
Then say it. You have five seconds.
Honestly...
What is wrong with this kid?
I've been thinking since we last talked.
The last time you came here, you started to say something. Remember?
I just figured that it would be a good idea to make sure my brother gets the message.

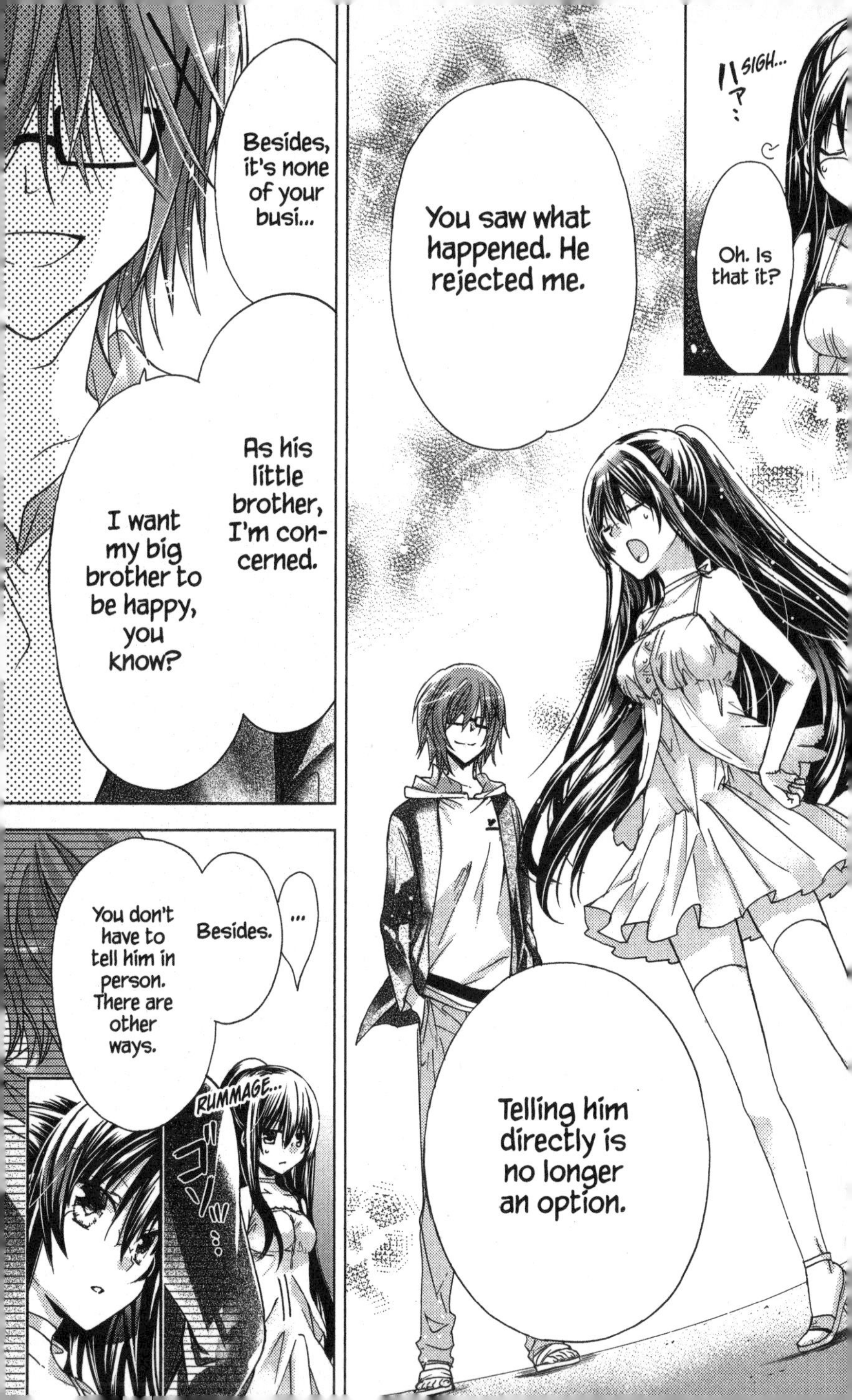
SIGH...
Oh. Is that it?
You saw what happened. He rejected me.
Telling him directly is no longer an option.
Besides, it's none of your busi...
As his little brother, I'm concerned.
I want my big brother to be happy, you know?
...
Besides.
You don't have to tell him in person. There are other ways.
RUMMAGE...

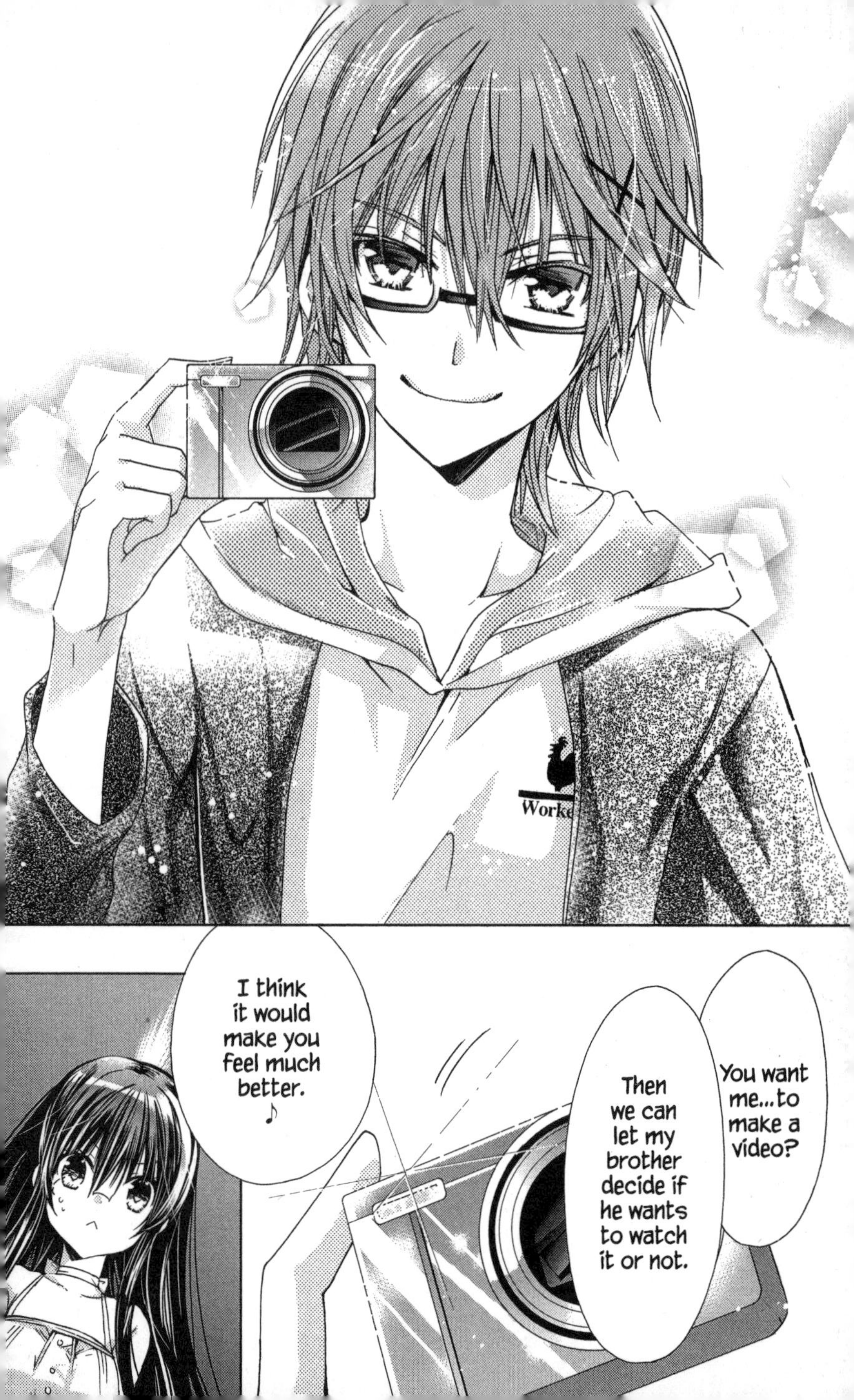
You want me...to make a video?
Then we can let my brother decide if he wants to watch it or not.
I think it would make you feel much better. ♪

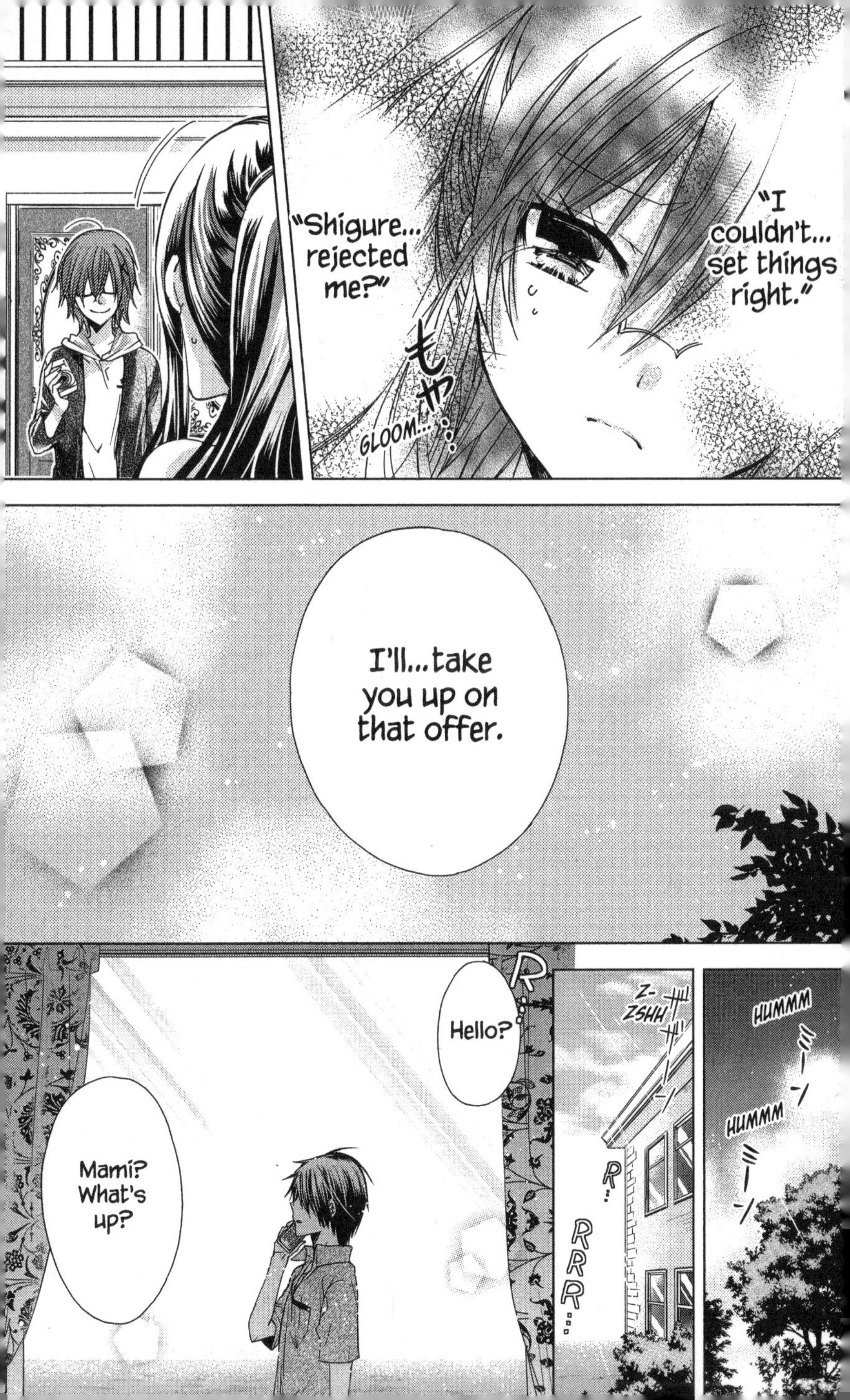
"I couldn't... set things right."
"Shigure... rejected me?"
もや
GLOOM...
I'll...take you up on that offer.
HUMMM
HUMMM
Z-ZSHH
R...
RRR...
R
Hello?
Mami? What's up?

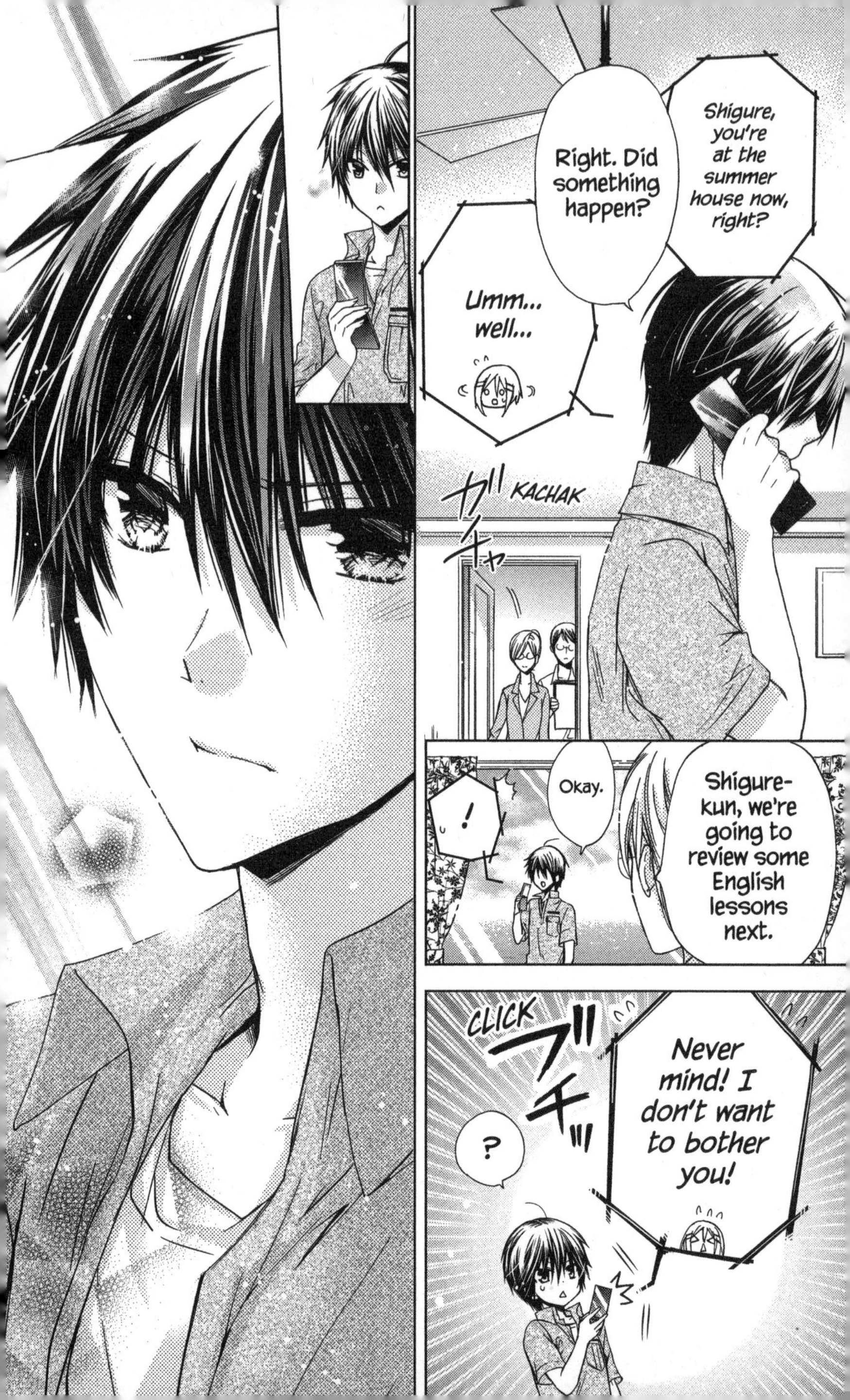
Shigure, you're at the summer house now, right?
Right. Did something happen?
Umm... well...
KACHAK
Shigure-kun, we're going to review some English lessons next.
Okay.
!
CLICK
Never mind! I don't want to bother you!
?

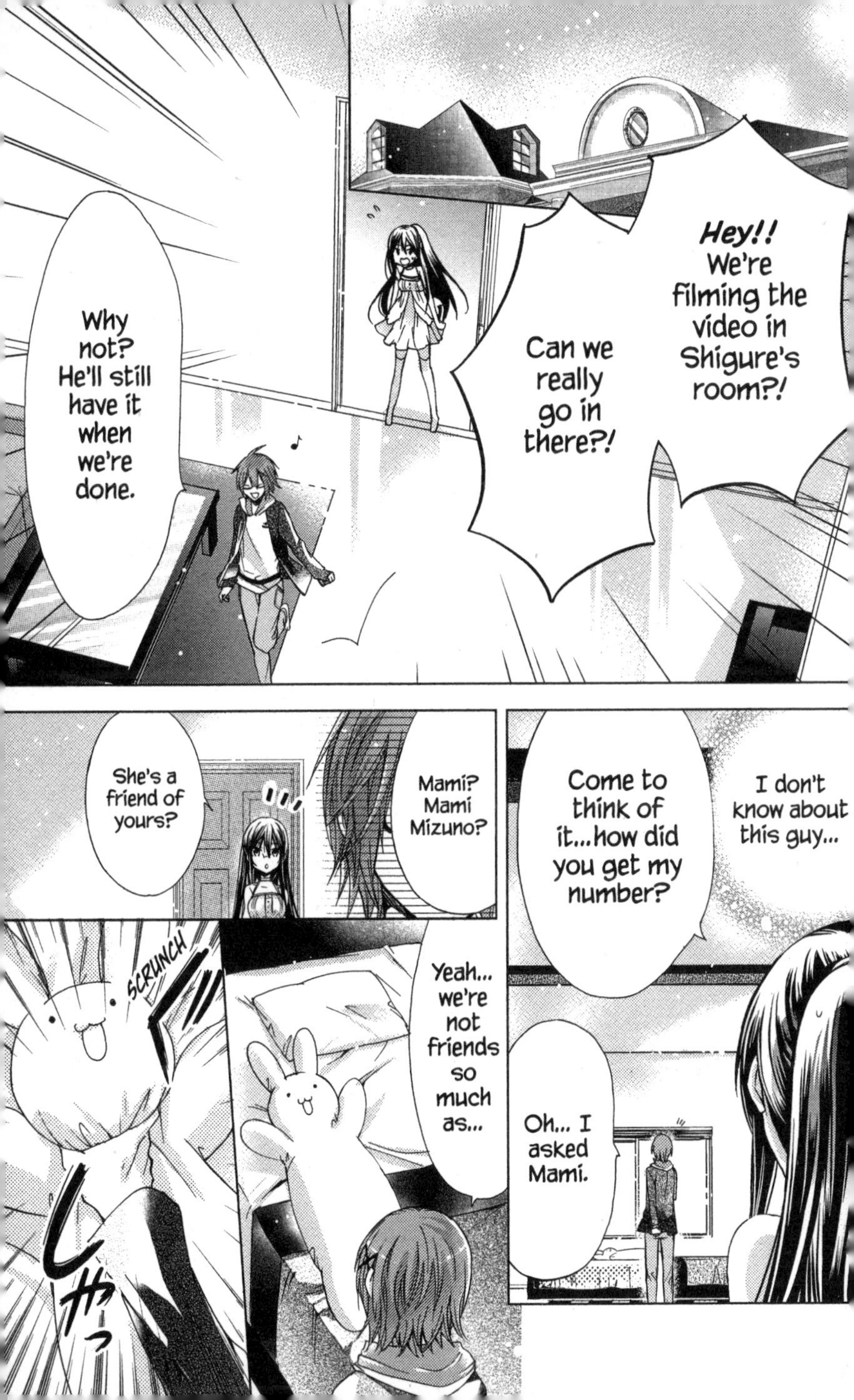
Hey!! We're filming the video in Shigure's room?!
Can we really go in there?!
Why not? He'll still have it when we're done.
I don't know about this guy...
Come to think of it...how did you get my number?
Oh... I asked Mami.
Mami? Mami Mizuno?
She's a friend of yours?
Yeah... we're not friends so much as...
SCRUNCH
しゅっ

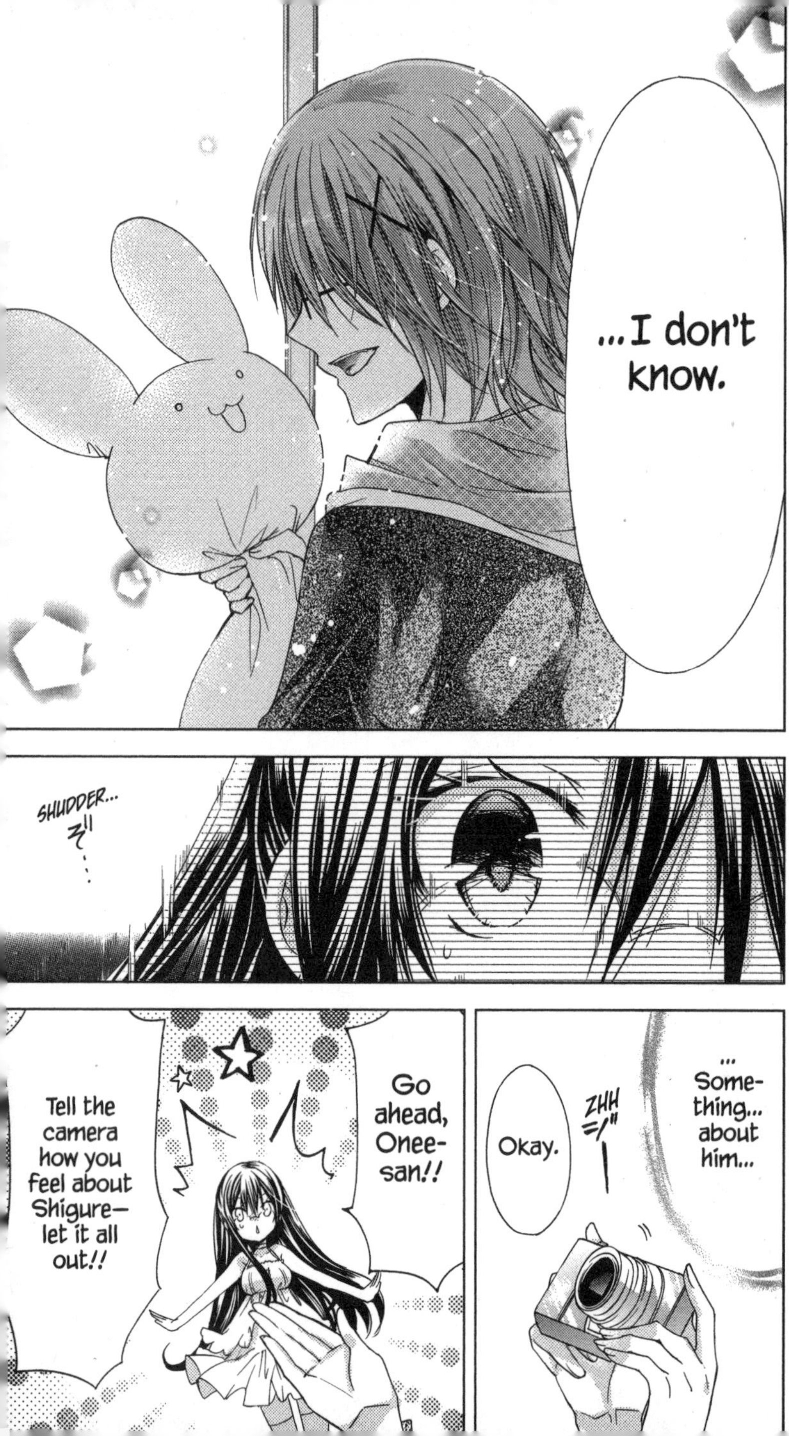
...I don't know.
SHUDDER...
...
Some-thing... about him...
ZHH
Okay.
Go ahead, Onee-san!!
Tell the camera how you feel about Shigure—let it all out!!

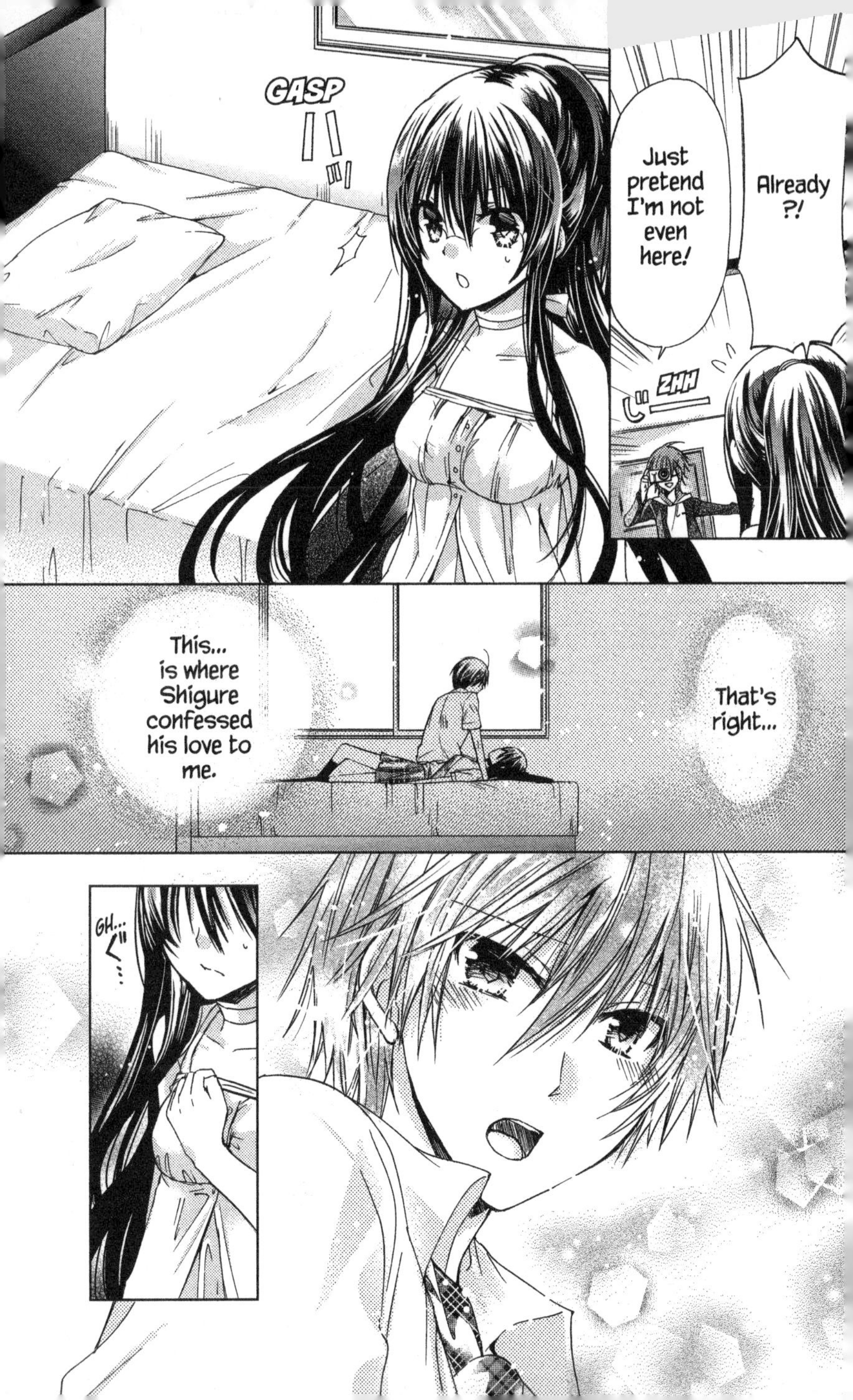
Already ?!
Just pretend I'm not even here!
ZHH
GASP
That's right...
This... is where Shigure confessed his love to me.
GH...

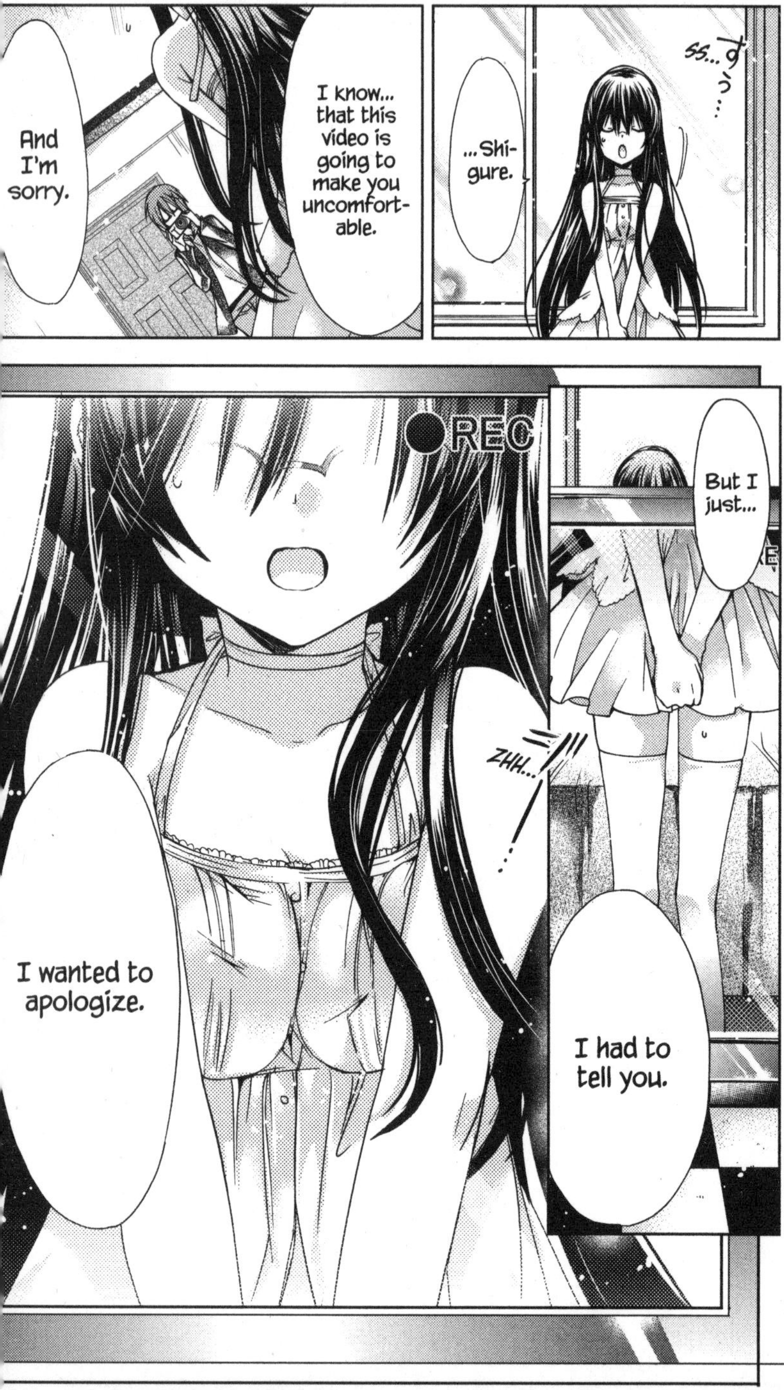
ss... すぅ…
...Shigure.
I know... that this video is going to make you uncomfortable.
And I'm sorry.
But I just...
I had to tell you.
REC
ZHH...
I wanted to apologize.

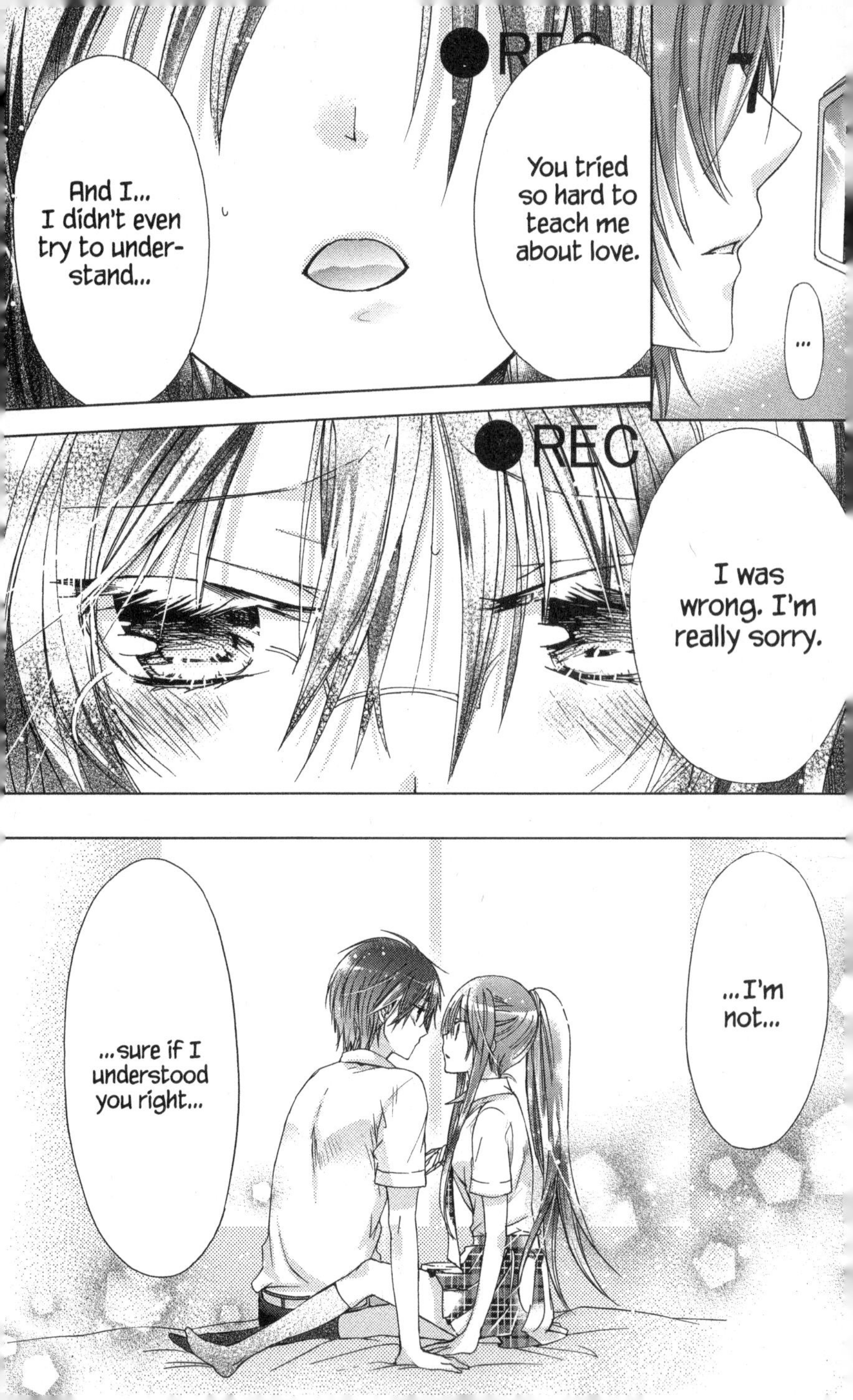
...
You tried so hard to teach me about love.
And I... I didn't even try to under-stand...
REC
I was wrong. I'm really sorry.
...I'm not...
...sure if I understood you right...

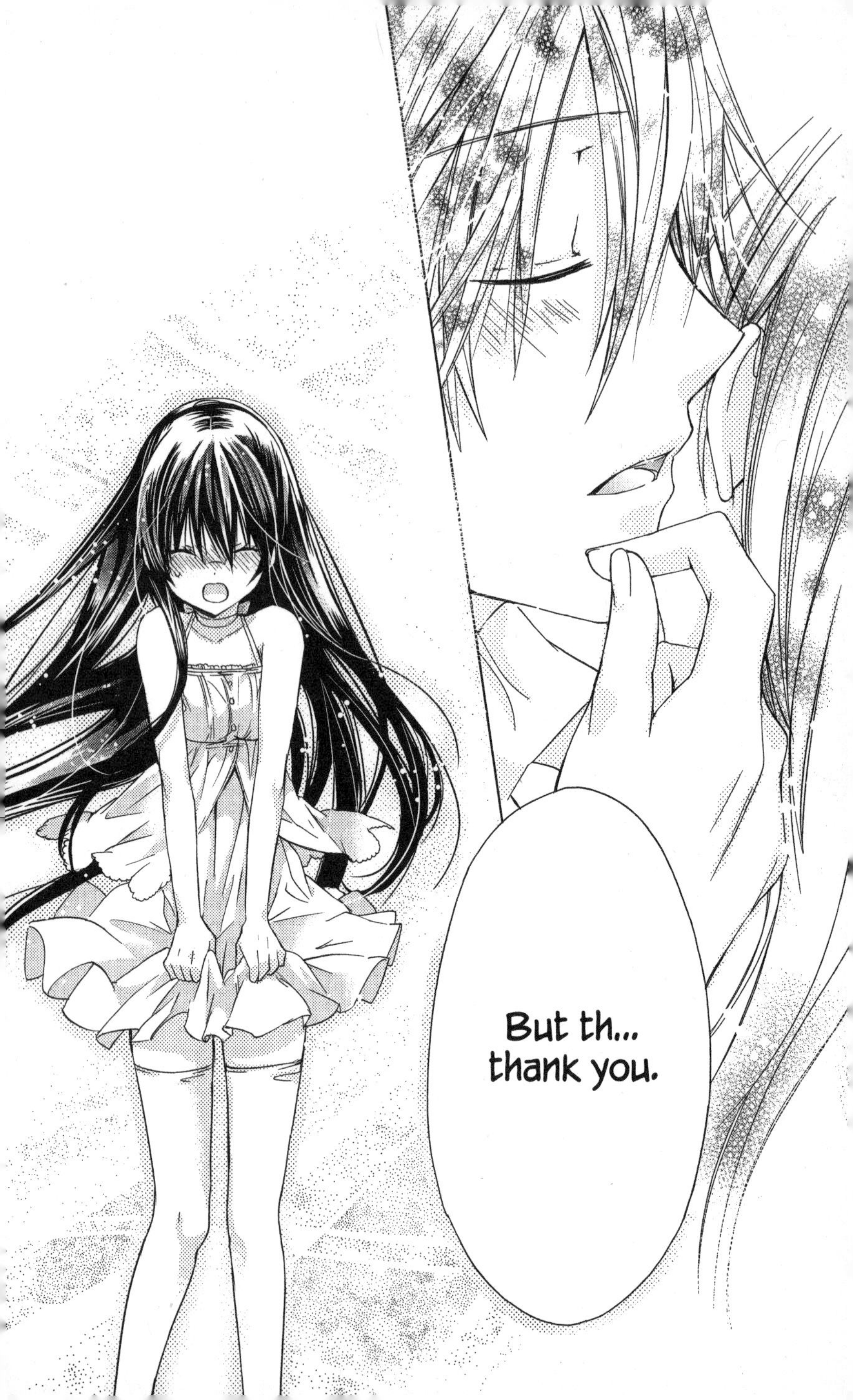
But th...
thank you.

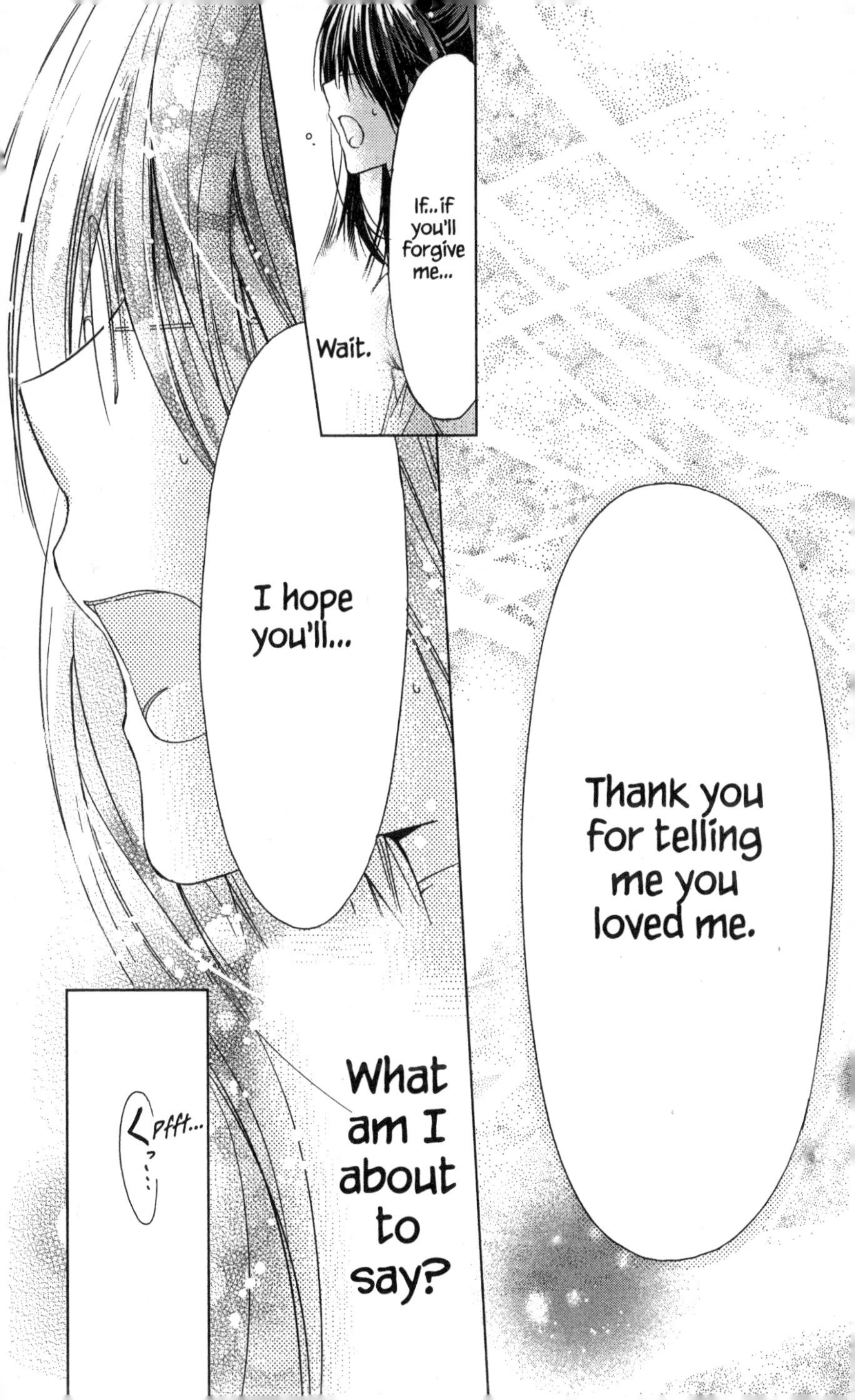
Thank you for telling me you loved me.
If...if you'll forgive me...
Wait.
I hope you'll...
What am I about to say?
pfft...

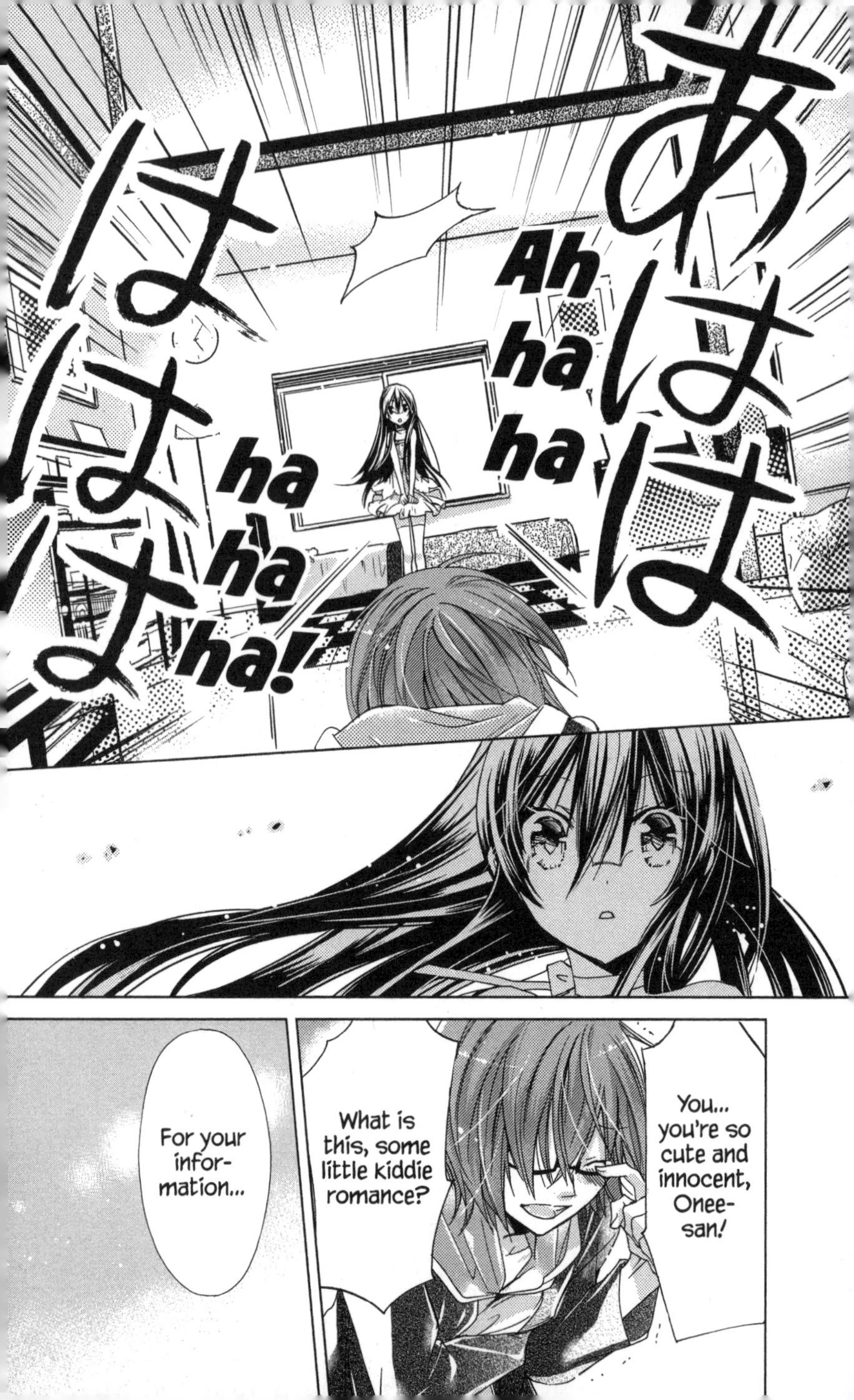
あはは
Ah ha ha ha
ははは
ha ha ha!
You... you're so cute and innocent, Onee-san!
What is this, some little kiddie romance?
For your information...

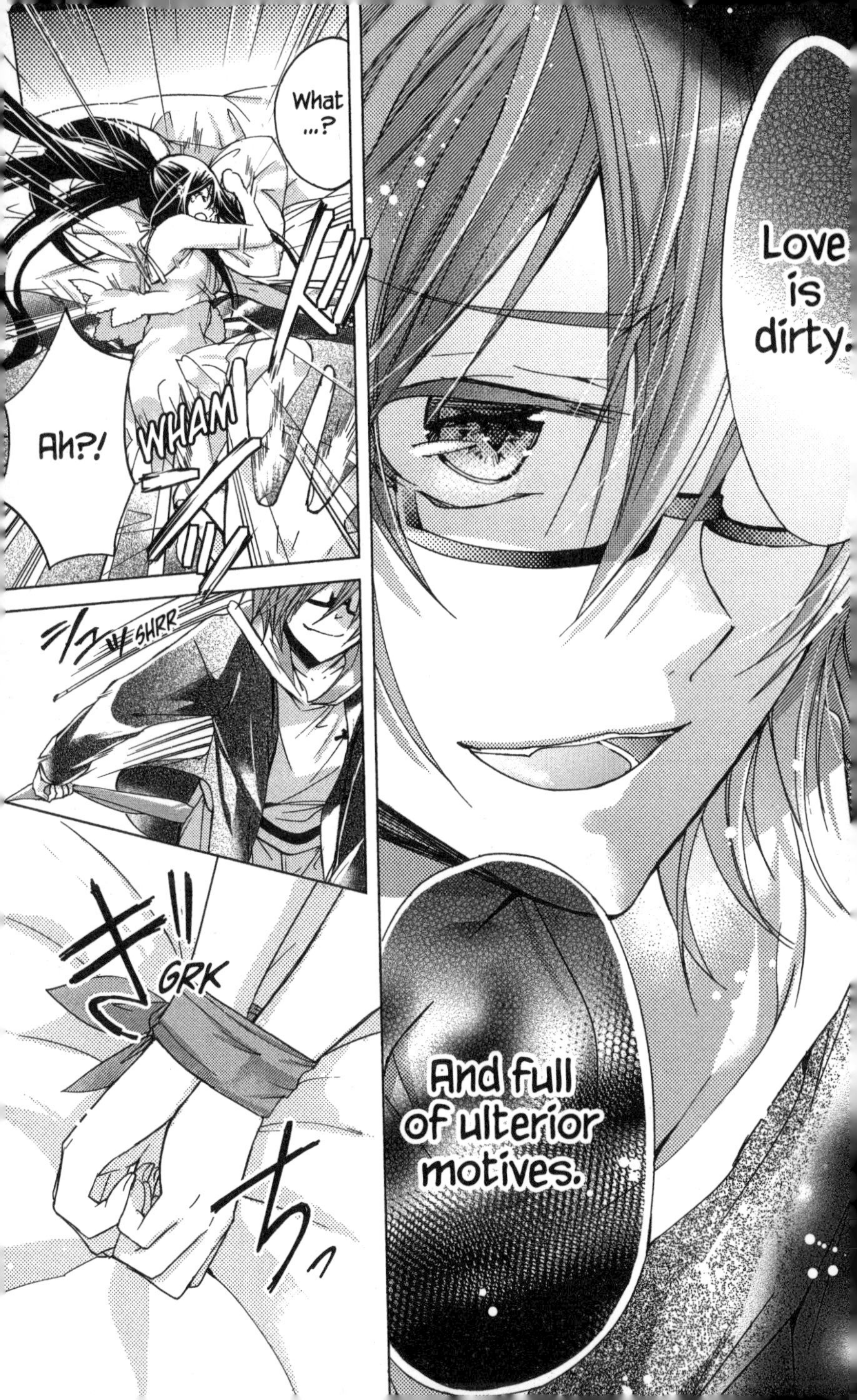
Love is dirty.
And full of ulterior motives.
What ...?
WHAM
Ah?!
シュ SHRR
GRK

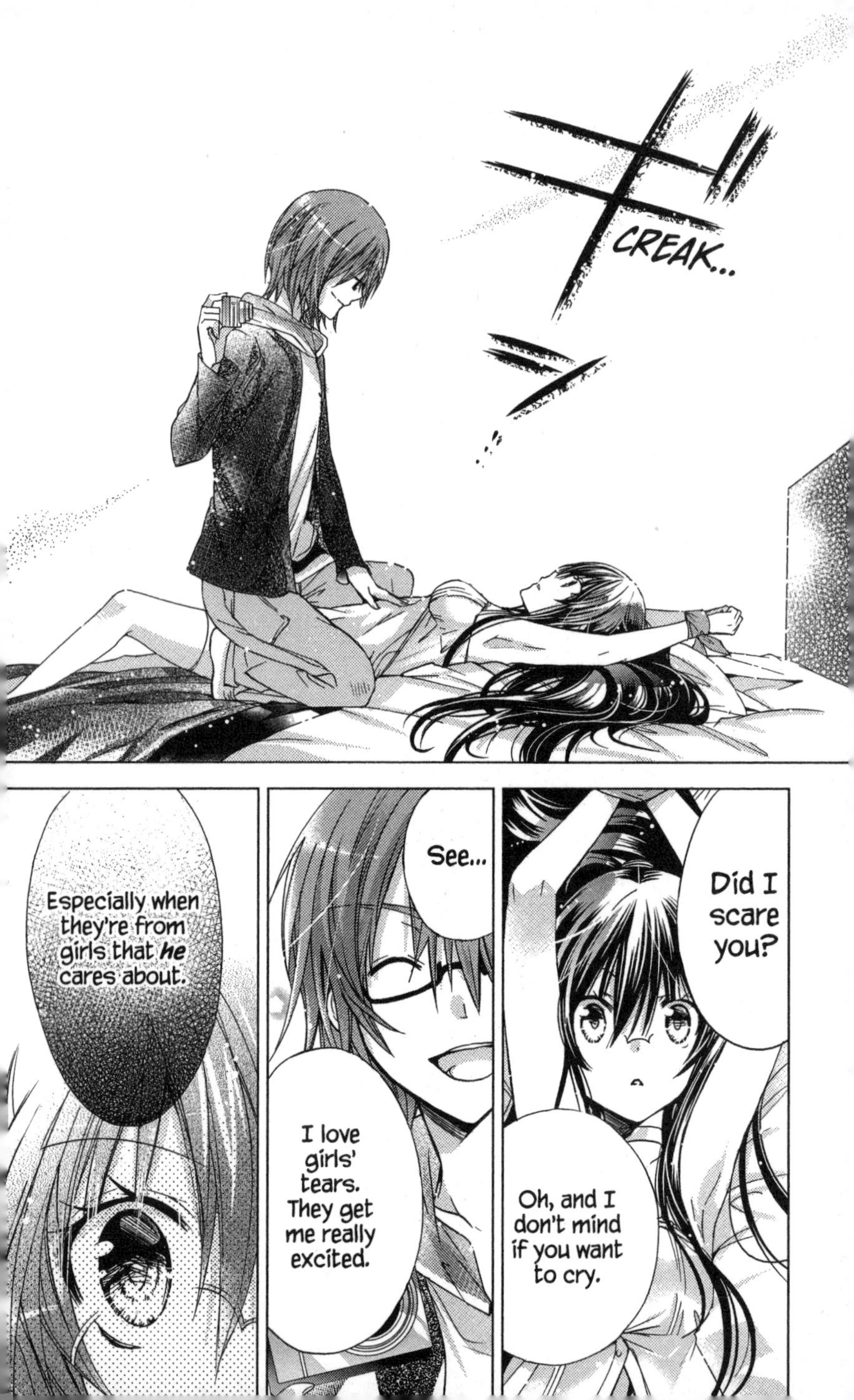
CREAK...
Did I scare you?
Oh, and I don't mind if you want to cry.
See...
I love girls' tears. They get me really excited.
Especially when they're from girls that *he* cares about.

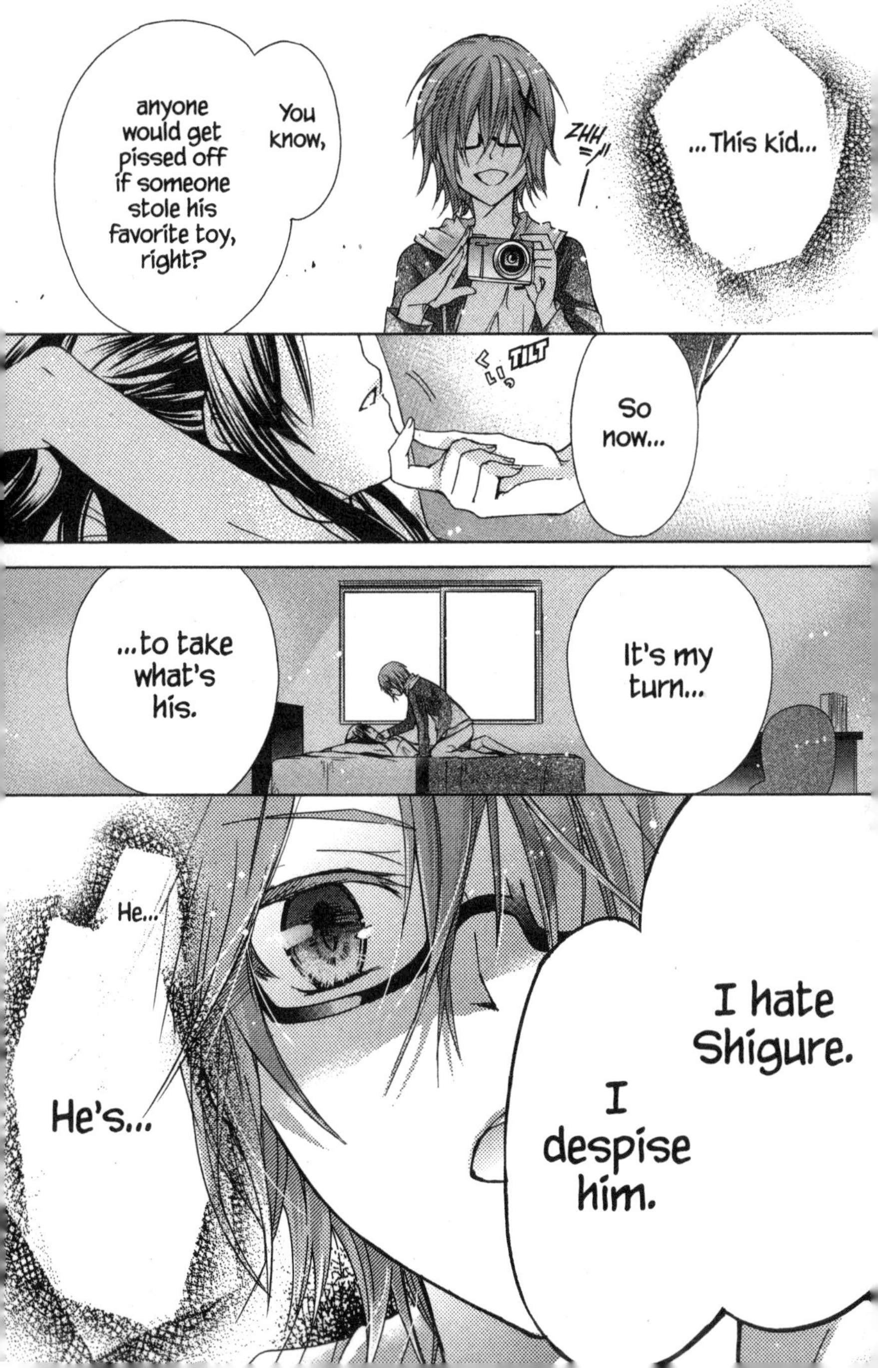
...This kid...
ZHH
You know,
anyone would get pissed off if someone stole his favorite toy, right?
TILT
So now...
It's my turn...
...to take what's his.
I hate Shigure.
I despise him.
He...
He's...

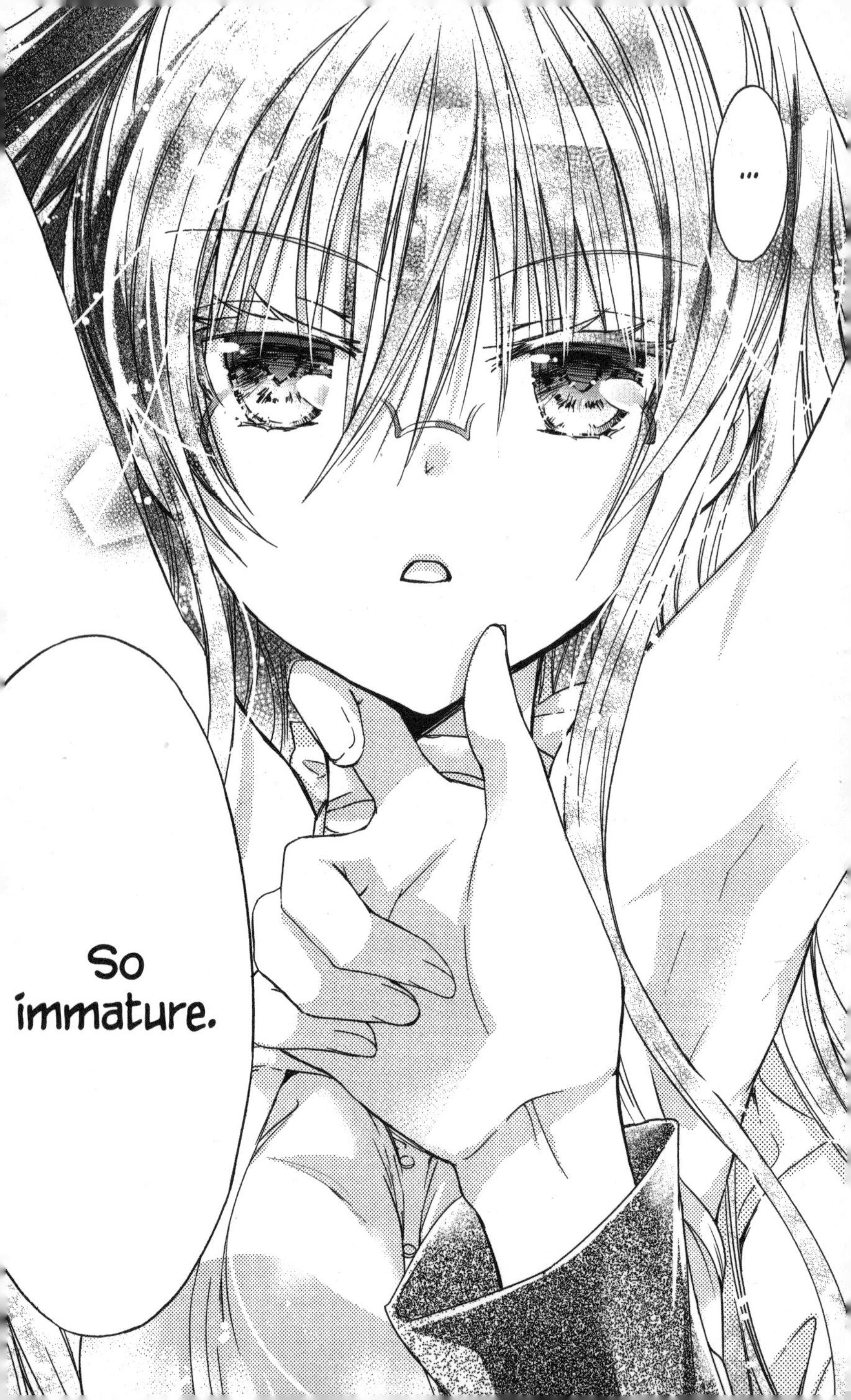
...
So immature.

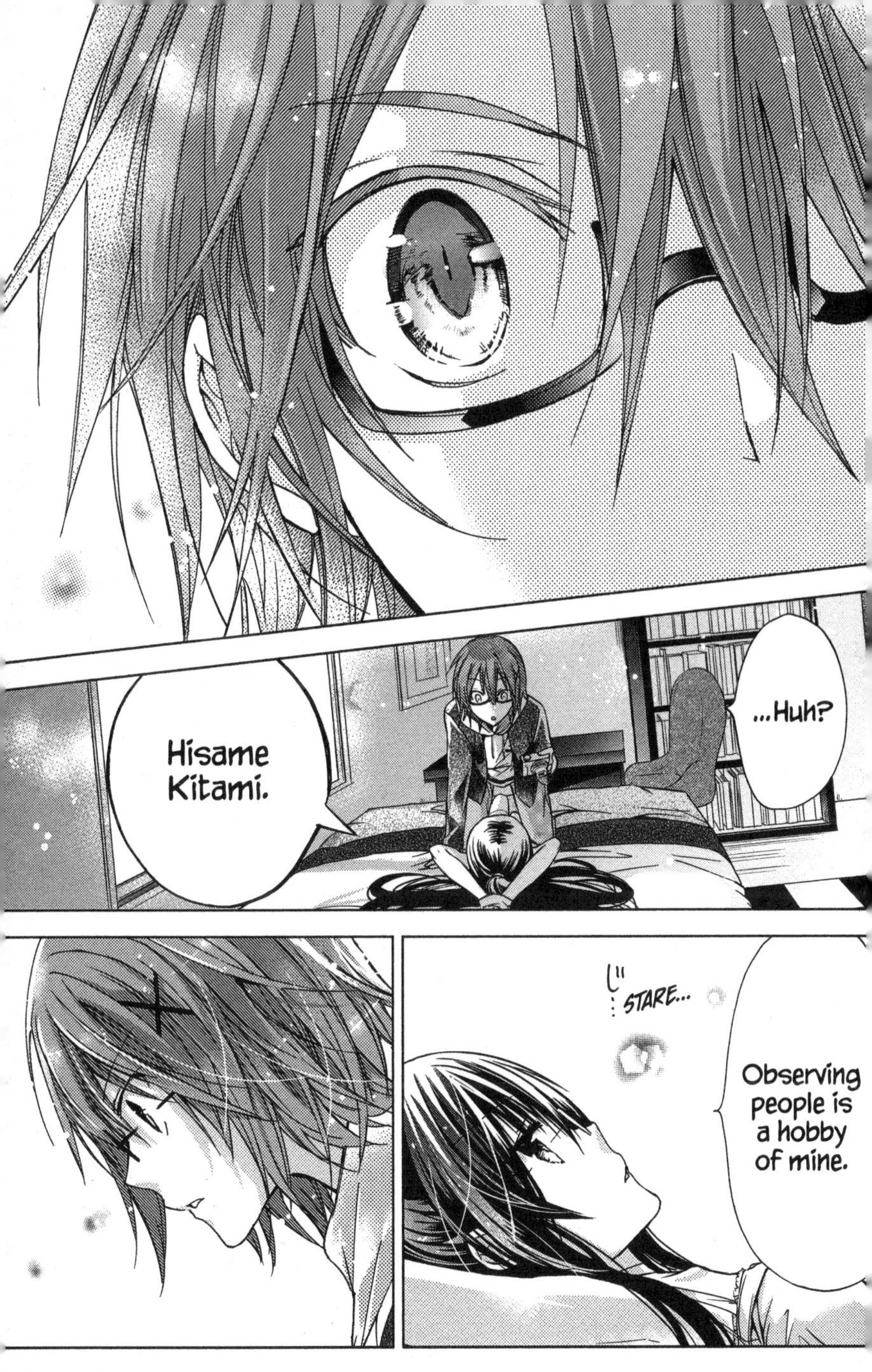
...Huh?
Hisame Kitami.
じ STARE...
Observing people is a hobby of mine.

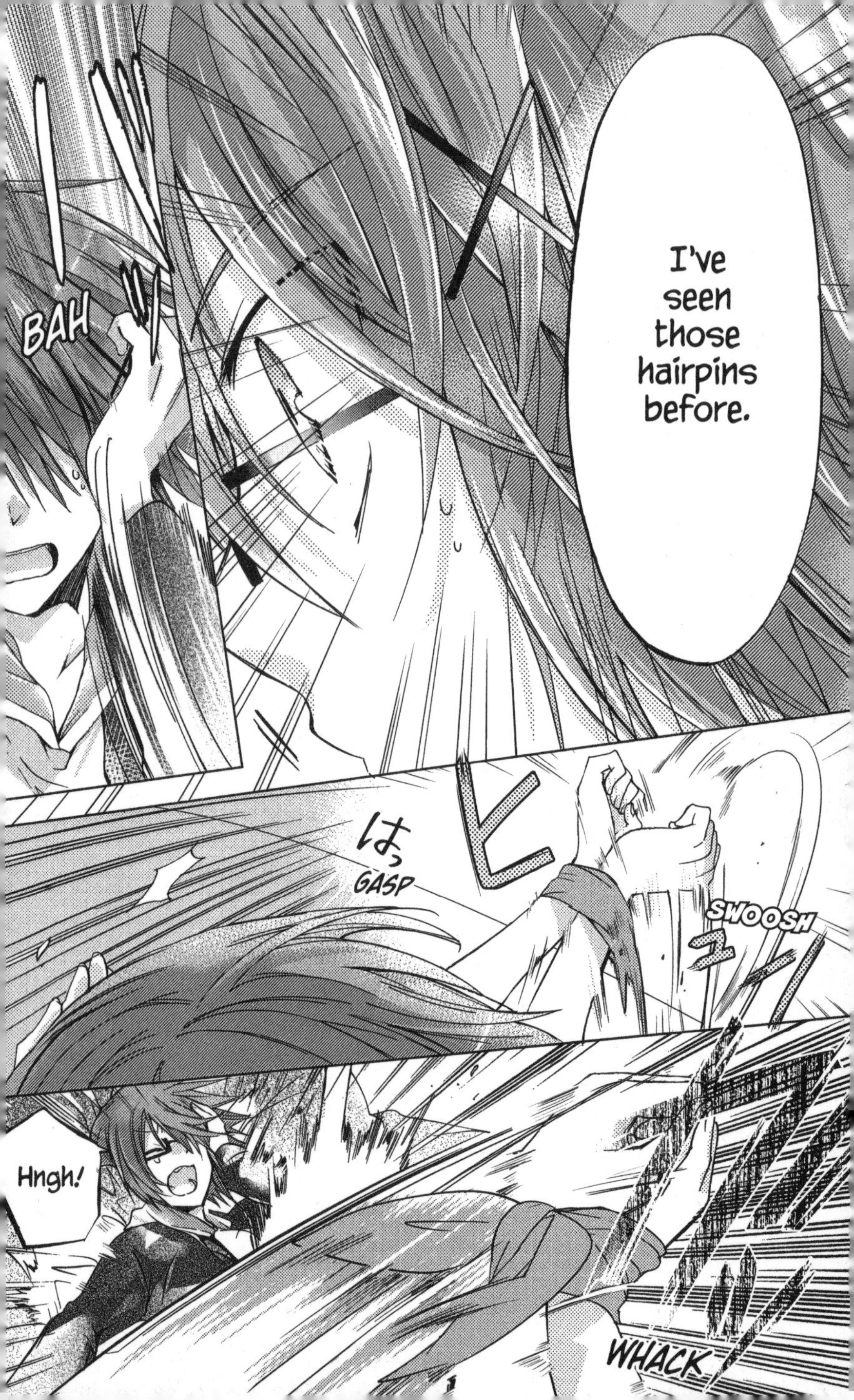
I've seen those hairpins before.
BAH
SWOOSH
はっ
GASP
Hngh!
WHACK

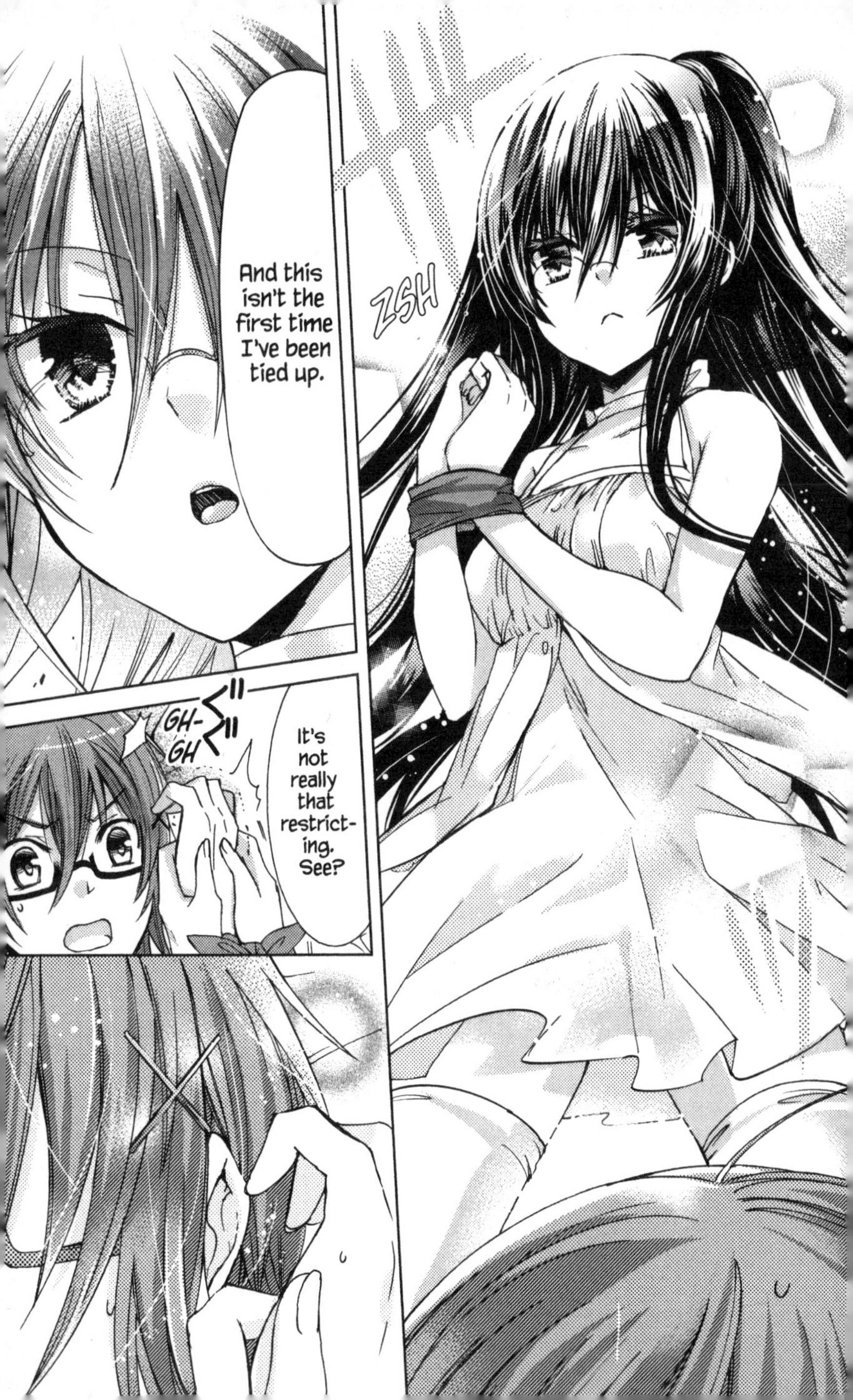
ZSH
And this isn't the first time I've been tied up.
It's not really that restrict-ing. See?
GH-GH

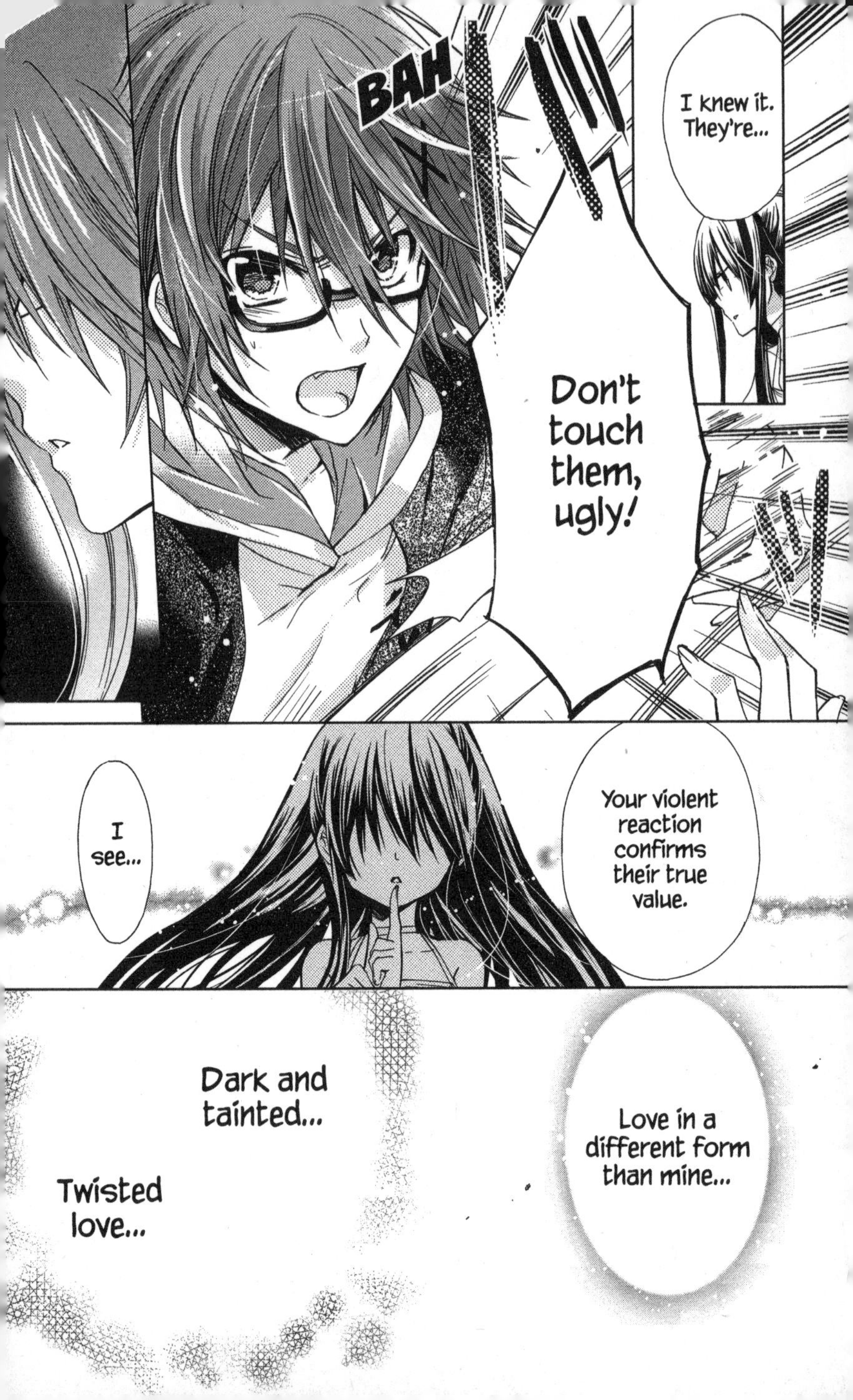
I knew it. They're...
BAH
Don't touch them, ugly!
Your violent reaction confirms their true value.
I see...
Love in a different form than mine...
Dark and tainted...
Twisted love...

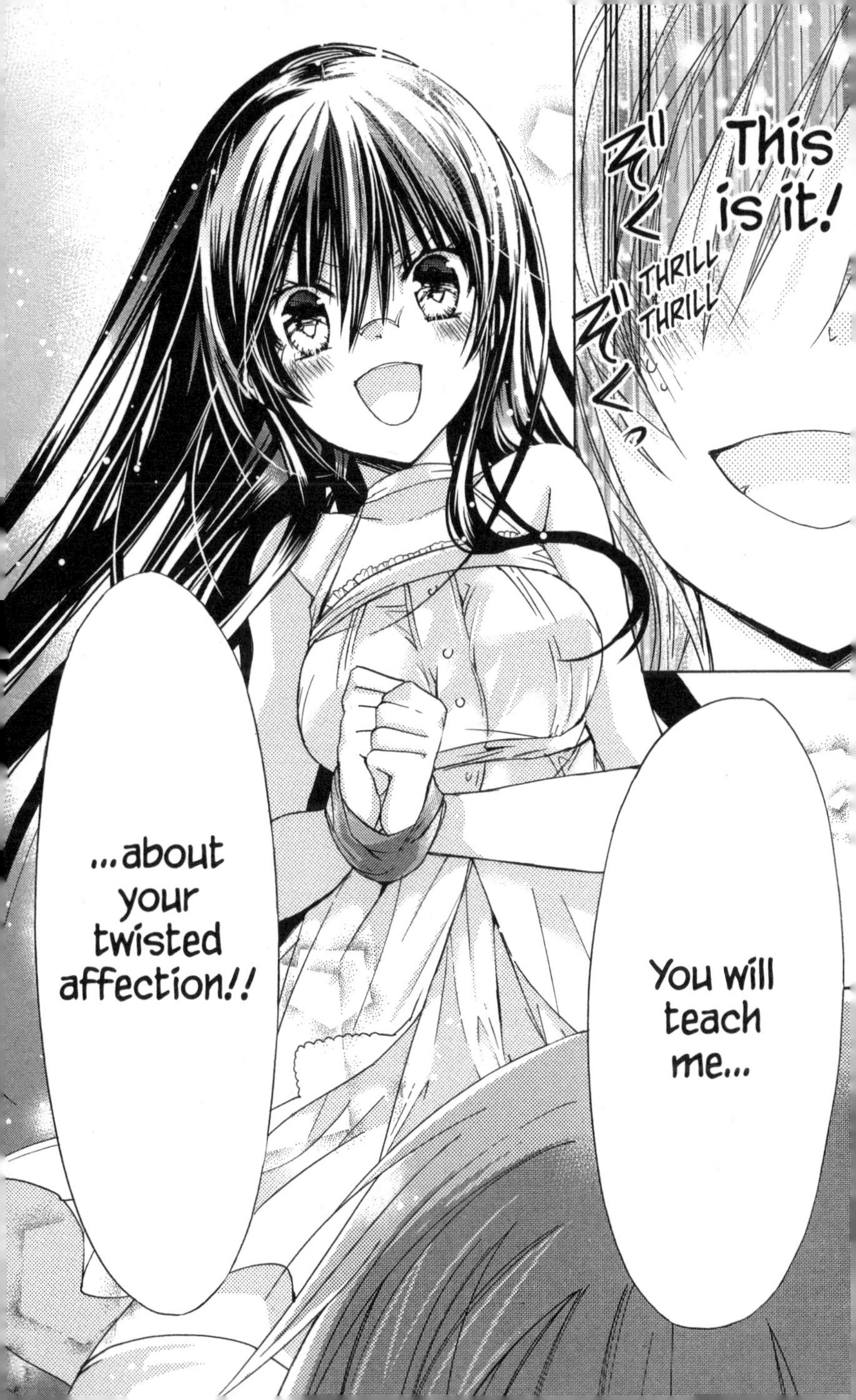
This is it!
ぞく
THRILL
ぞくっ
THRILL
You will teach me...
...about your twisted affection!!

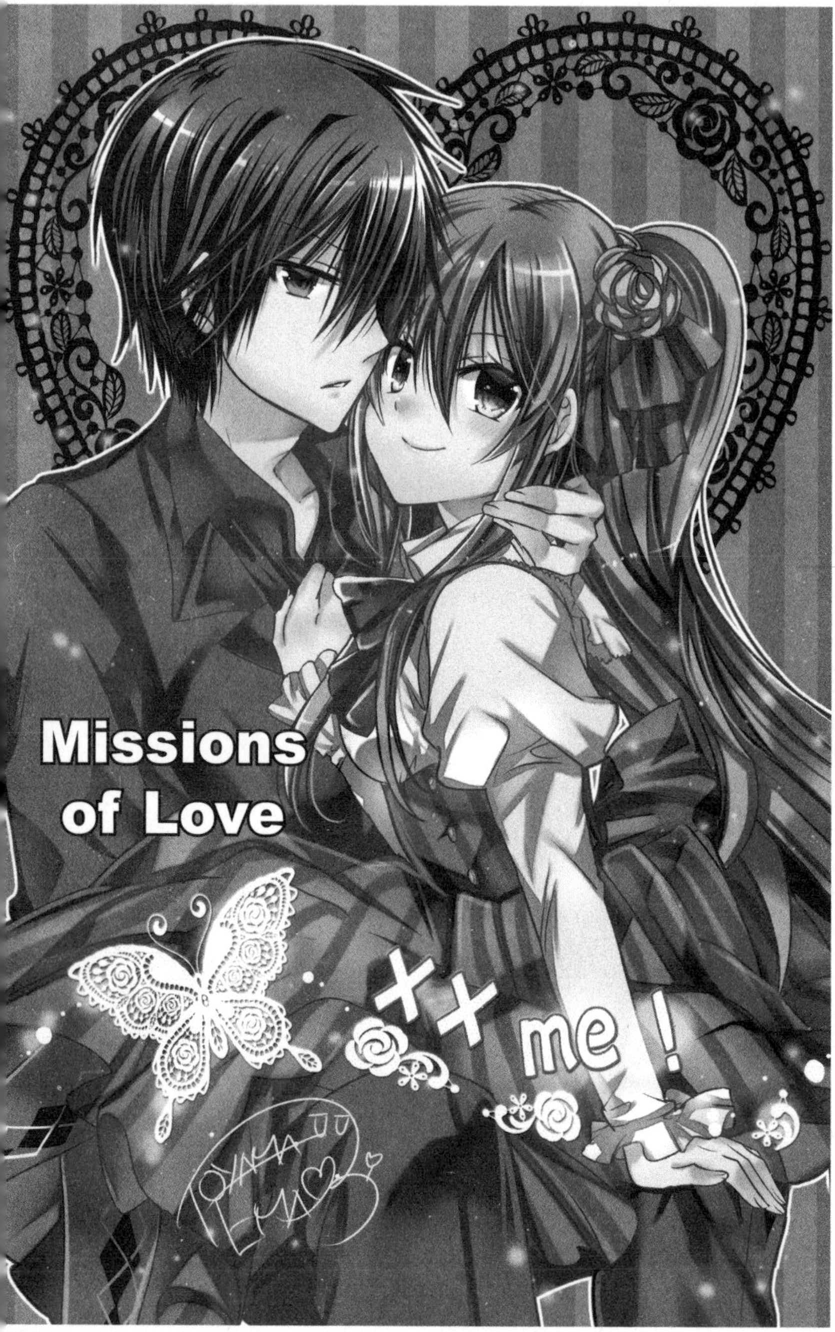
Missions of Love
×× me!

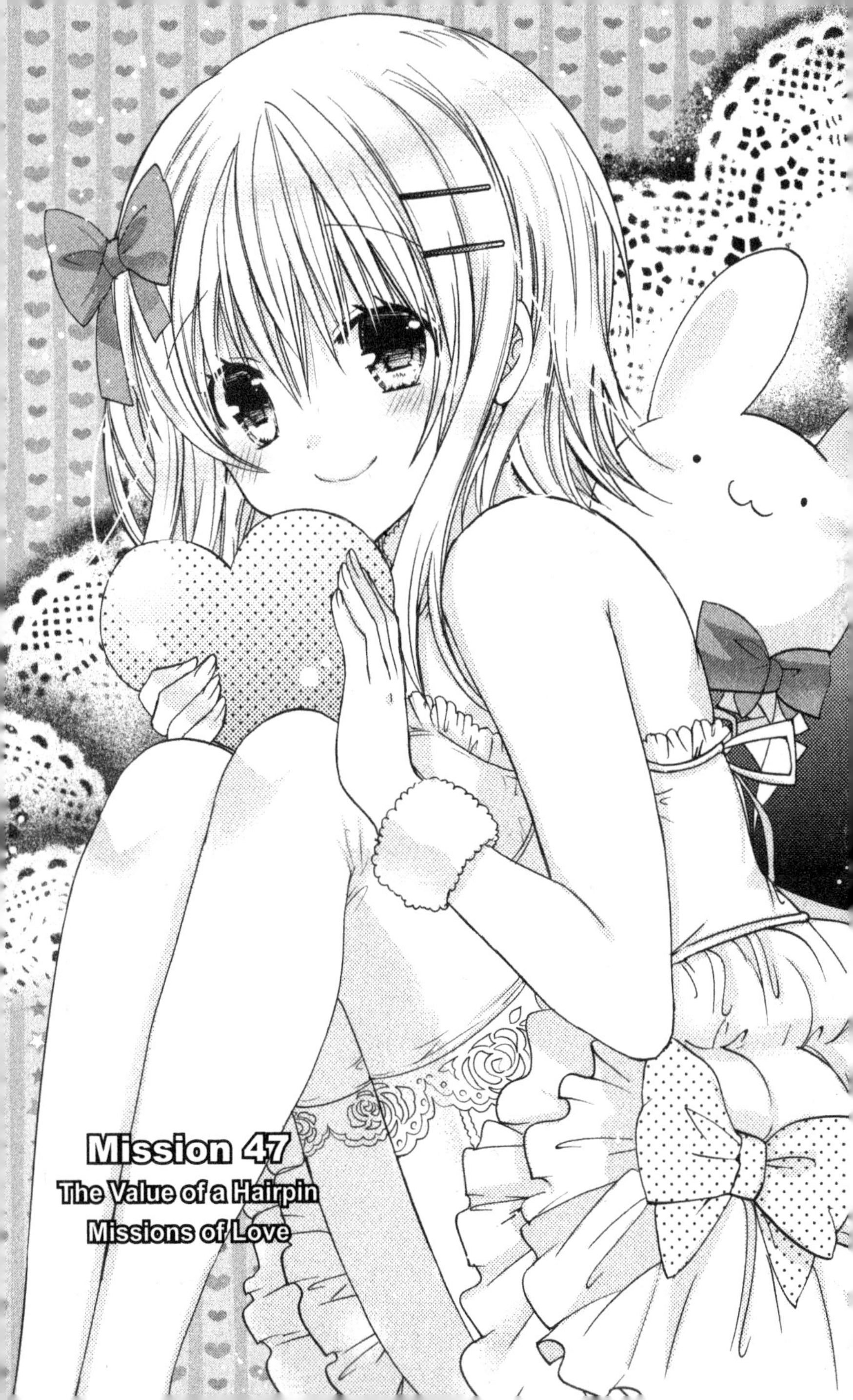
Mission 47
The Value of a Hairpin
Missions of Love

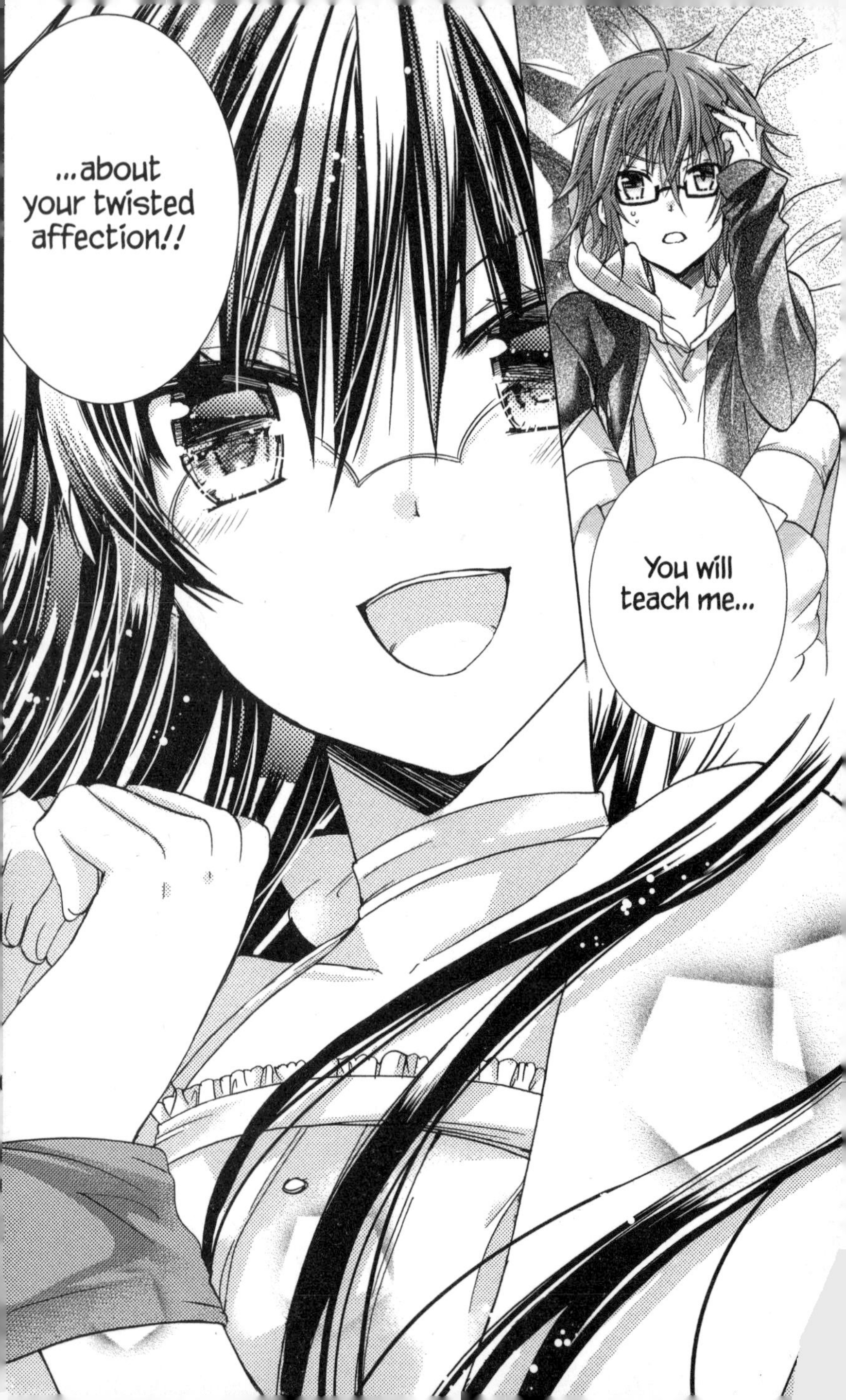
You will teach me...
...about your twisted affection!!

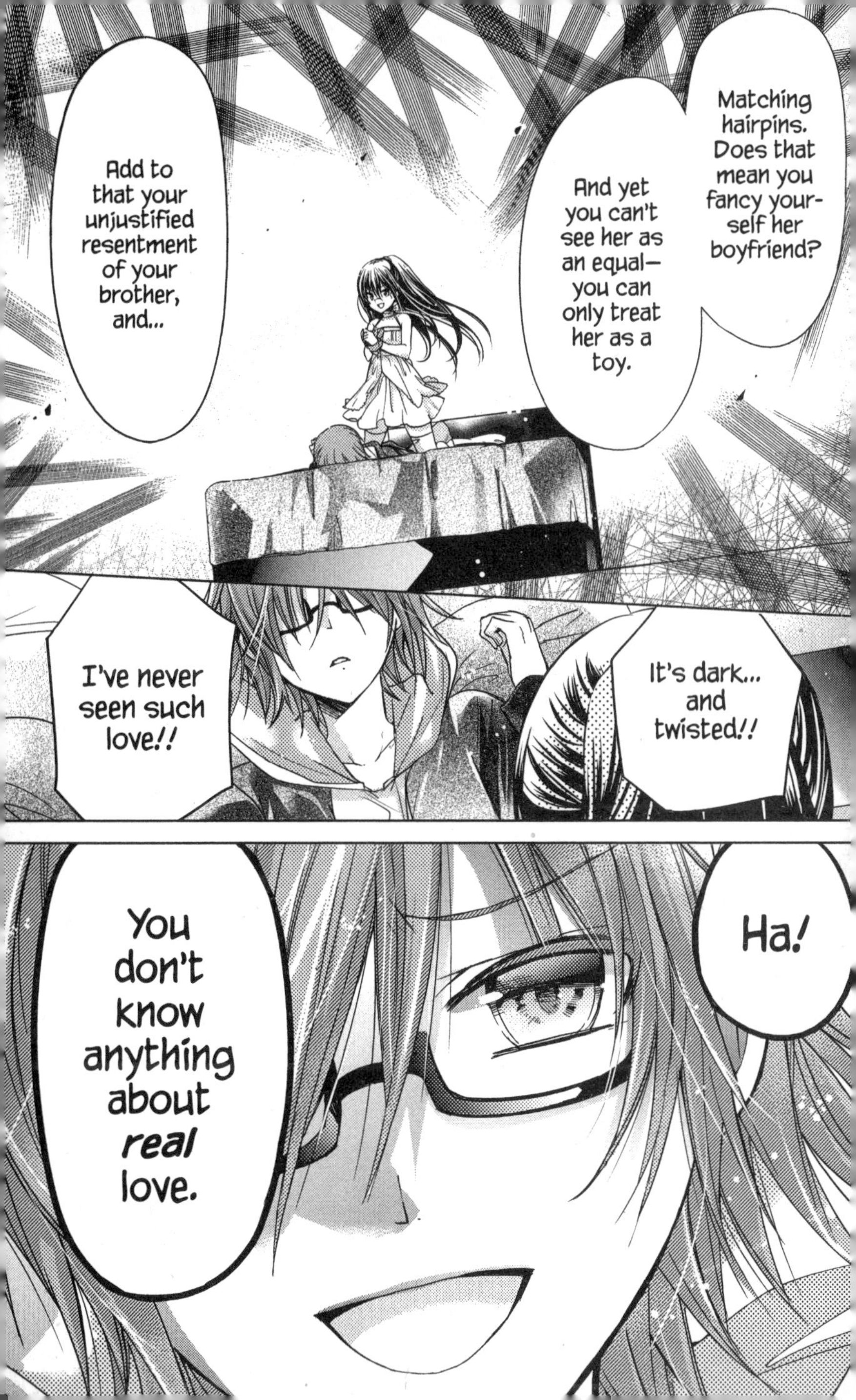
Matching hairpins. Does that mean you fancy your-self her boyfriend?
And yet you can't see her as an equal—you can only treat her as a toy.
Add to that your unjustified resentment of your brother, and...
It's dark... and twisted!!
I've never seen such love!!
Ha!
You don't know anything about *real* love.

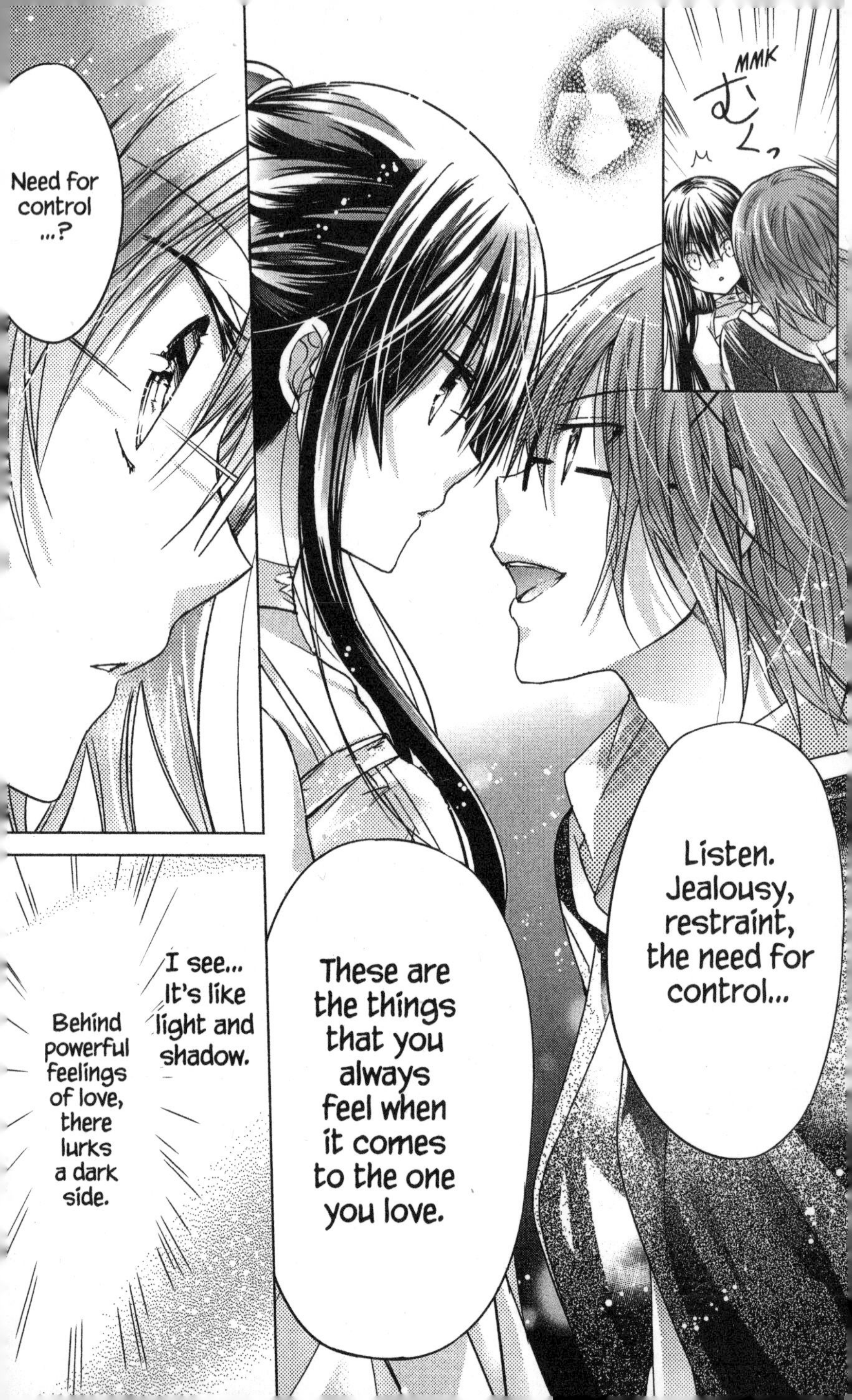
MMK
むくっ
Listen. Jealousy, restraint, the need for control...
These are the things that you always feel when it comes to the one you love.
Need for control ...?
I see... It's like light and shadow.
Behind powerful feelings of love, there lurks a dark side.

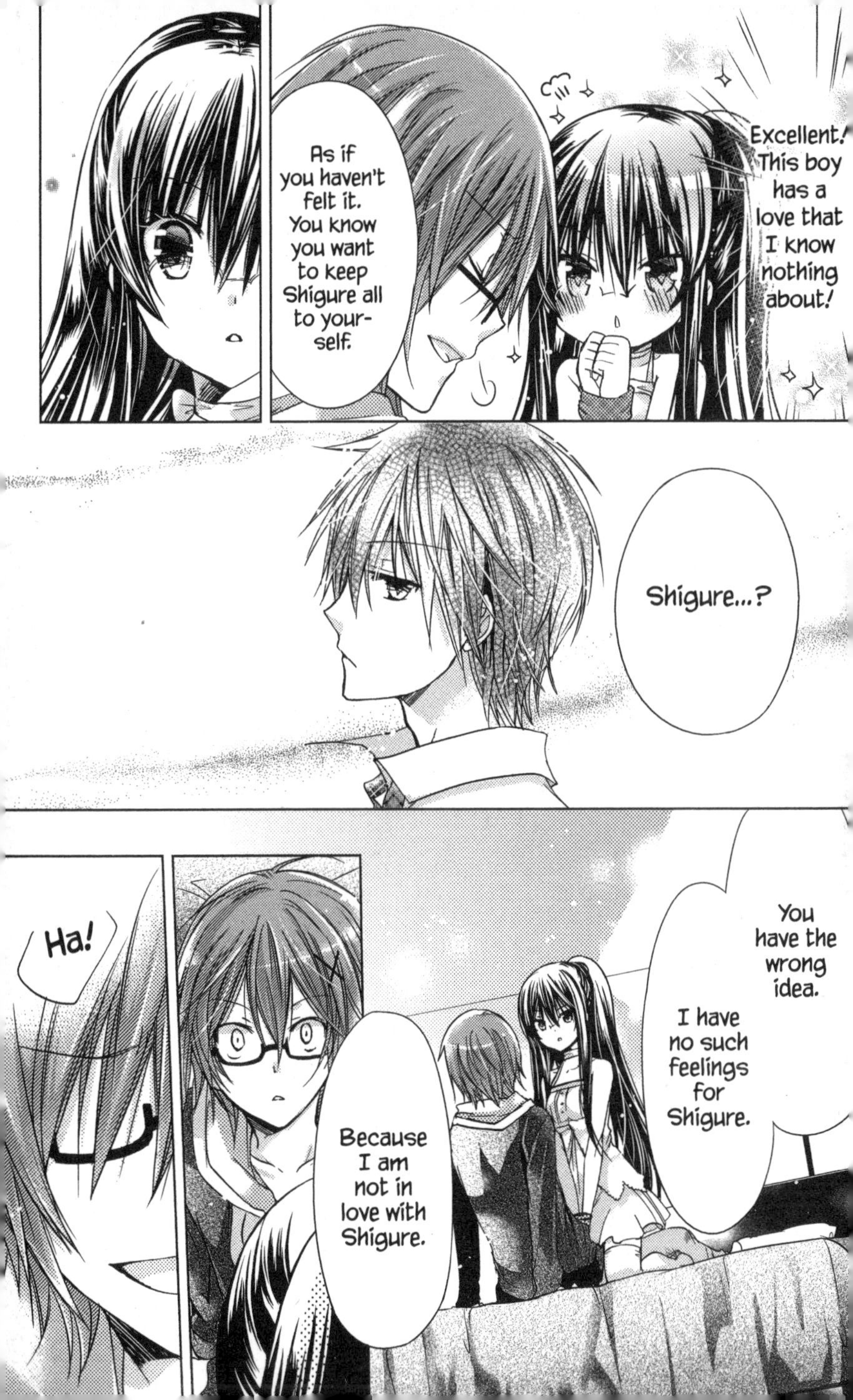
Excellent! This boy has a love that I know nothing about!
As if you haven't felt it. You know you want to keep Shigure all to your-self.
Shigure...?
You have the wrong idea.
I have no such feelings for Shigure.
Because I am not in love with Shigure.
Ha!

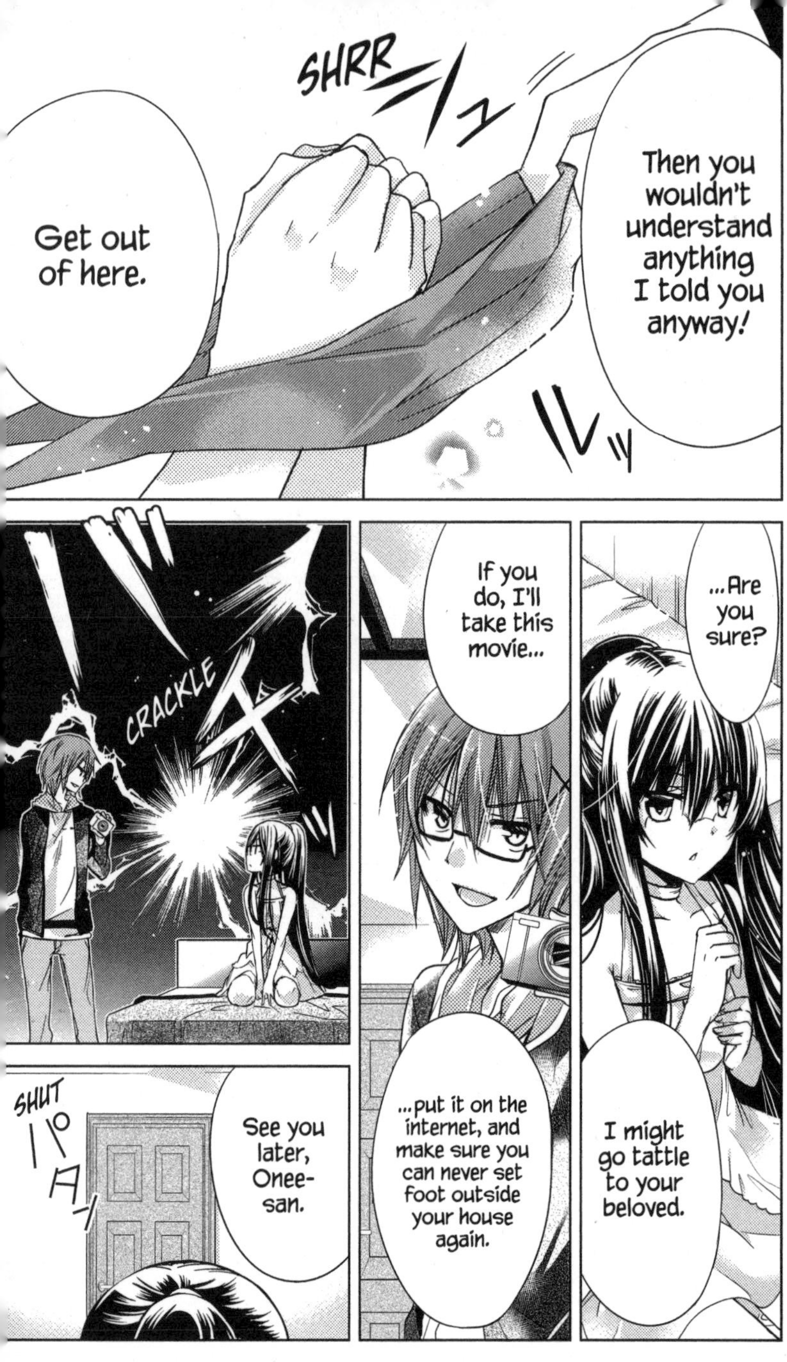
Then you wouldn't understand anything I told you anyway!
SHRR
Get out of here.
...Are you sure?
I might go tattle to your beloved.
If you do, I'll take this movie...
...put it on the internet, and make sure you can never set foot outside your house again.
CRACKLE
See you later, Onee-san.
SHUT

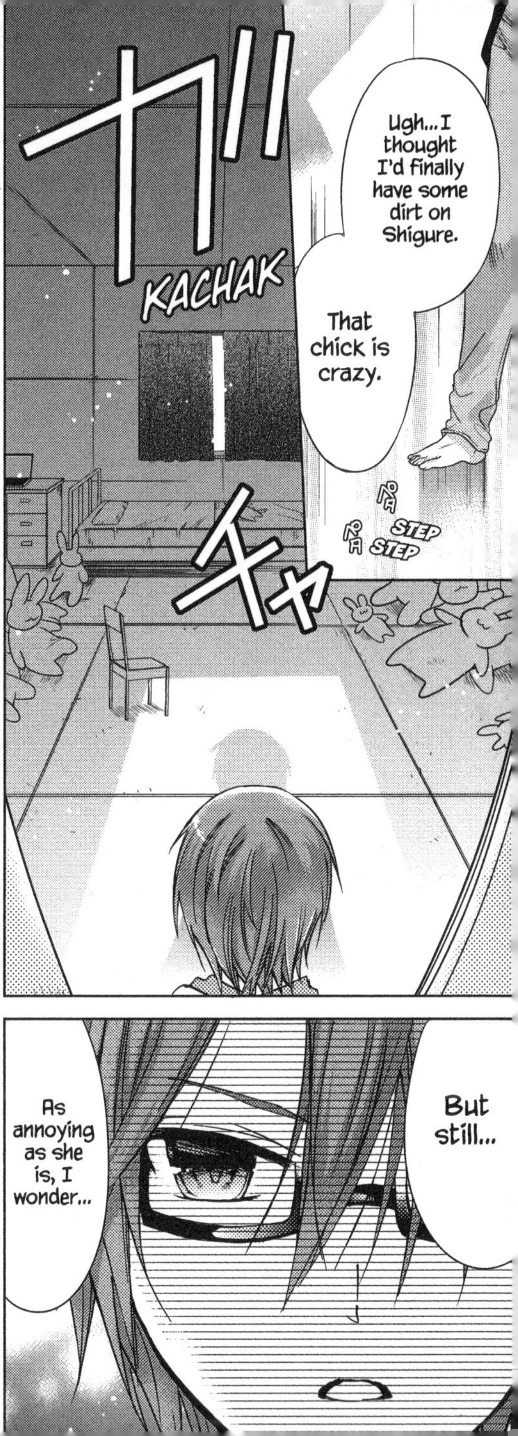
KACHAK
Ugh...I thought I'd finally have some dirt on Shigure.
That chick is crazy.
STEP STEP
But still...
As annoying as she is, I wonder...

Touchy-Feely ♡ Snow Yukina

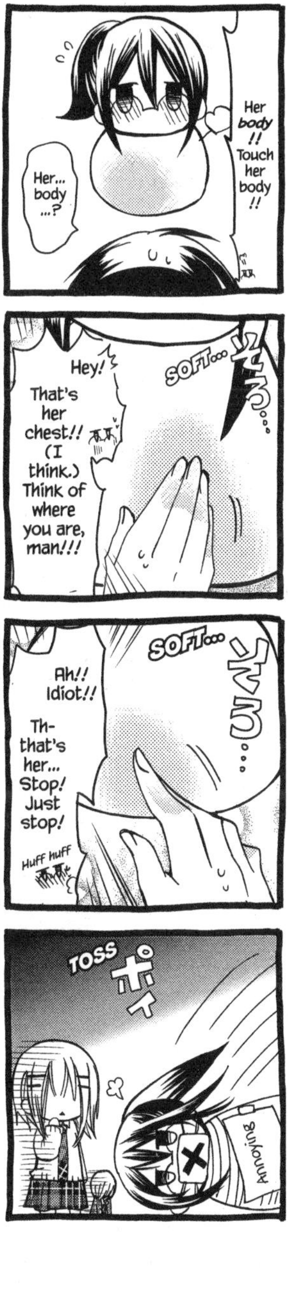
Her *body*!! Touch her body!!
Her... body...?
SOFT...
Hey! That's her chest!! (I think.) Think of where you are, man!!!
SOFT...
Ah!! Idiot!!
Th-that's her... Stop! Just stop!
Huff huff
TOSS
Annoying

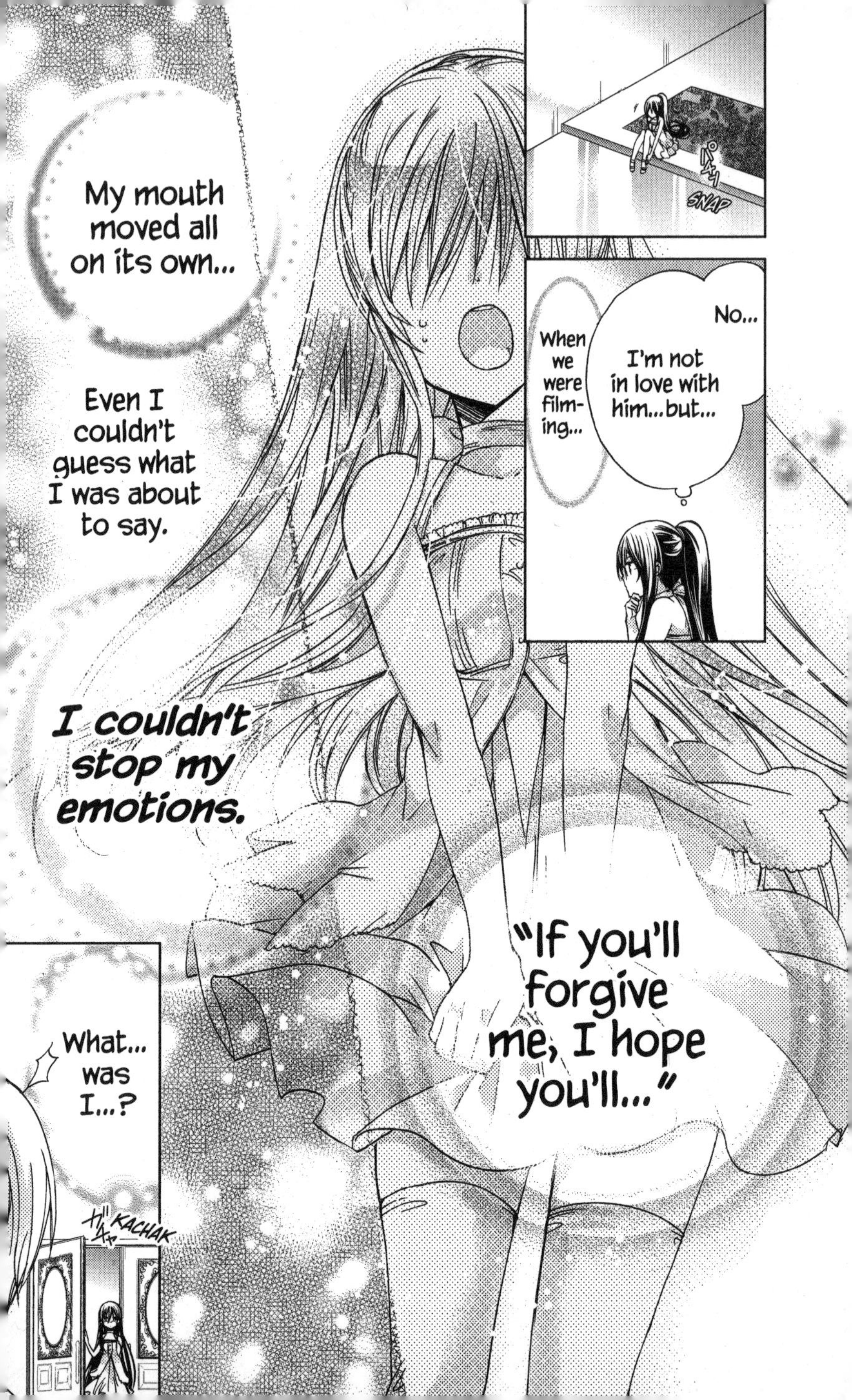
SNAP
No...
I'm not in love with him...but...
When we were film-ing...
My mouth moved all on its own...
Even I couldn't guess what I was about to say.
I couldn't stop my emotions.
"If you'll forgive me, I hope you'll..."
What... was I...?
KACHAK

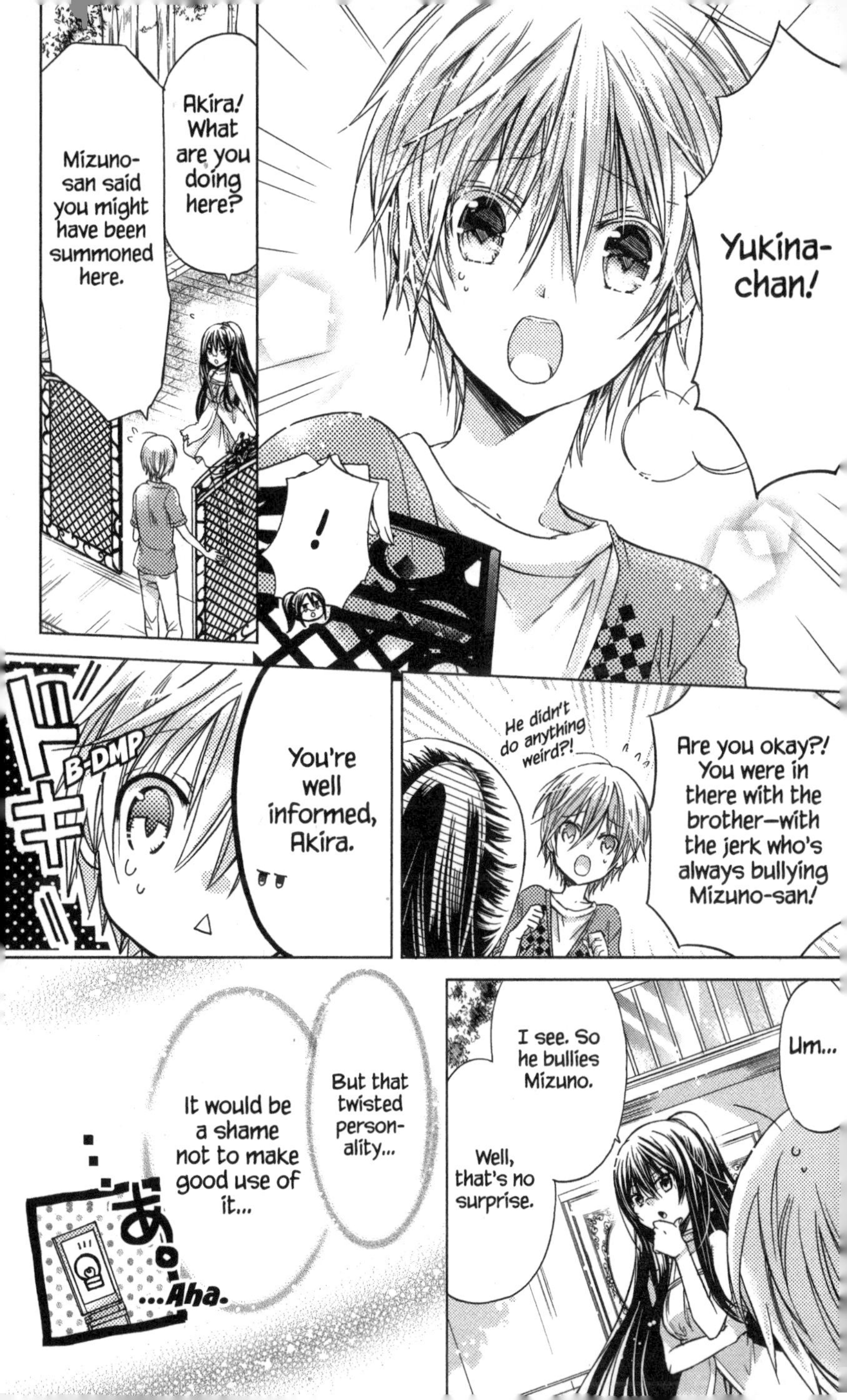
Yukina-chan!
!
Akira! What are you doing here?
Mizuno-san said you might have been summoned here.
Are you okay?! You were in there with the brother—with the jerk who's always bullying Mizuno-san!
He didn't do anything weird?!
You're well informed, Akira.
B-DMP
Um...
I see. So he bullies Mizuno.
Well, that's no surprise.
But that twisted personality...
It would be a shame not to make good use of it...
あ。
...Aha.

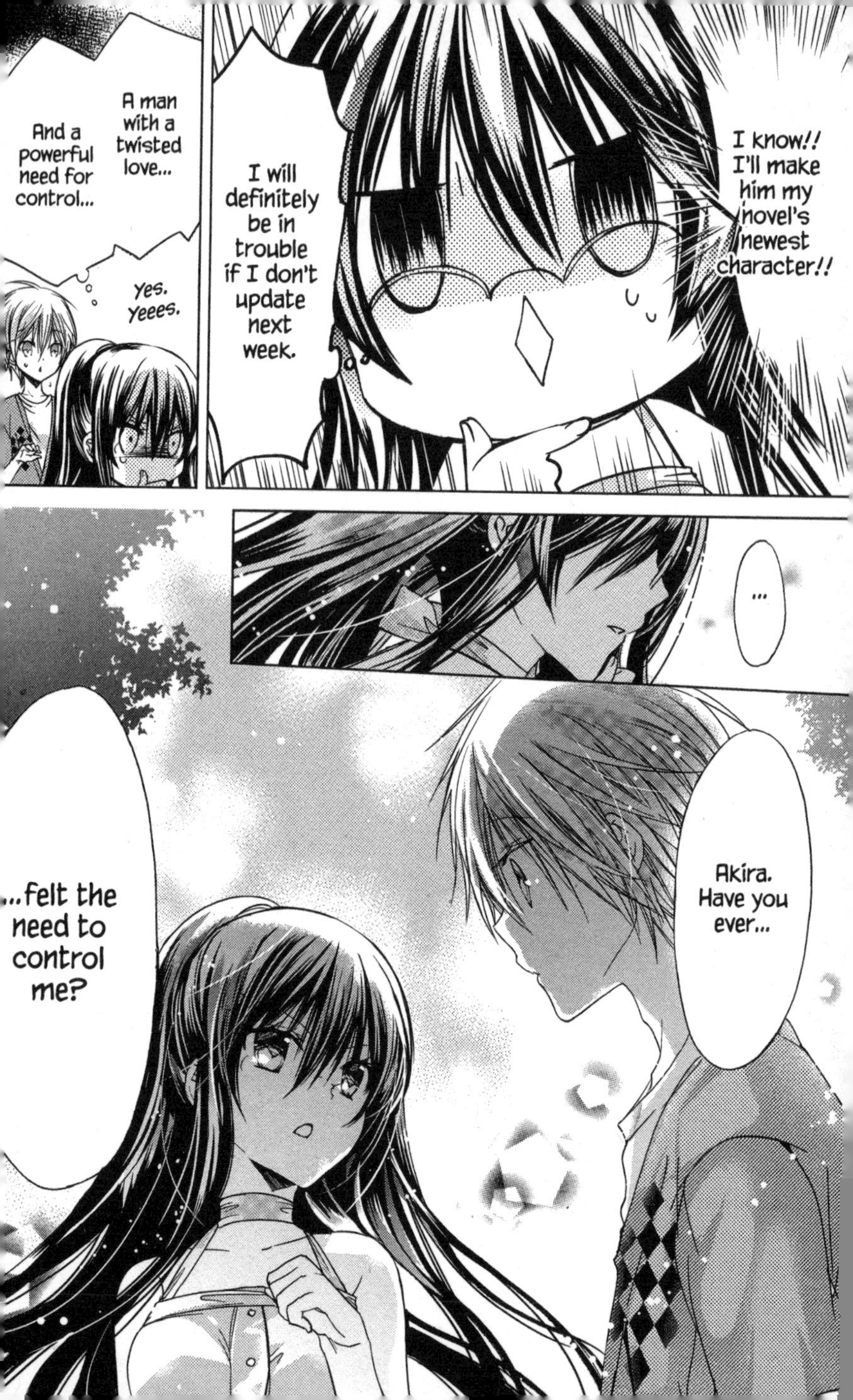
I know!! I'll make him my novel's newest character!!
I will definitely be in trouble if I don't update next week.
A man with a twisted love...
And a powerful need for control...
Yes. Yeees.
...
Akira. Have you ever...
...felt the need to control me?

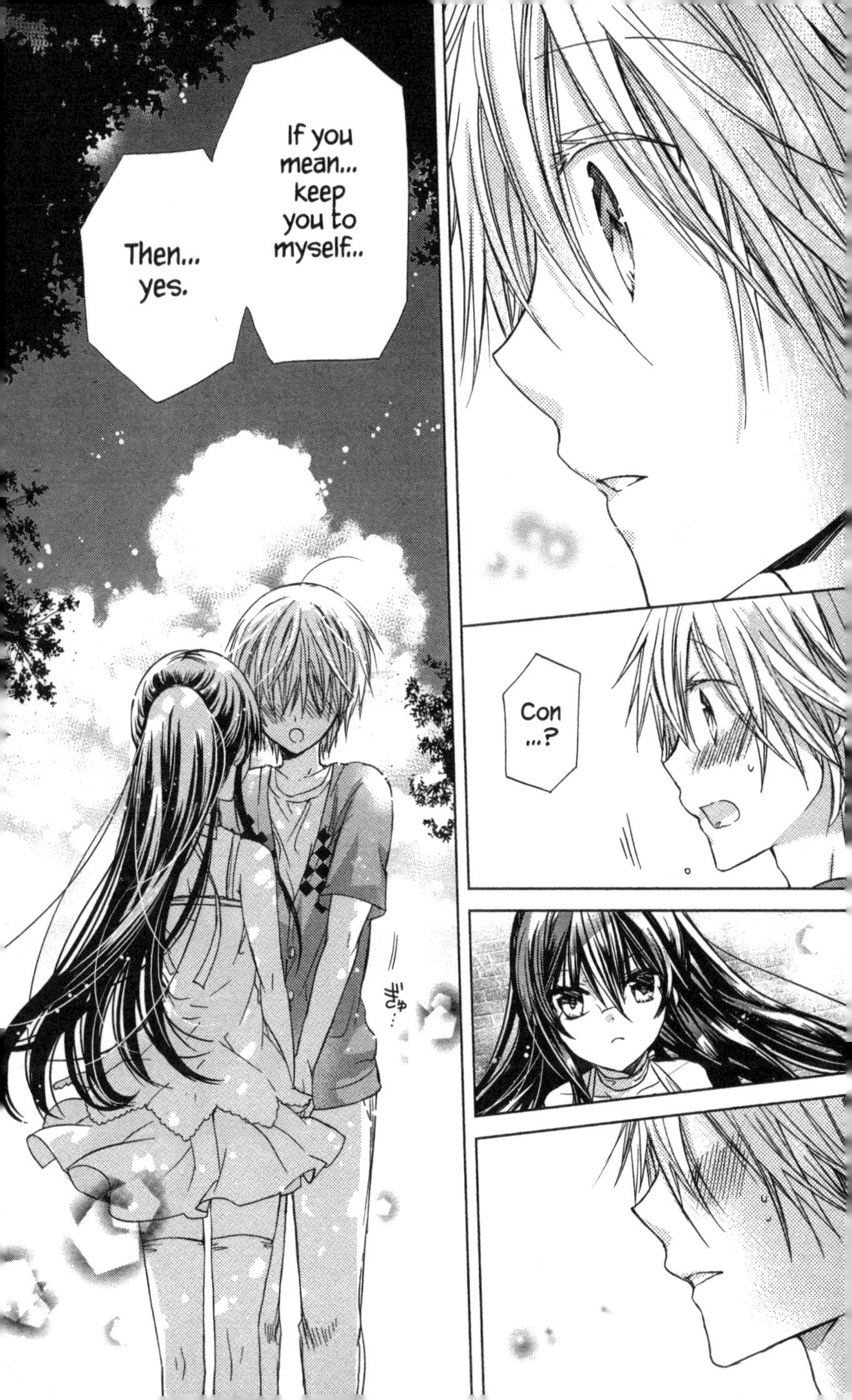
Con ...?
If you mean... keep you to myself...
Then... yes.
ぎゅ…

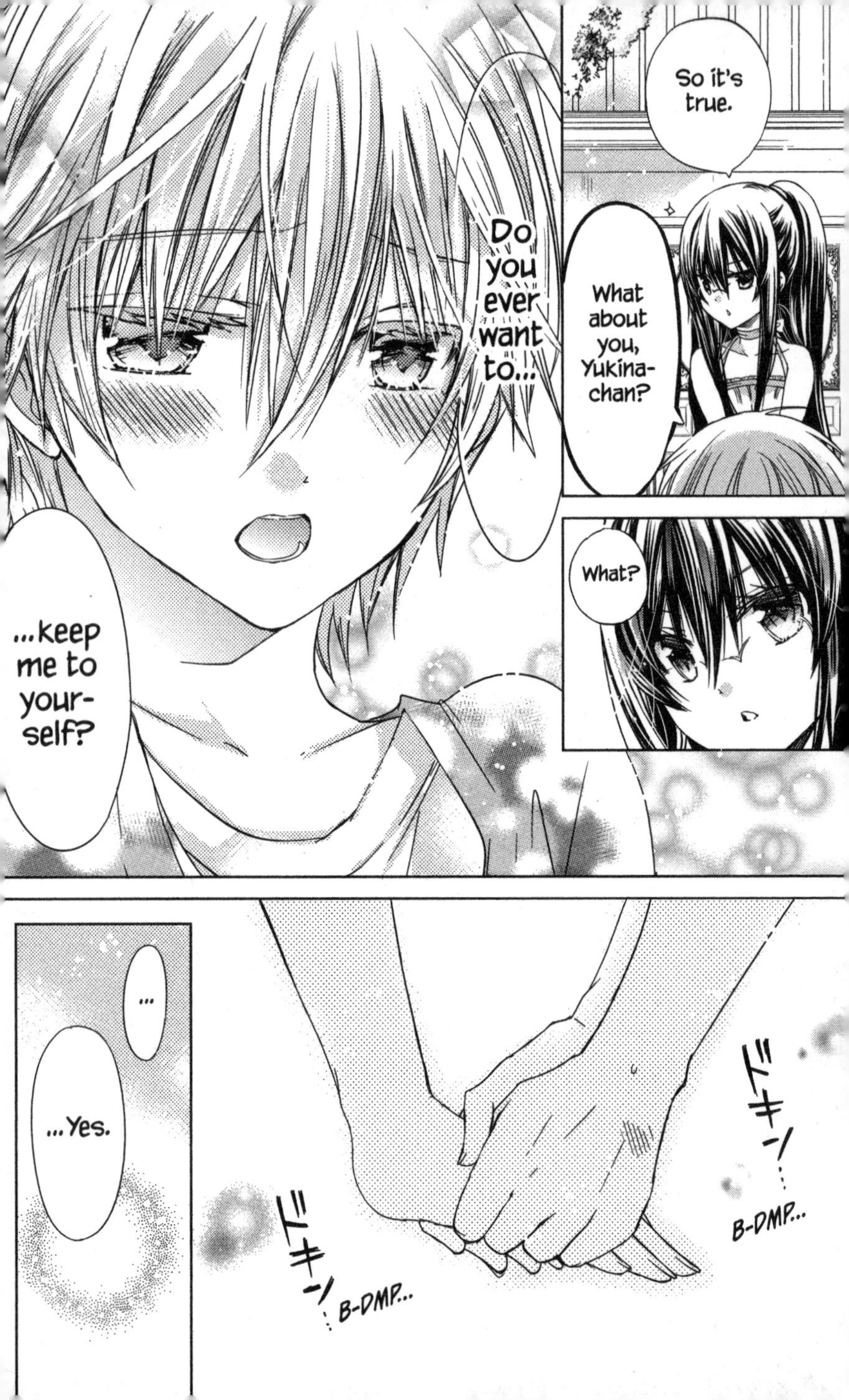
So it's true.
What about you, Yukina-chan?
What?
Do you ever want to...
...keep me to your-self?
ドキン B-DMP...
ドキン B-DMP...
...
...Yes.

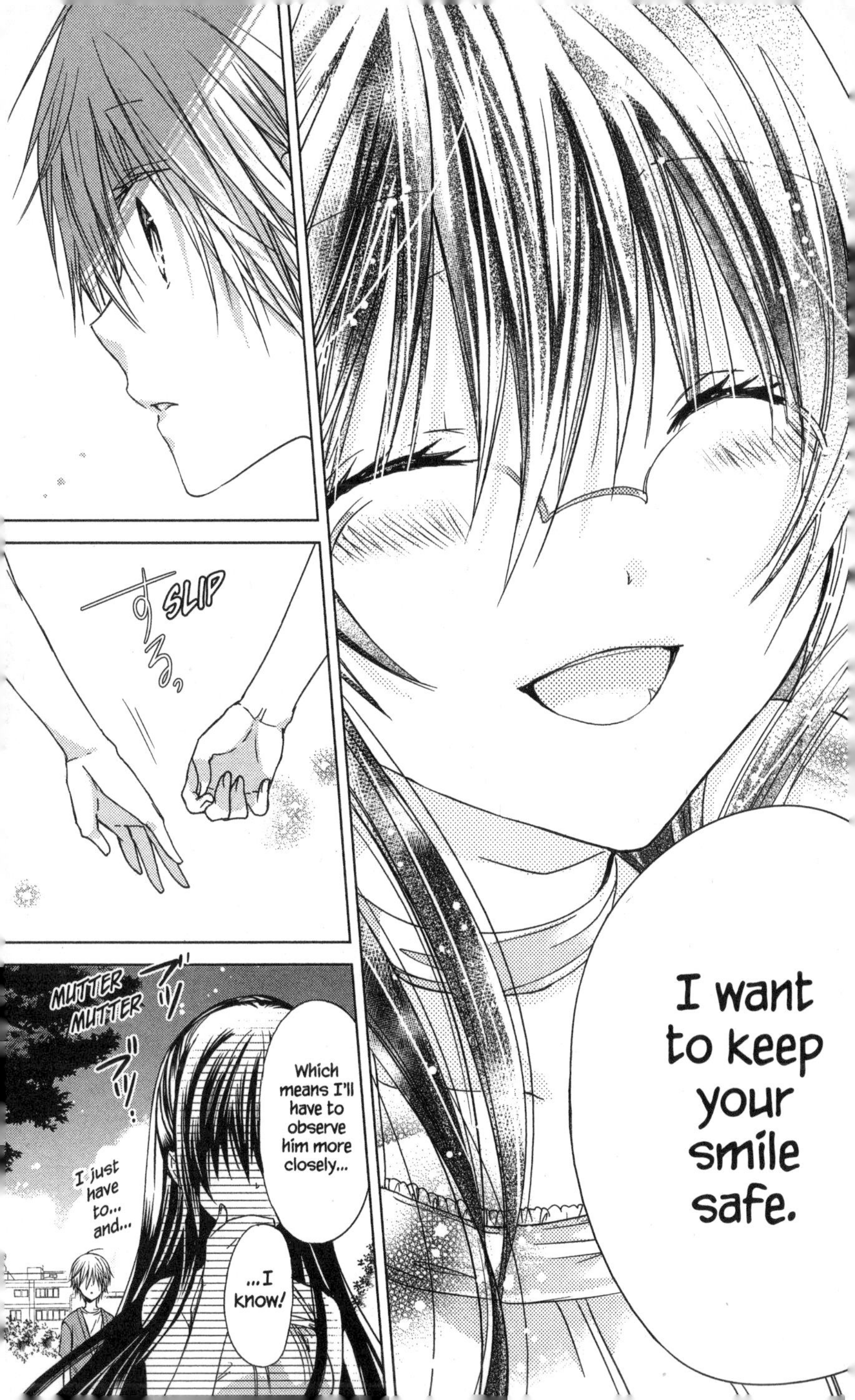
I want to keep your smile safe.
SLIP
MUTTER MUTTER
Which means I'll have to observe him more closely...
...I know!
I just have to... and...

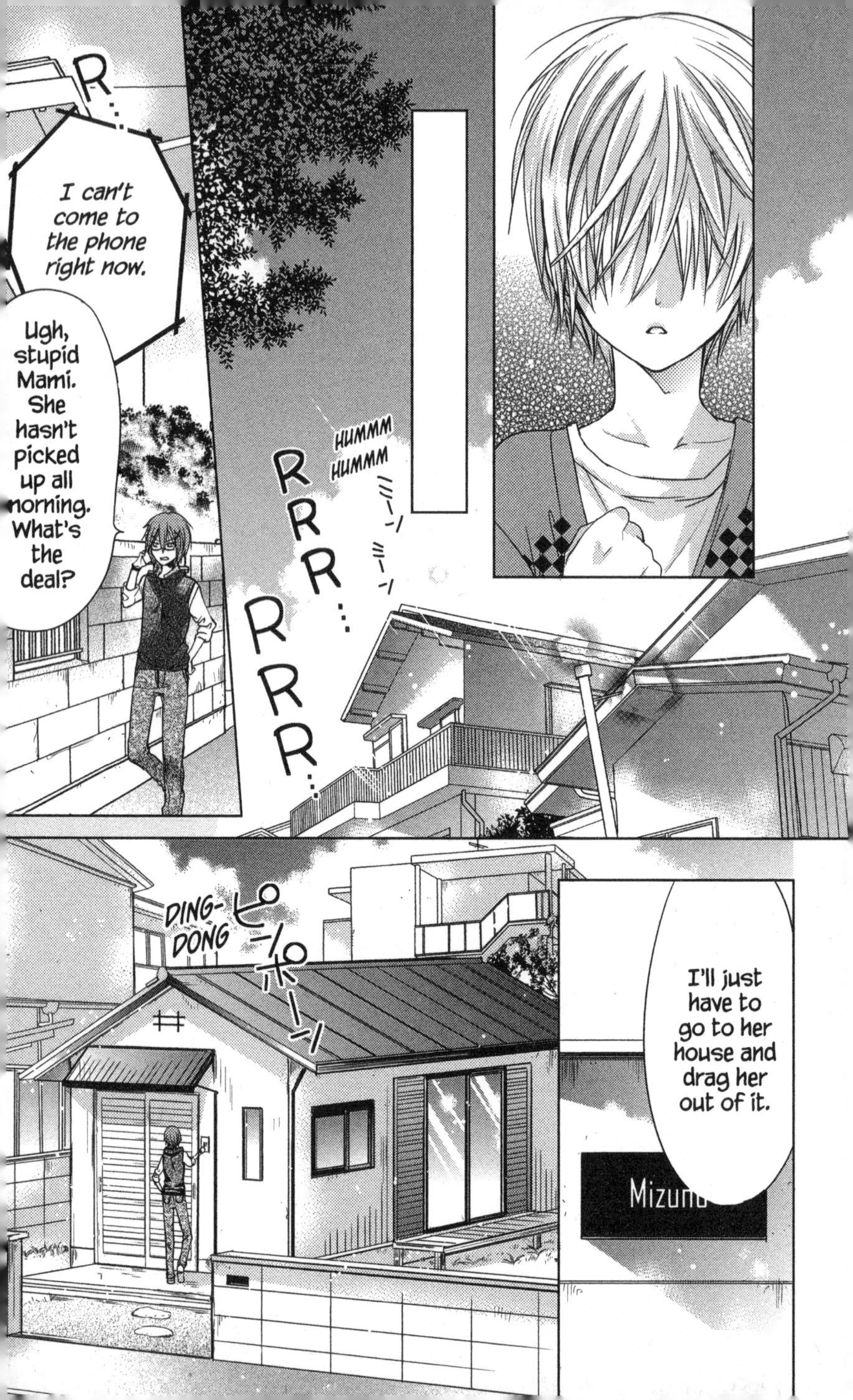
HUMMM HUMMM
RRR...
RRR...
R...
I can't come to the phone right now.
Ugh, stupid Mami. She hasn't picked up all morning. What's the deal?
I'll just have to go to her house and drag her out of it.
Mizuno
DING-DONG

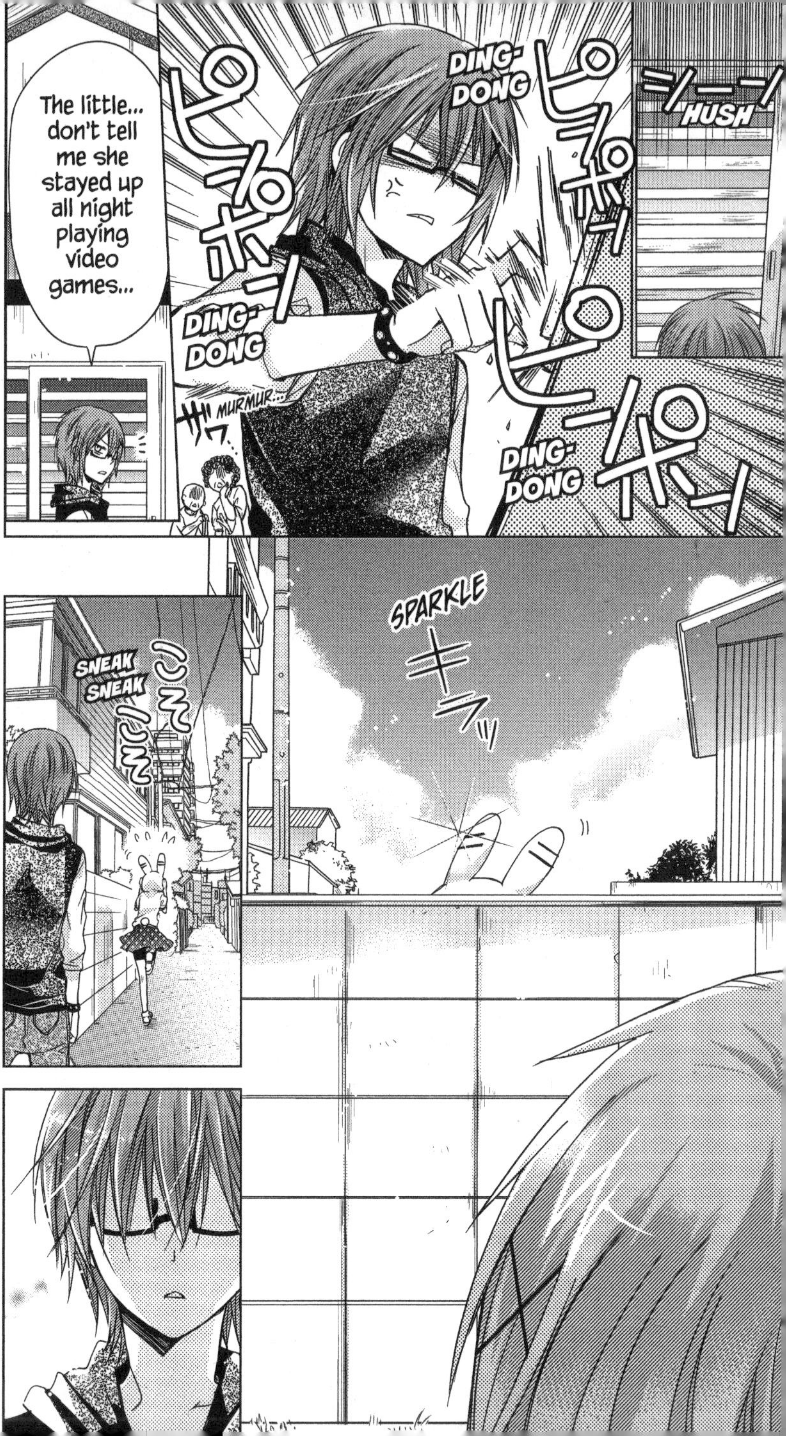
ピンポーン
DING-DONG
ピンポーン
DING-DONG
ピンポーン
DING-DONG
シーン
HUSH
The little... don't tell me she stayed up all night playing video games...
ザワ
MURMUR...
キラッ
SPARKLE
こそこそ
SNEAK SNEAK

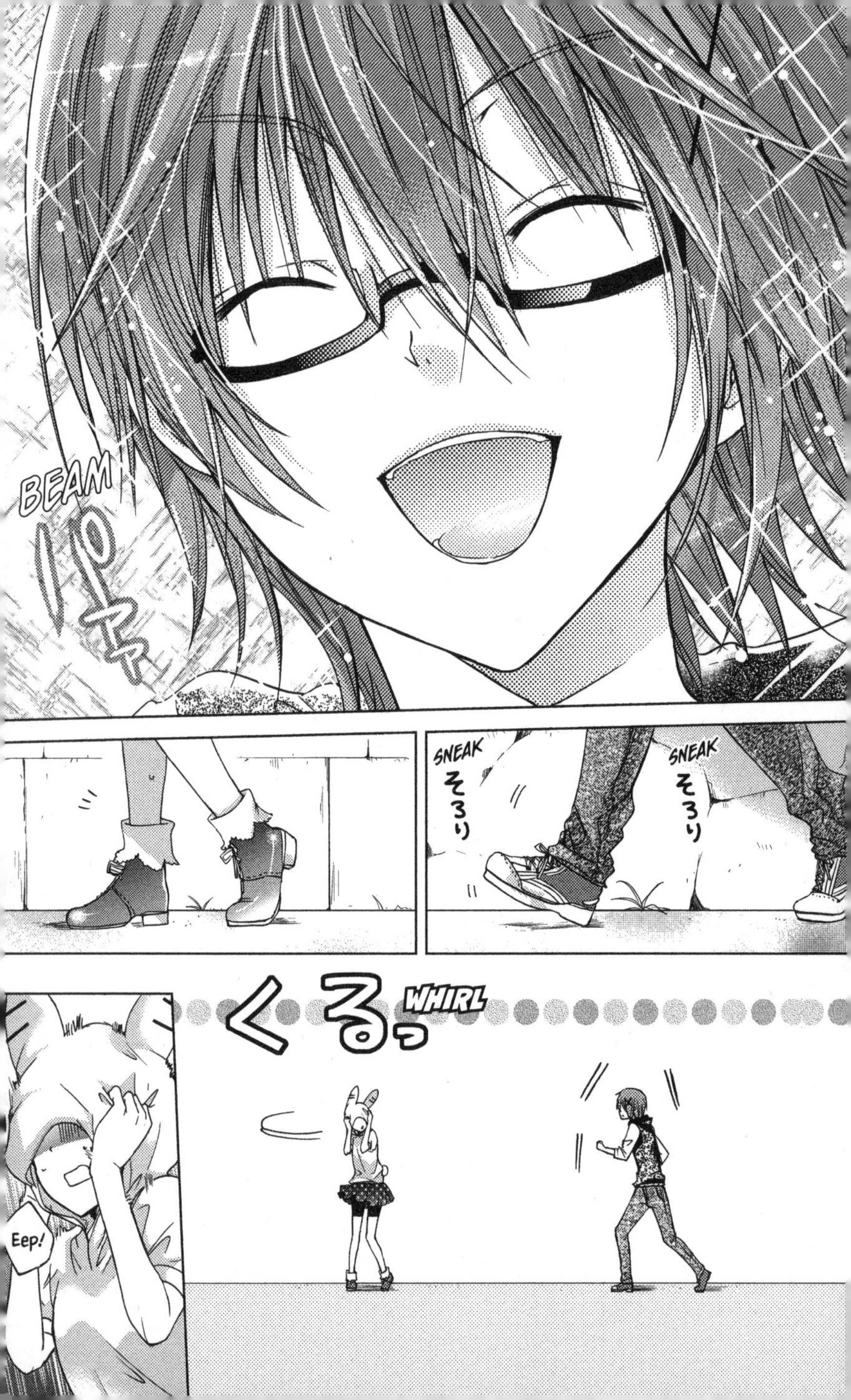
BEAM
パァァ
SNEAK
そろり
SNEAK
そろり
くるっ
WHIRL
Eep!

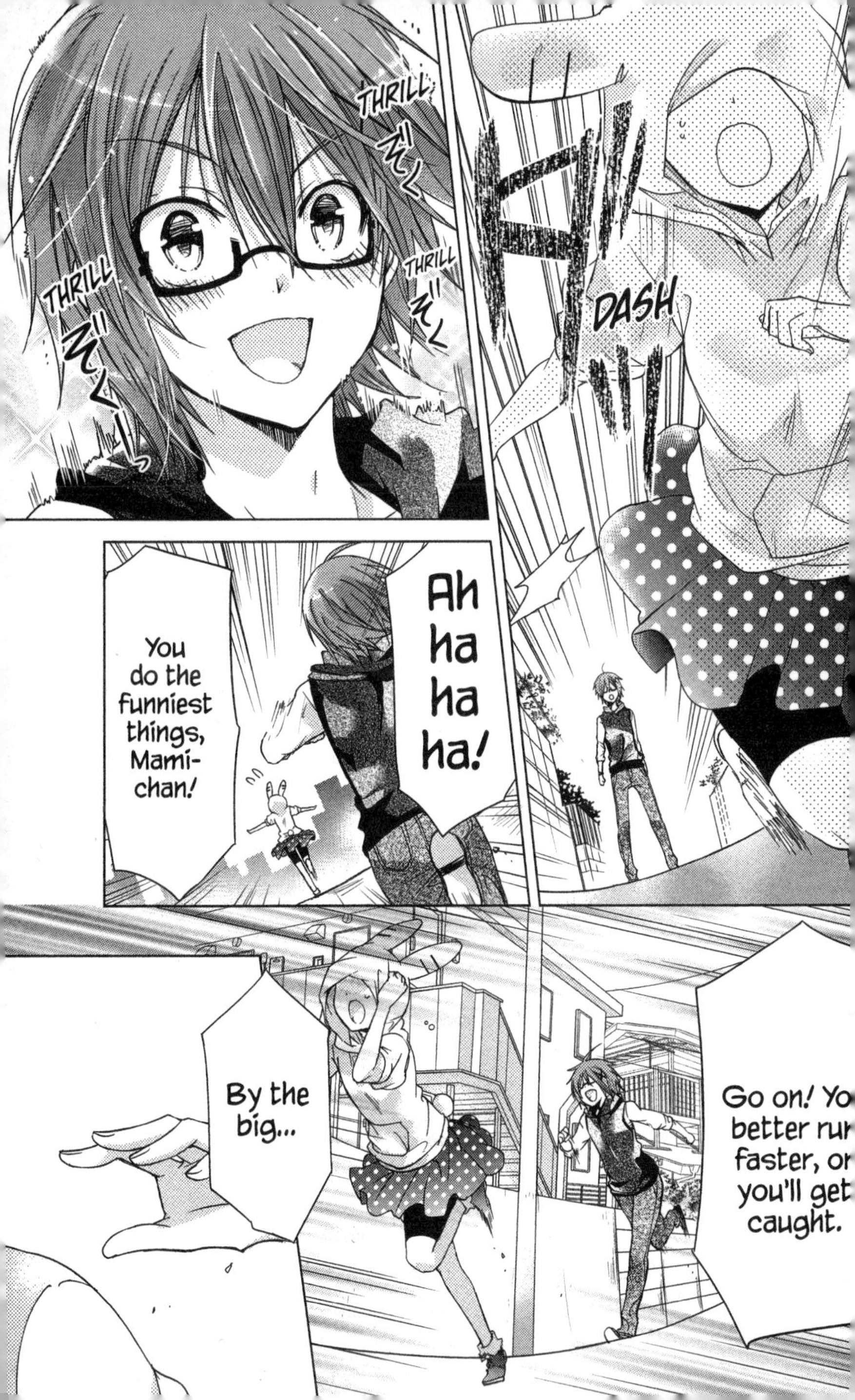
DASH
THRILL
THRILL
THRILL
Ah ha ha ha!
You do the funniest things, Mami-chan!
Go on! Yo better ru faster, or you'll get caught.
By the big...

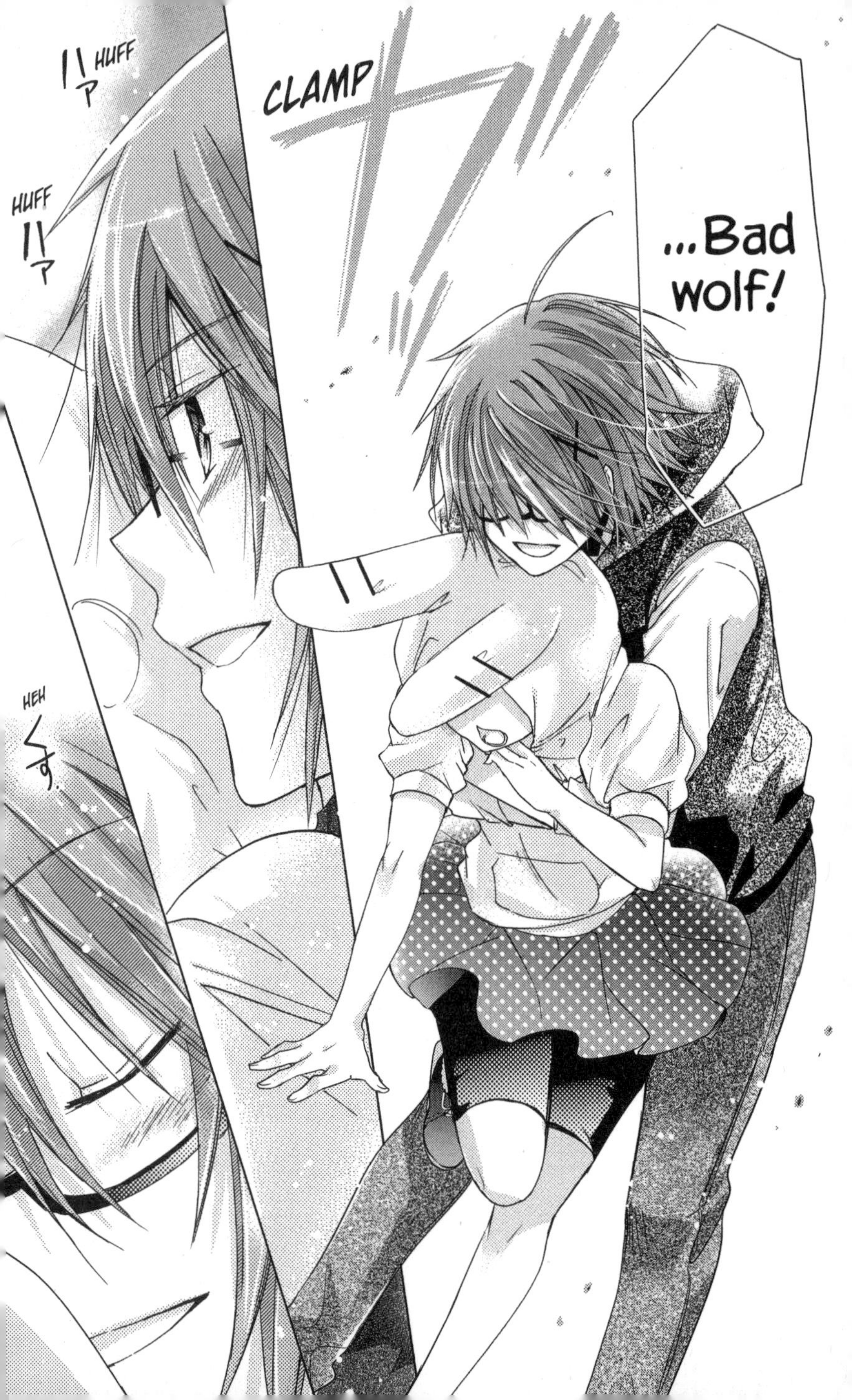
...Bad wolf!
CLAMP
ハァ HUFF
HUFF ハァ
HEH くす

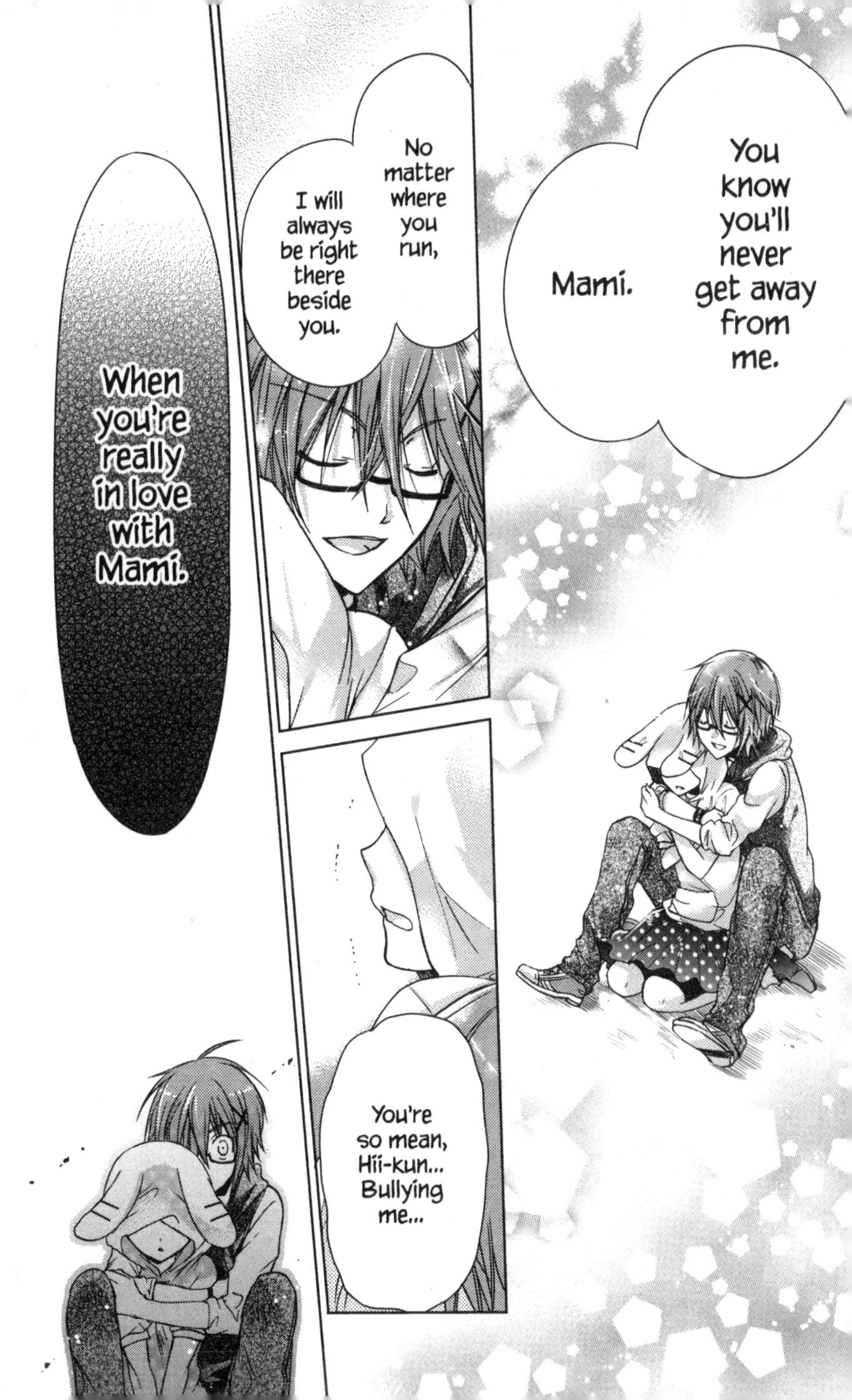
You know you'll never get away from me.
Mami.
No matter where you run,
I will always be right there beside you.
You're so mean, Hii-kun... Bullying me...
When you're really in love with Mami.

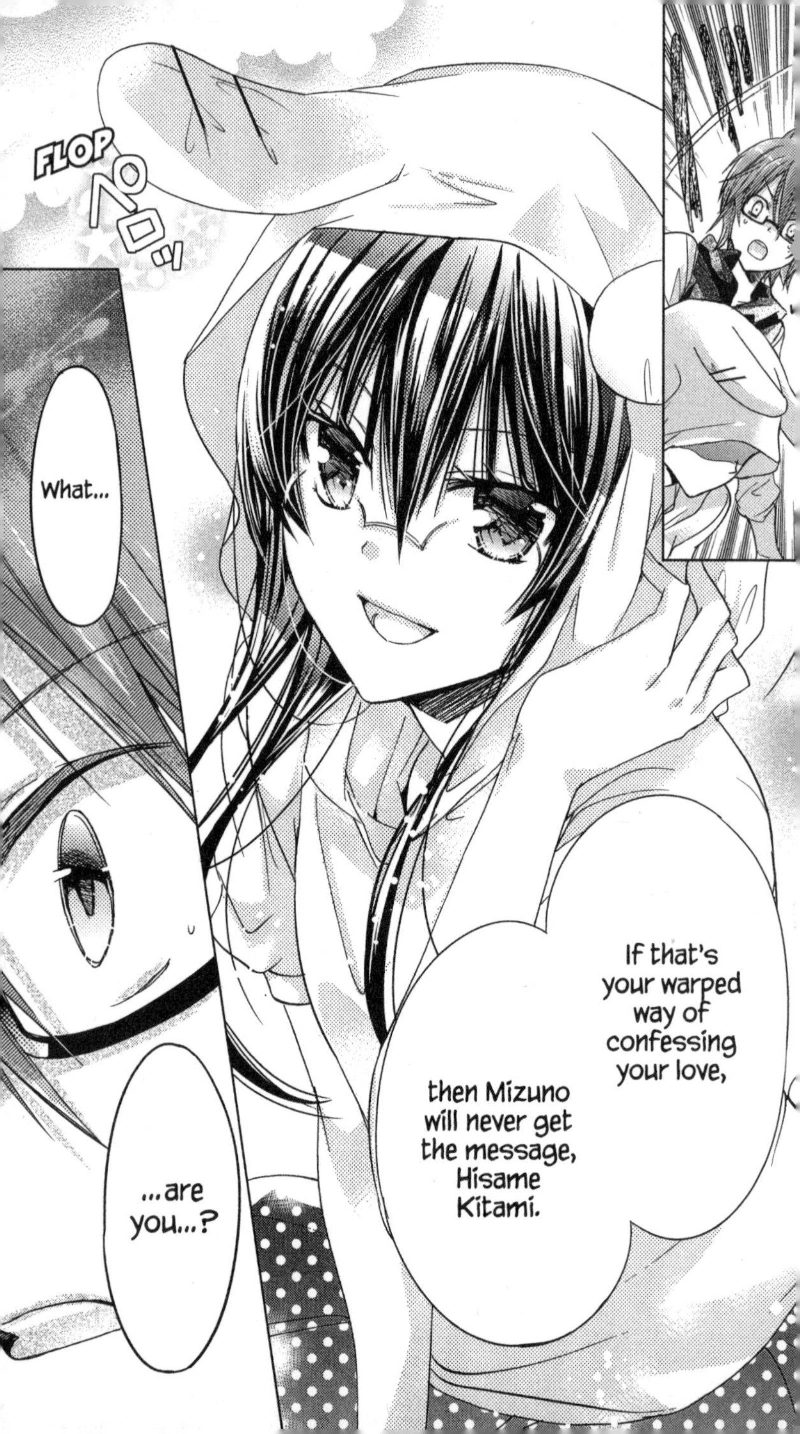
FLOP
ヘロッ
If that's your warped way of confessing your love,
then Mizuno will never get the message, Hisame Kitami.
What...
...are you...?

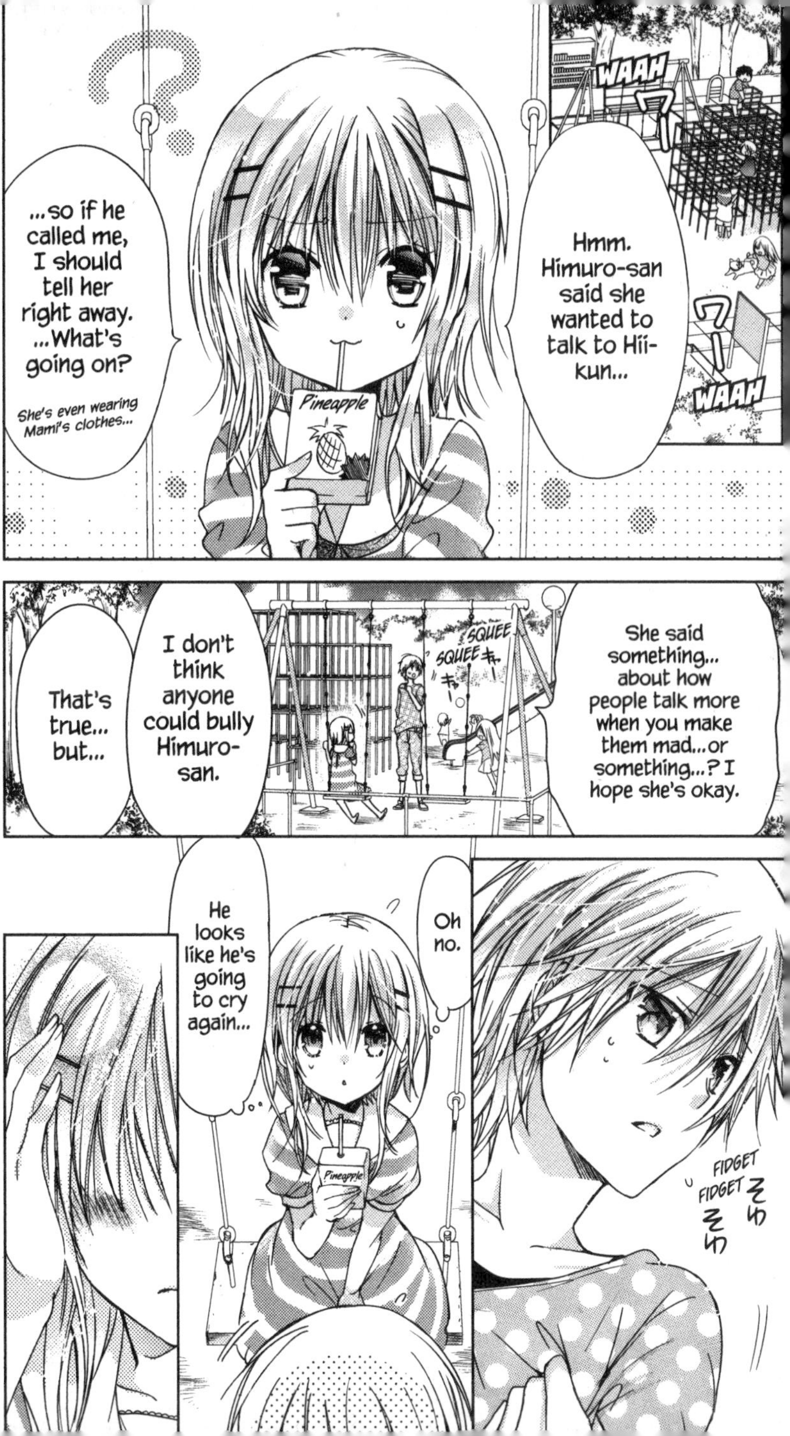
WAAH
ワー
WAAH
ワー
Hmm. Himuro-san said she wanted to talk to Hii-kun...
...so if he called me, I should tell her right away. ...What's going on?
She's even wearing Mami's clothes...
Pineapple
She said something... about how people talk more when you make them mad...or something...? I hope she's okay.
SQUEE
SQUEE
キャー
キャ
I don't think anyone could bully Himuro-san.
That's true... but...
FIDGET
FIDGET
そわそわ
Oh no.
He looks like he's going to cry again...
Pineapple

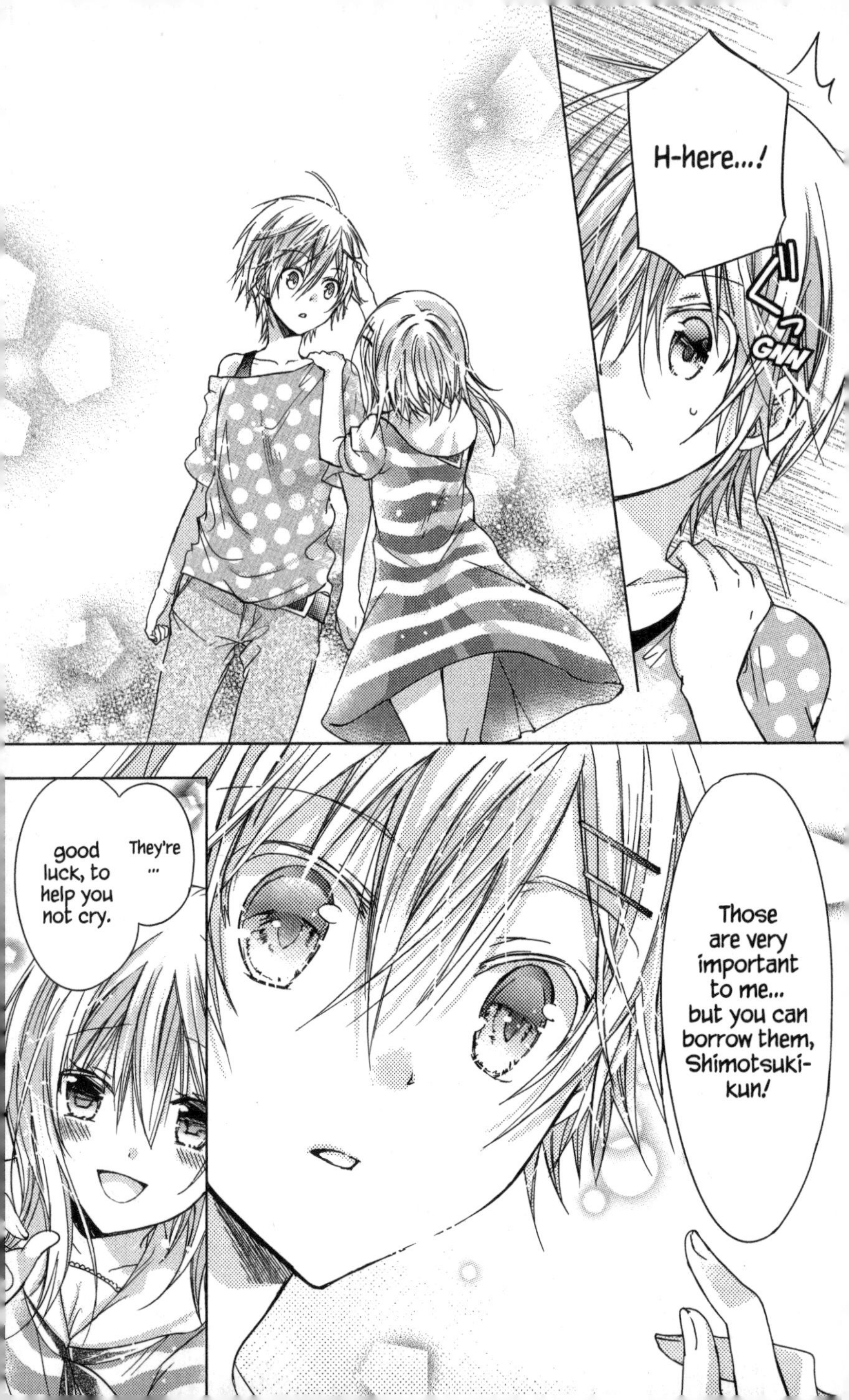
H-here...!
GNN
Those are very important to me... but you can borrow them, Shimotsuki-kun!
They're... good luck, to help you not cry.

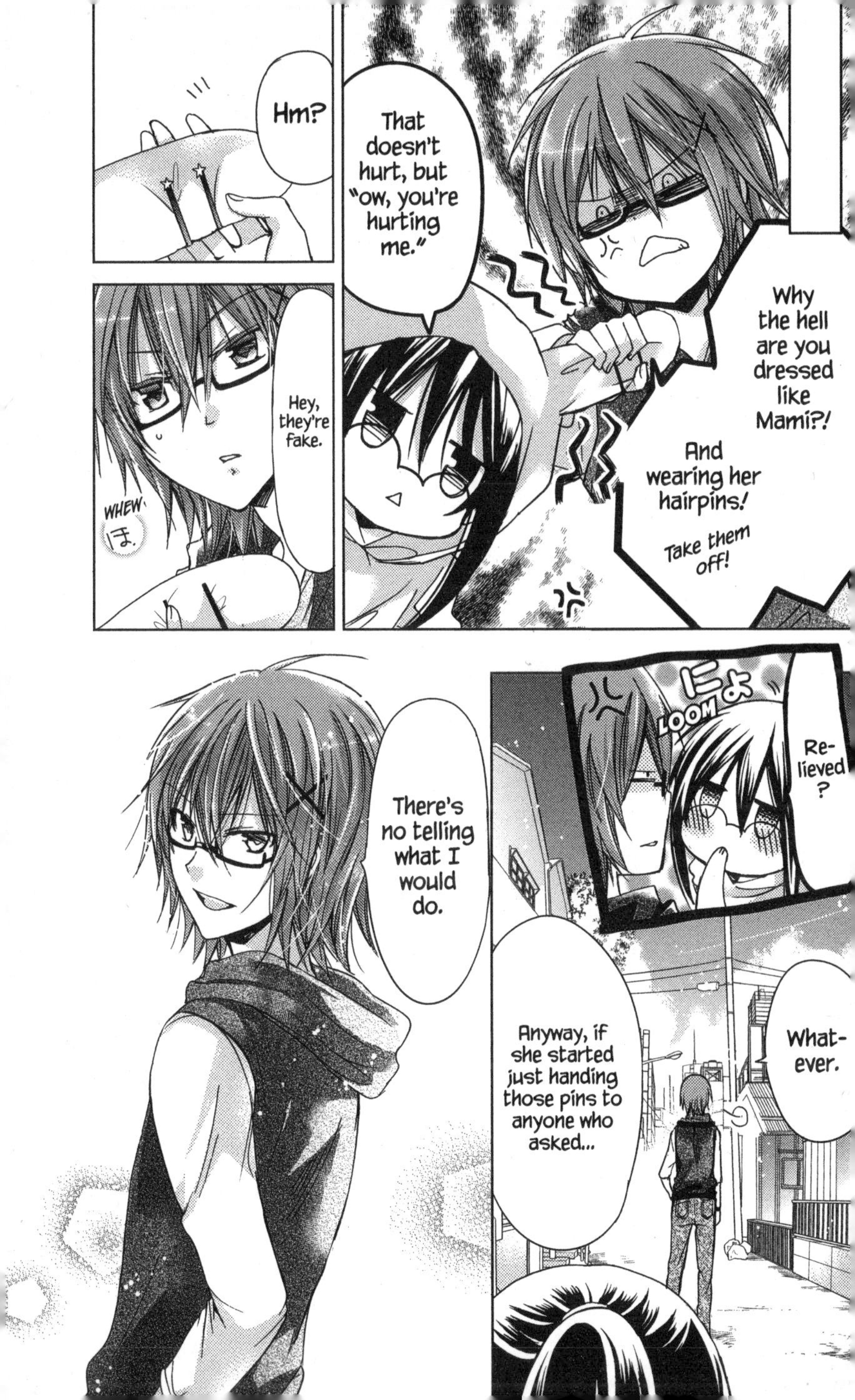
Why the hell are you dressed like Mami?!
And wearing her hairpins!
Take them off!
That doesn't hurt, but "ow, you're hurting me."
Hm?
Hey, they're fake.
WHEW
ほ.
にょ
LOOM
Re-lieved?
What-ever.
Anyway, if she started just handing those pins to anyone who asked...
There's no telling what I would do.

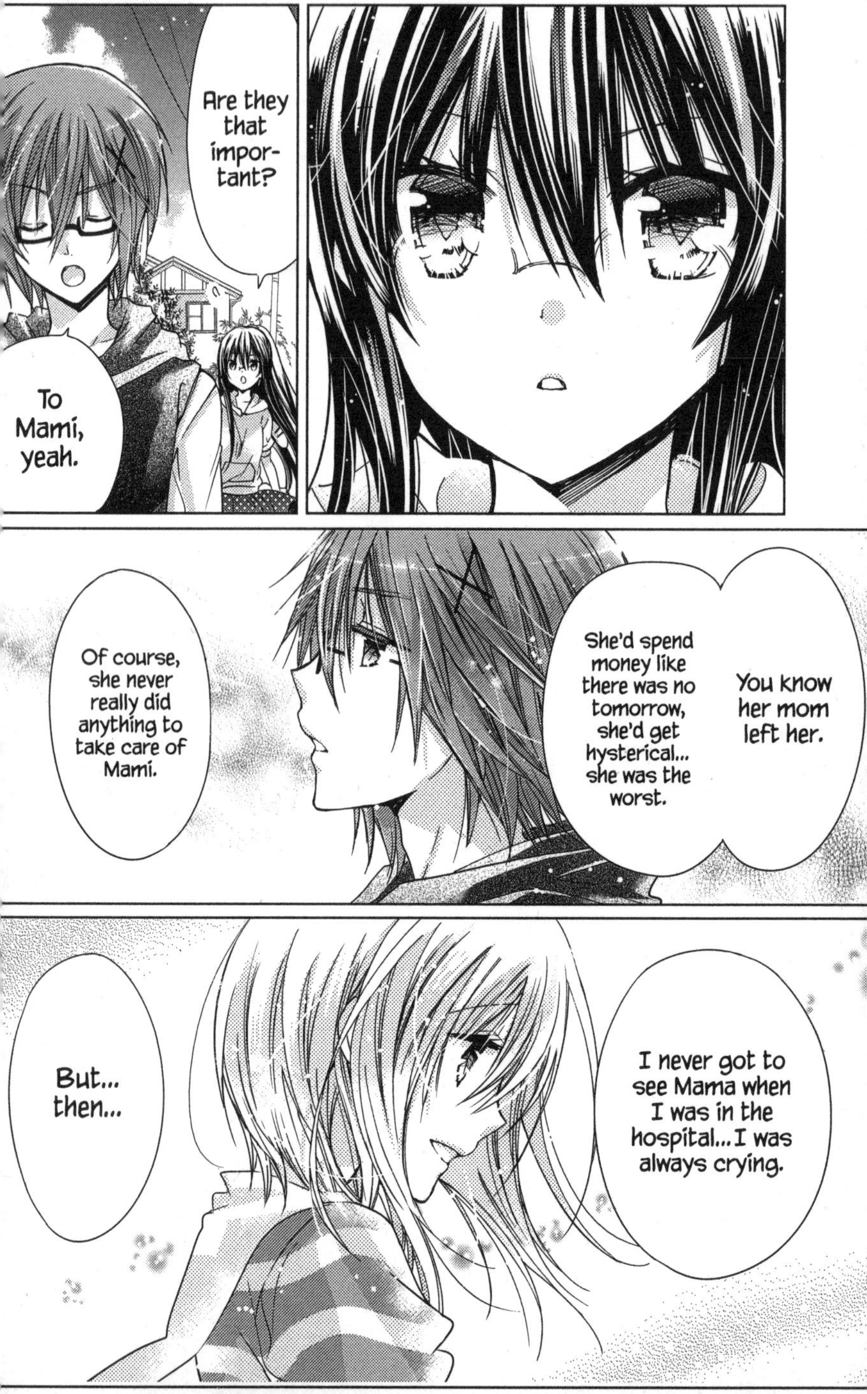
Are they that impor-tant?
To Mami, yeah.
You know her mom left her.
She'd spend money like there was no tomorrow, she'd get hysterical... she was the worst.
Of course, she never really did anything to take care of Mami.
I never got to see Mama when I was in the hospital... I was always crying.
But... then...

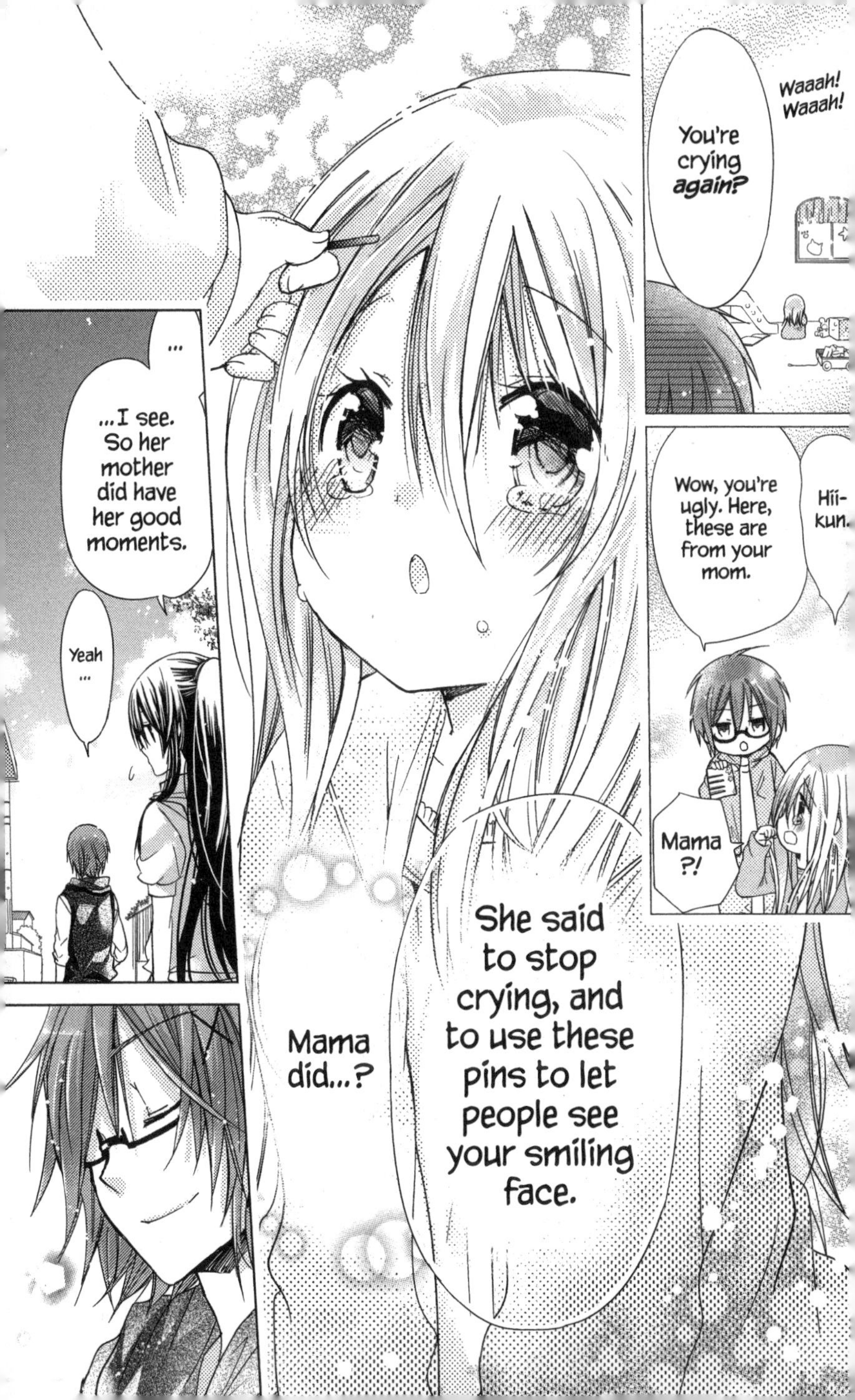
Waaah! Waaah!
You're crying *again?*
Hii-kun.
Wow, you're ugly. Here, these are from your mom.
Mama?!
She said to stop crying, and to use these pins to let people see your smiling face.
Mama did...?
...
...I see. So her mother did have her good moments.
Yeah...

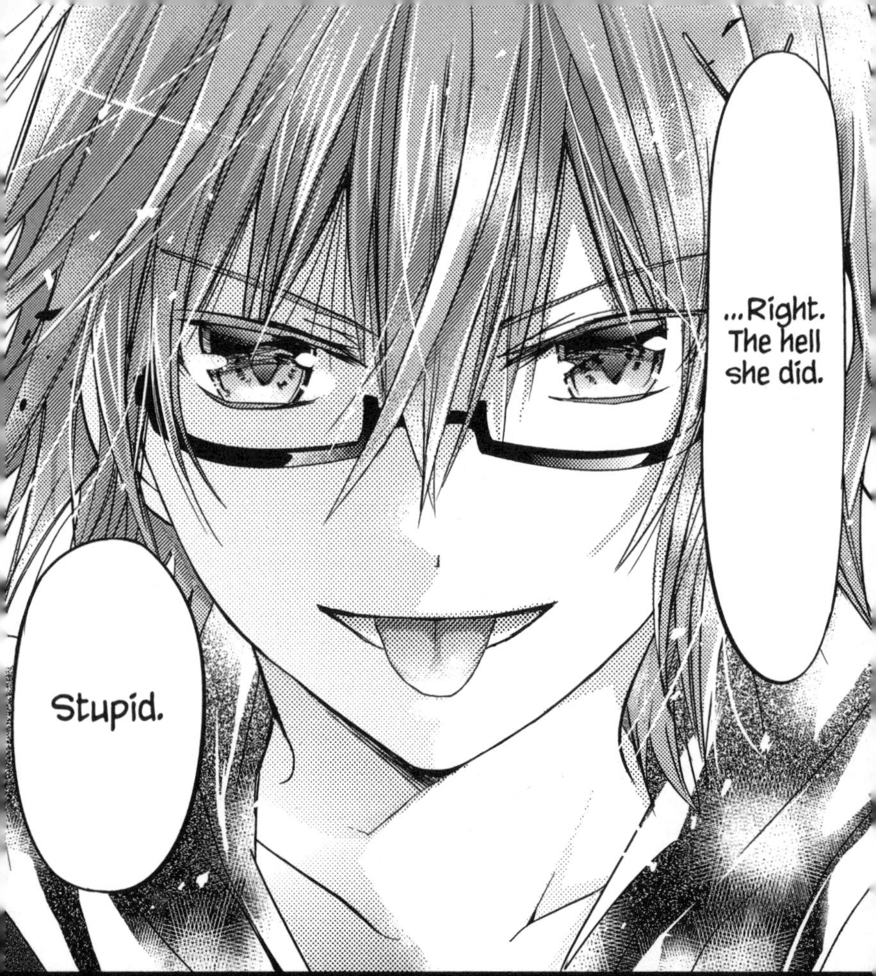
...Right. The hell she did.
Stupid.
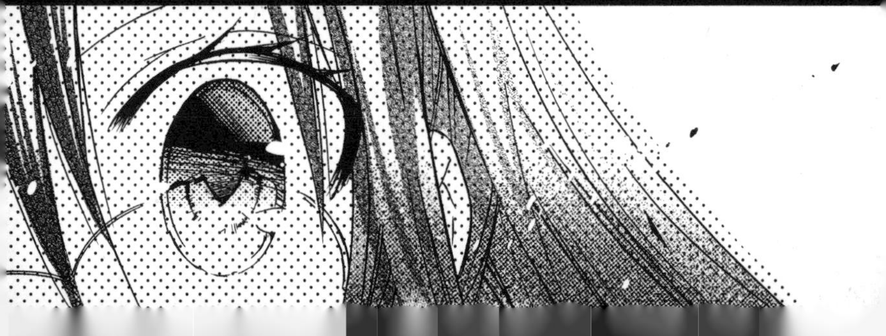

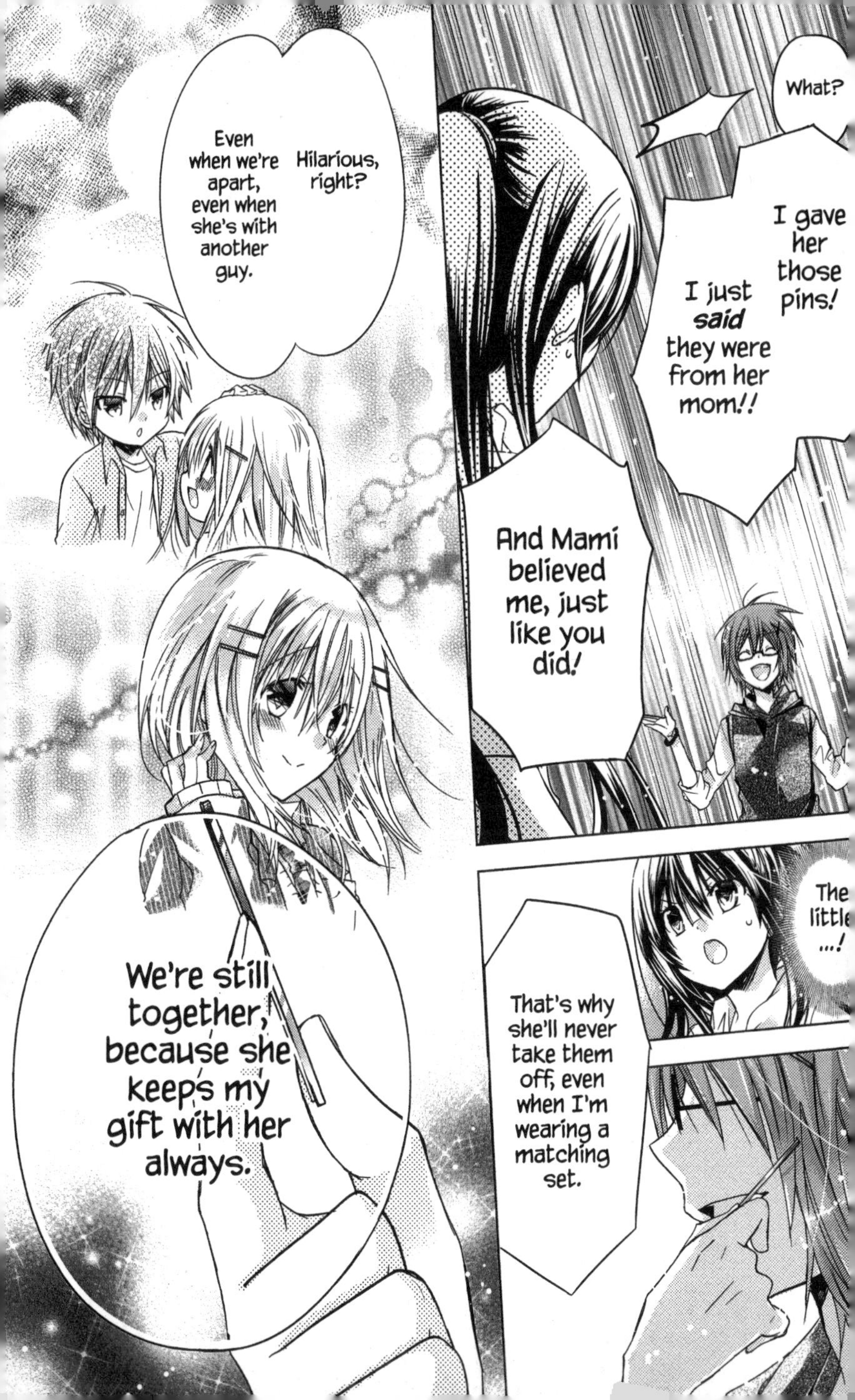
What?
I gave her those pins!
I just *said* they were from her mom!!
And Mami believed me, just like you did!
The little...!
That's why she'll never take them off, even when I'm wearing a matching set.
Hilarious, right?
Even when we're apart, even when she's with another guy.
We're still together, because she keeps my gift with her always.

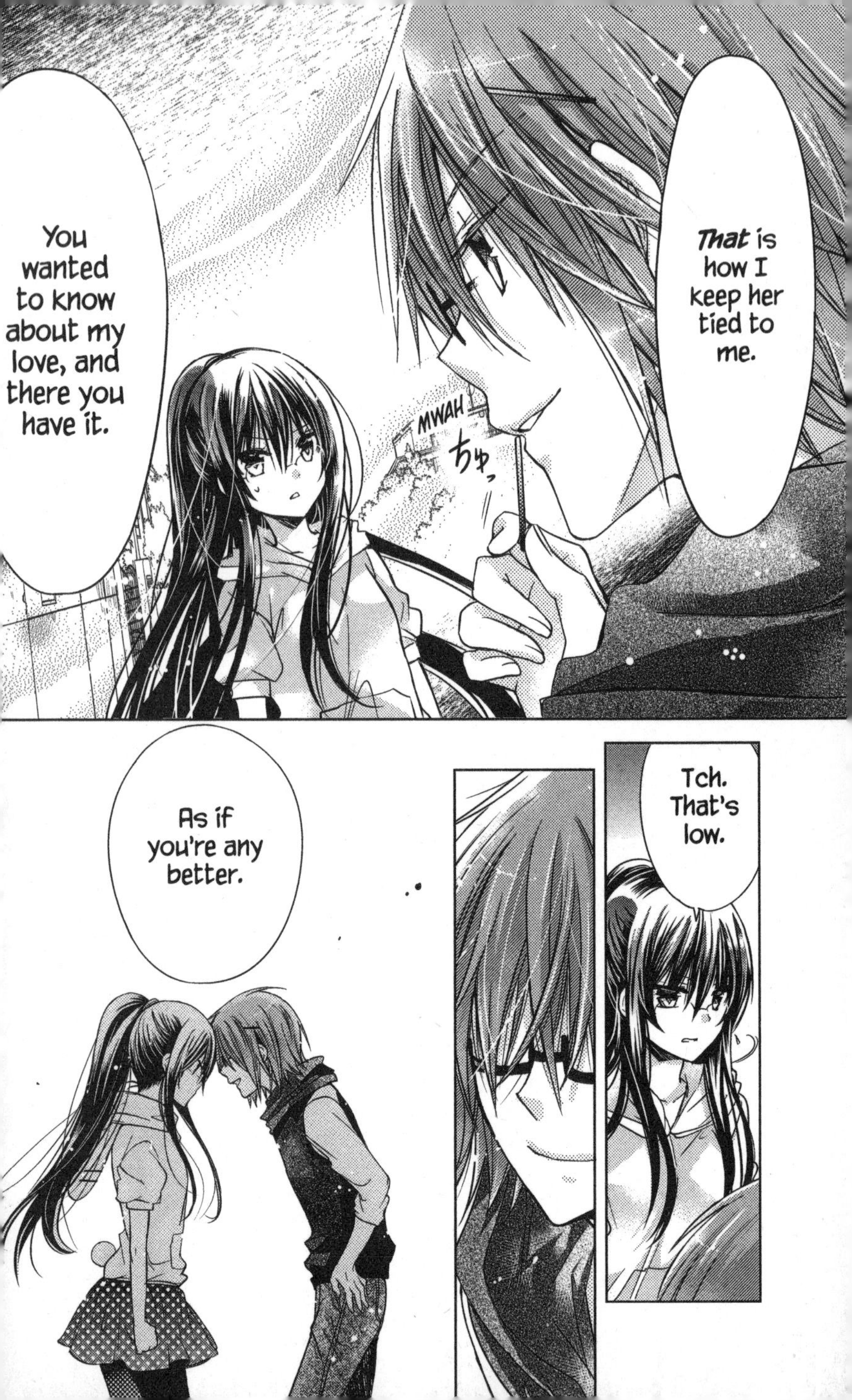
That is how I keep her tied to me.
MWAH
ちゅっ
You wanted to know about my love, and there you have it.
Tch. That's low.
As if you're any better.

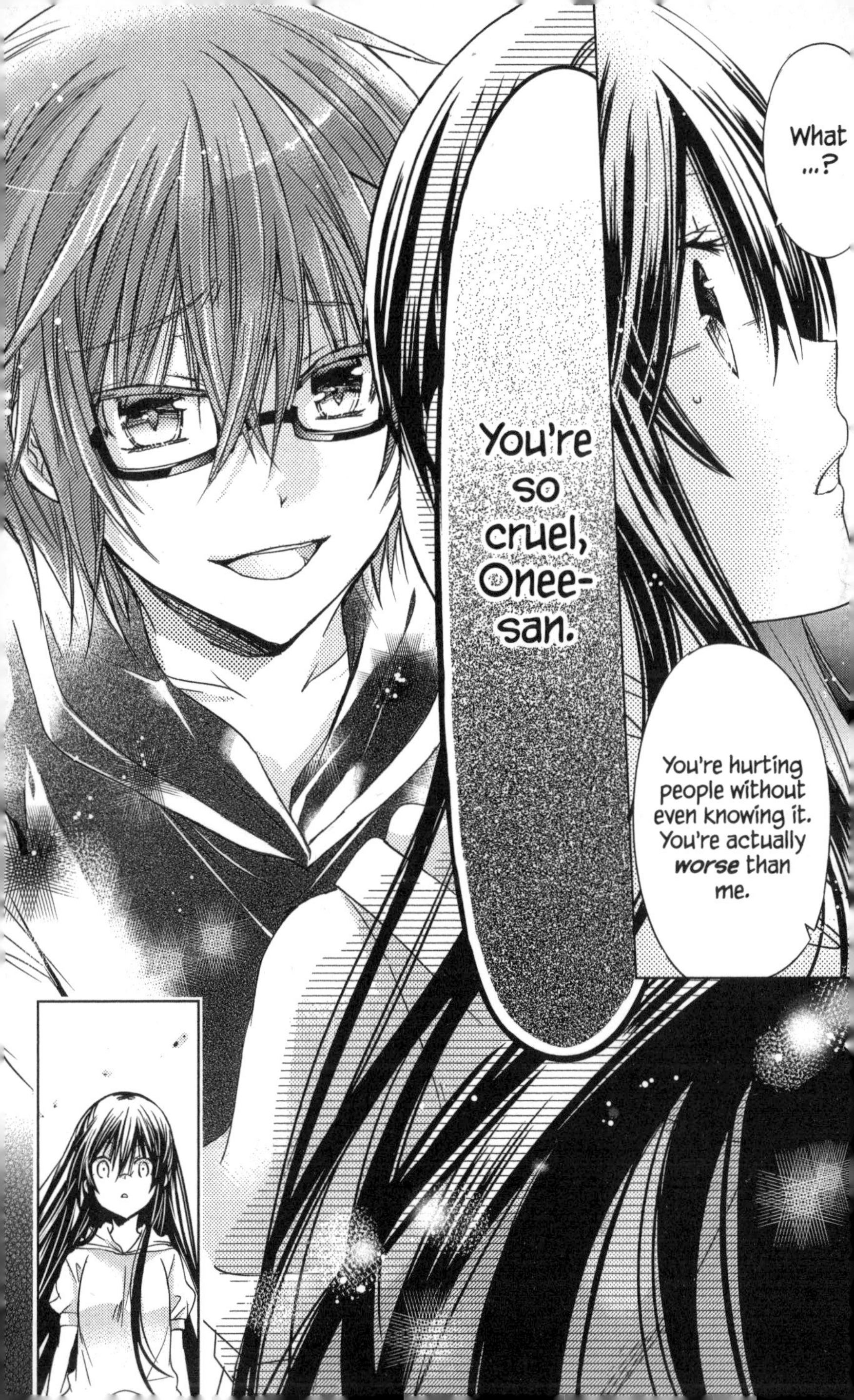
What ...?
You're so cruel, Onee-san.
You're hurting people without even knowing it. You're actually *worse* than me.

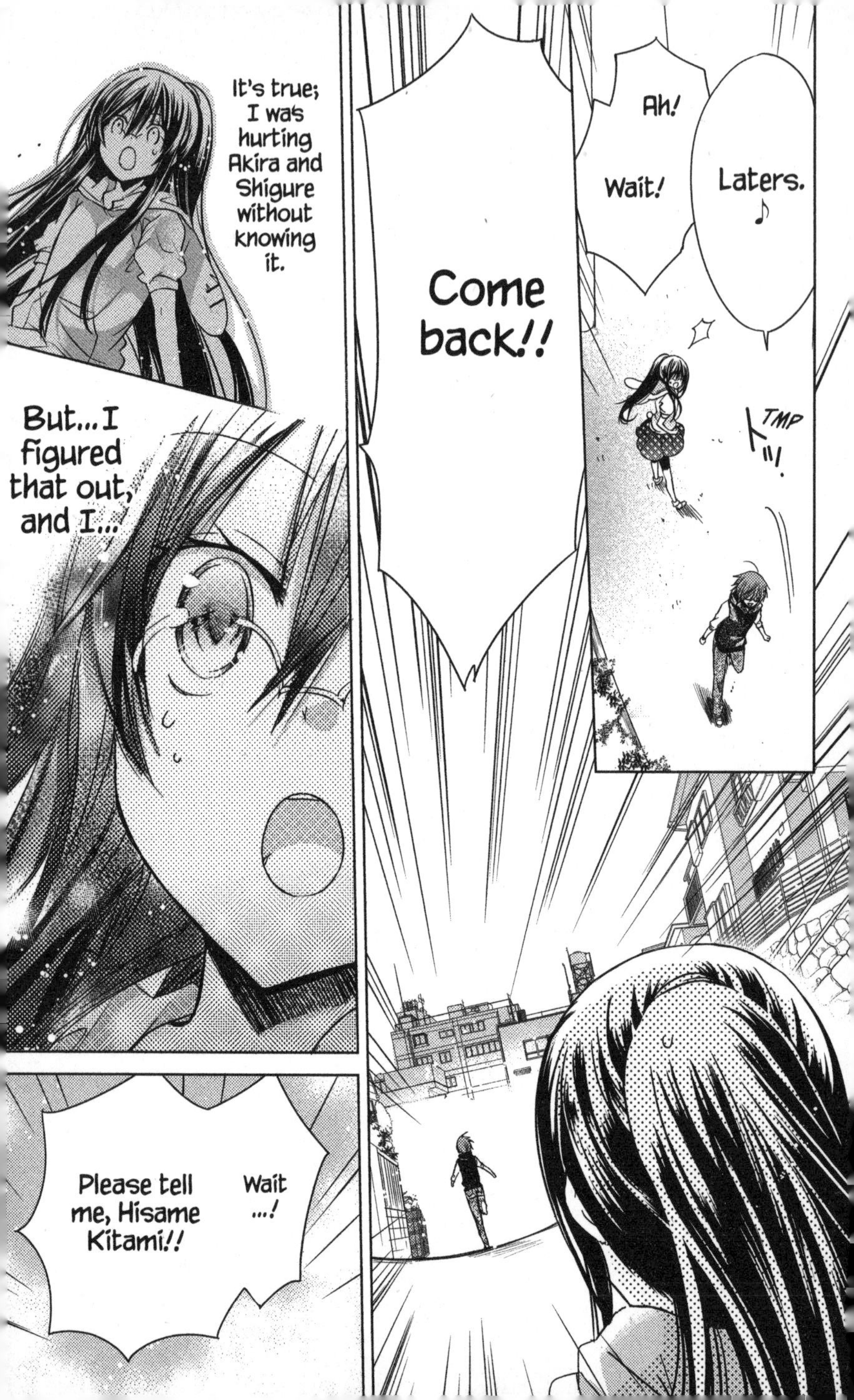

Laters. ♪
Ah!
Wait!
TMP
Come back!!
It's true; I was hurting Akira and Shigure without knowing it.
But...I figured that out, and I...
Wait...!
Please tell me, Hisame Kitami!!

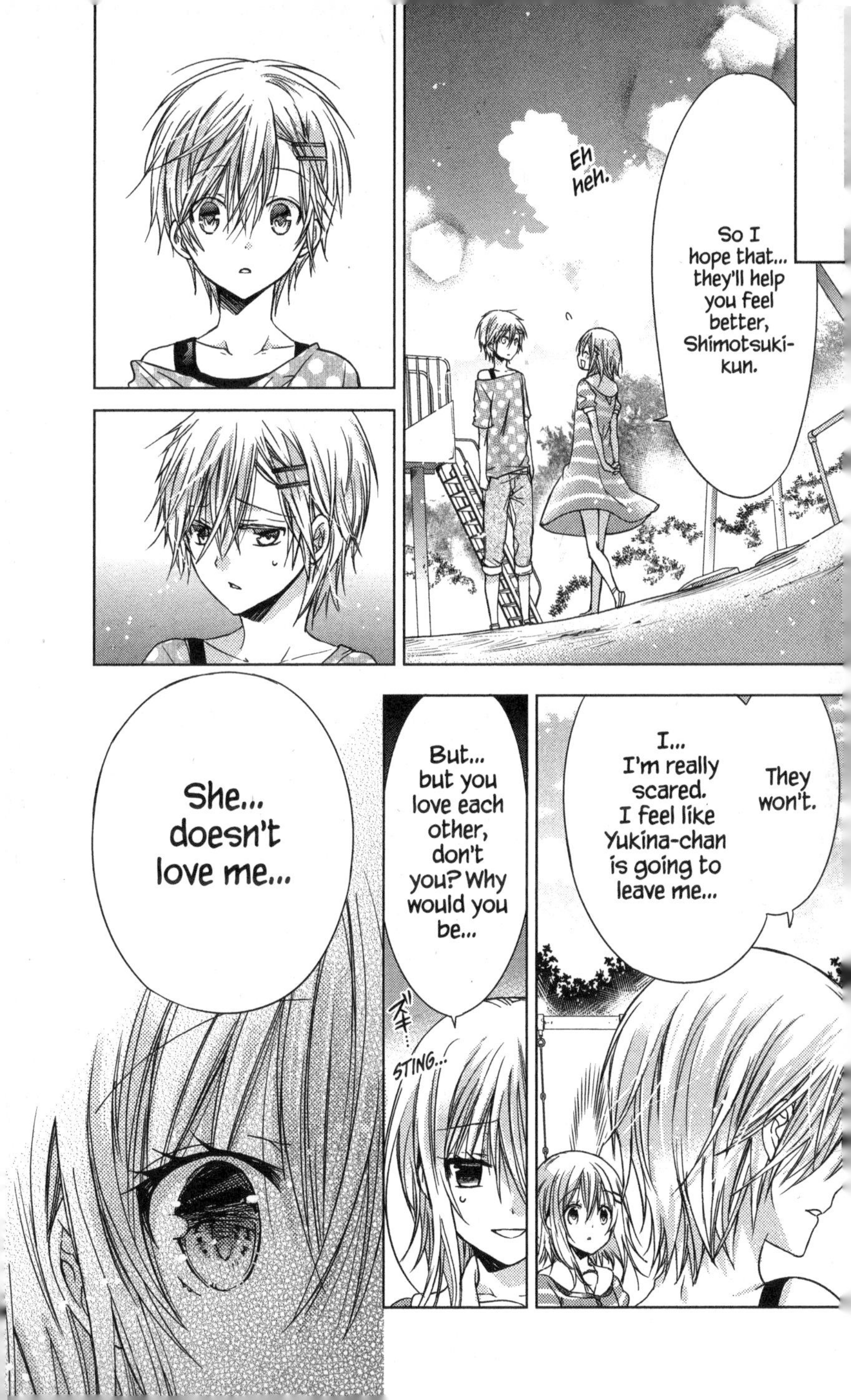
So I hope that... they'll help you feel better, Shimotsuki-kun.
Eh heh.
They won't.
I... I'm really scared. I feel like Yukina-chan is going to leave me...
But... but you love each other, don't you? Why would you be...
ズキ...
STING...
She... doesn't love me...

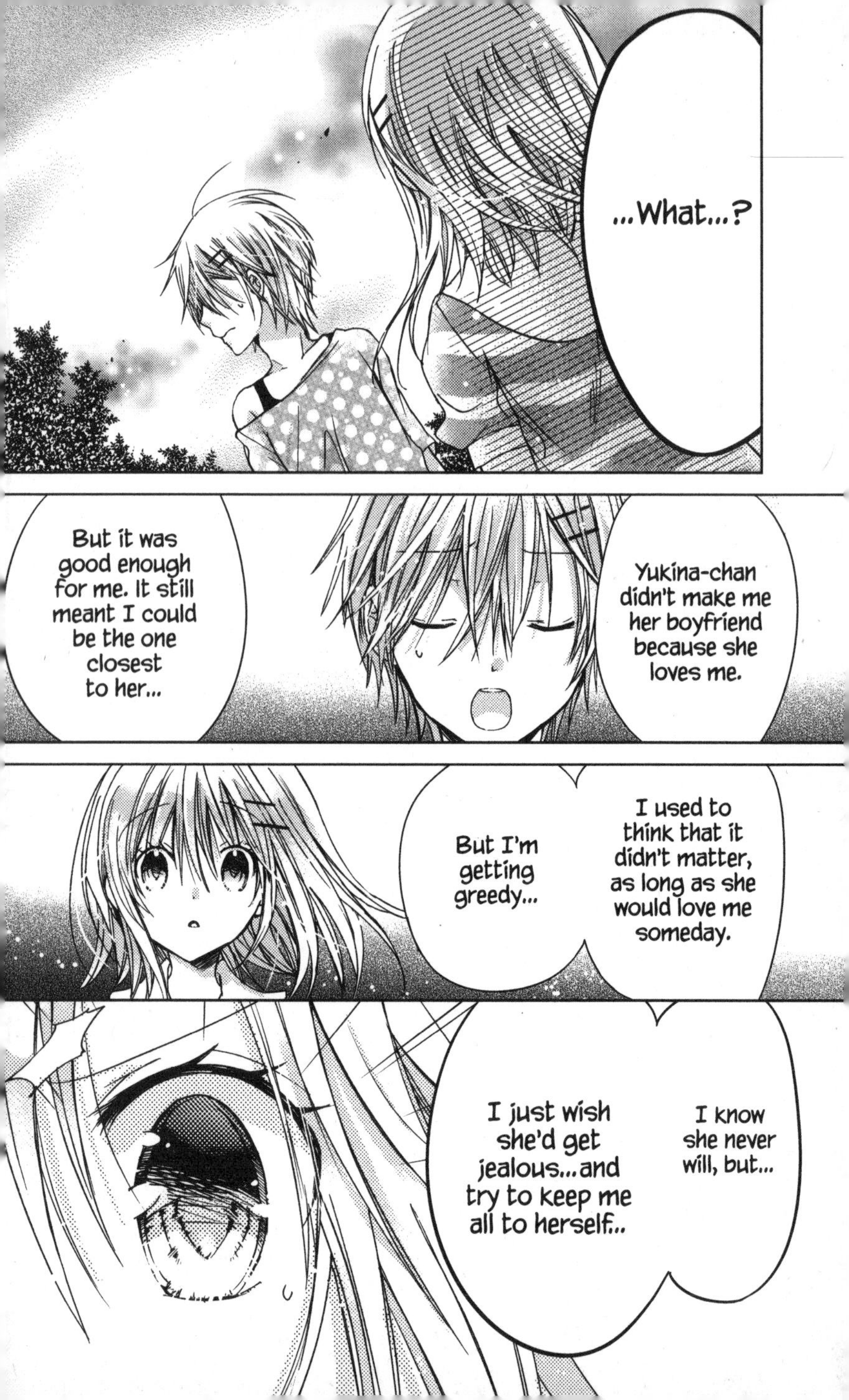

...What...?
Yukina-chan didn't make me her boyfriend because she loves me.
But it was good enough for me. It still meant I could be the one closest to her...
I used to think that it didn't matter, as long as she would love me someday.
But I'm getting greedy...
I know she never will, but...
I just wish she'd get jealous...and try to keep me all to herself...

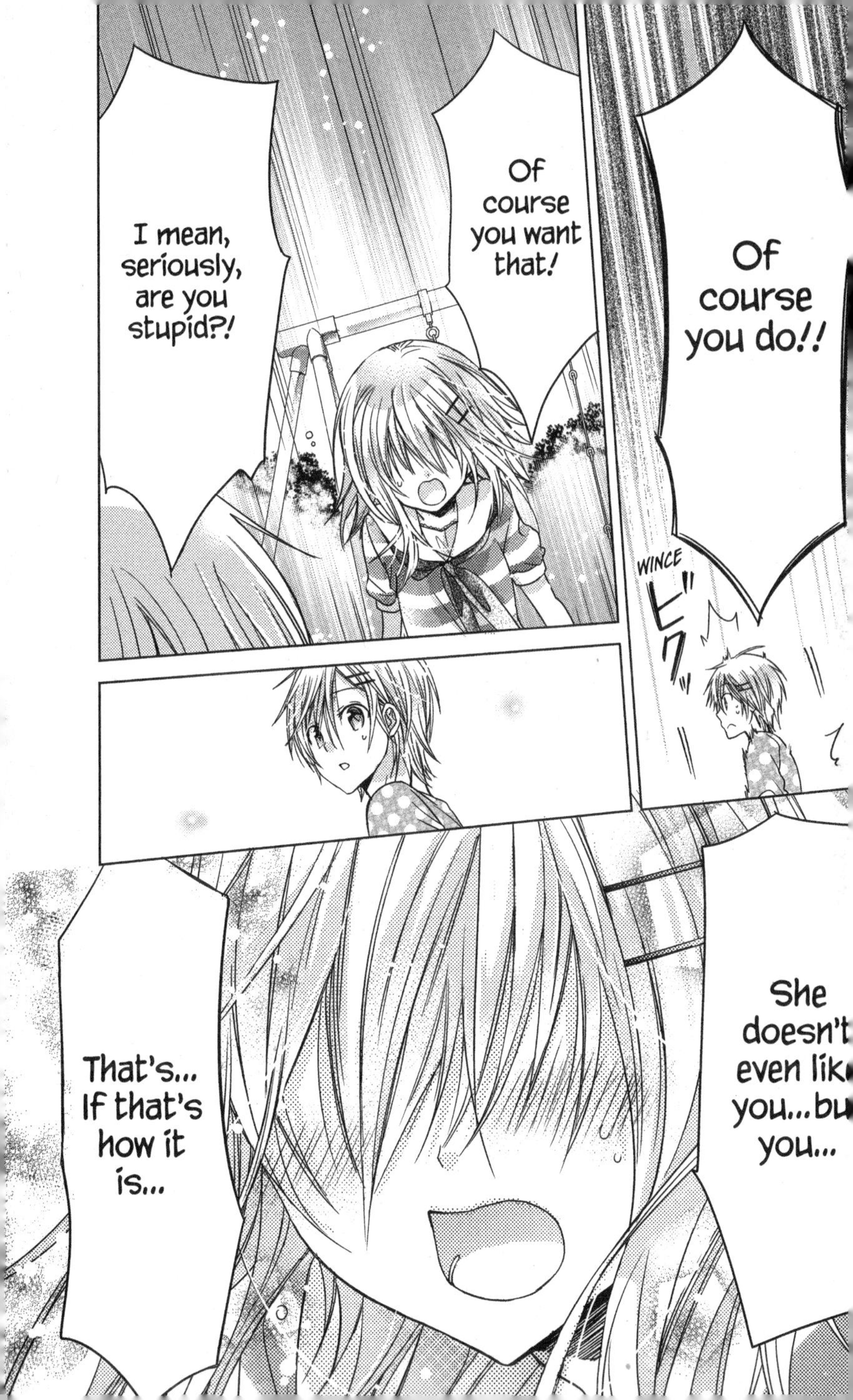
Of course you do!!
WINCE
ビクッ
Of course you want that!
I mean, seriously, are you stupid?!
She doesn't even lik you...bu you...
That's... If that's how it is...

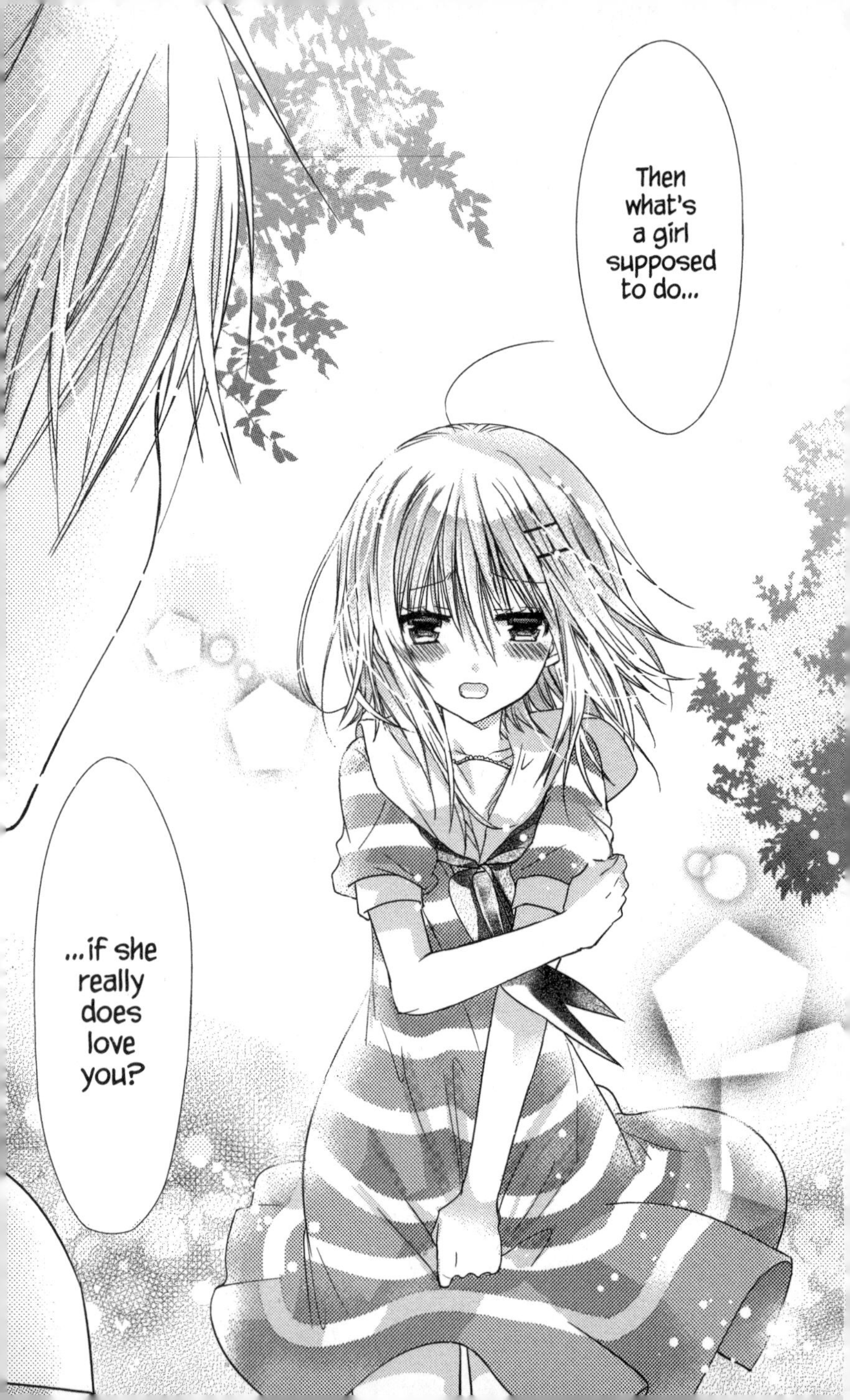
Then what's a girl supposed to do...
...if she really does love you?

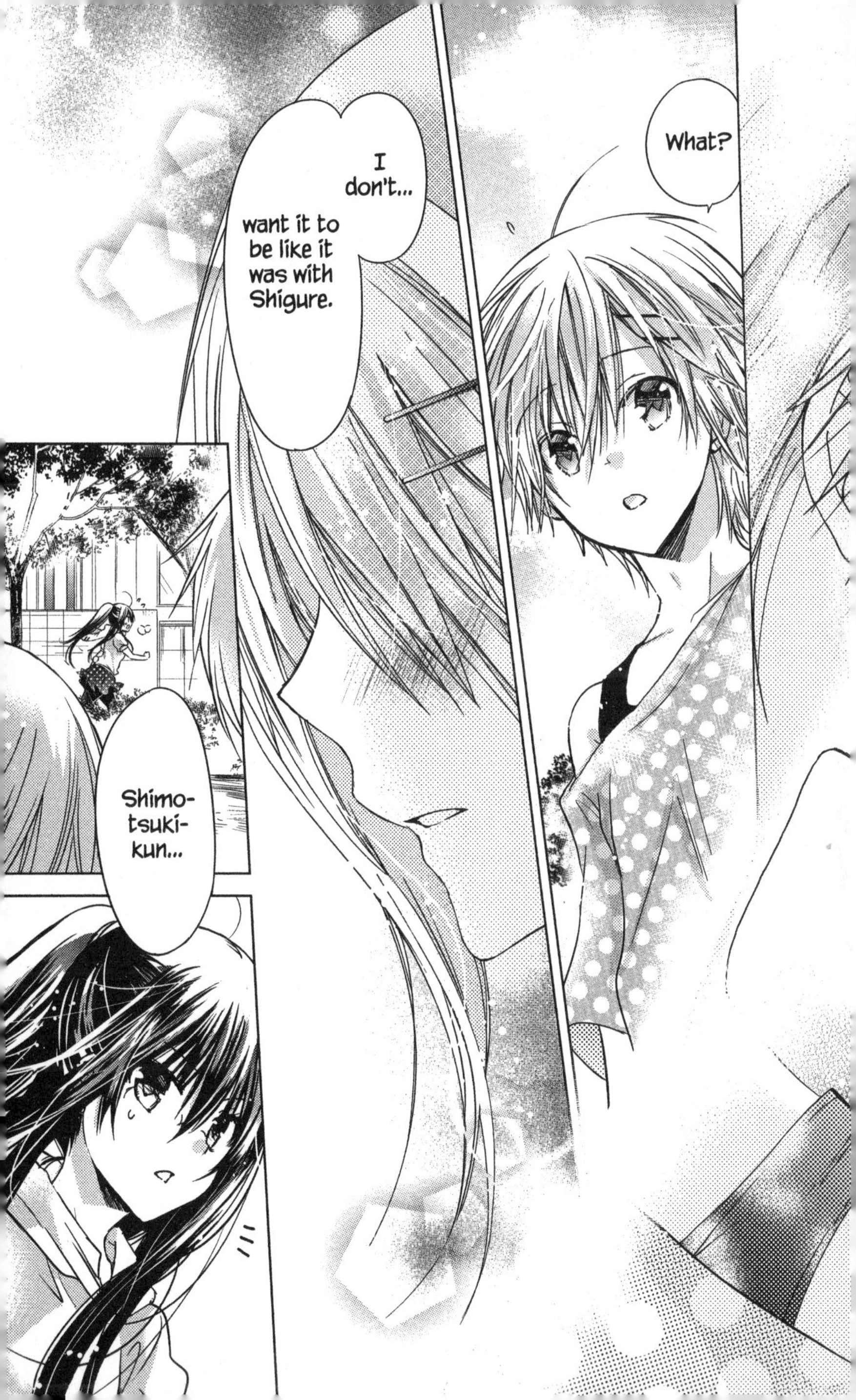
What?
I don't...
want it to be like it was with Shigure.
Shimo-tsuki-kun...

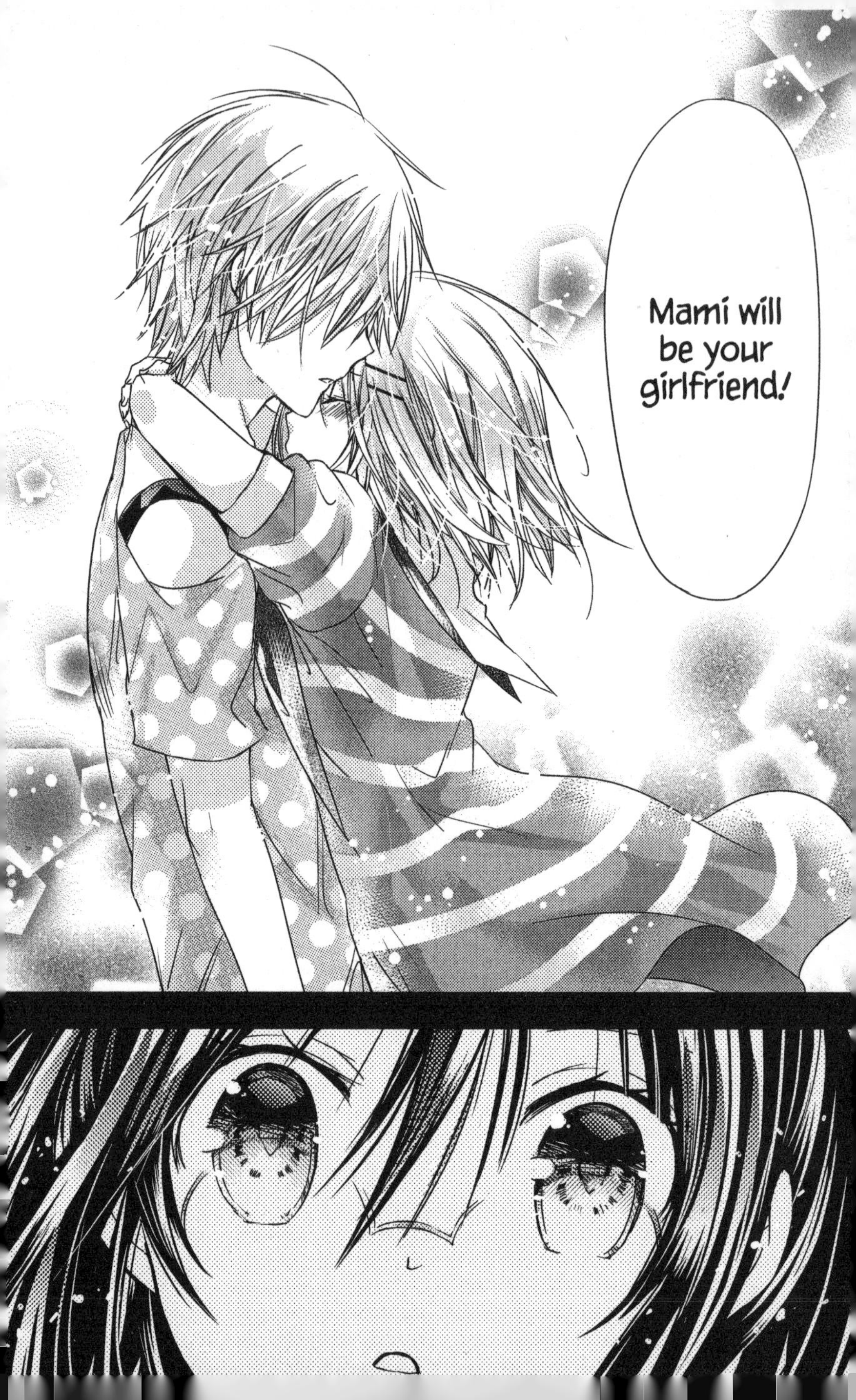
Mami will be your girlfriend!

Mission 48
Tactical Romance Missions of Love

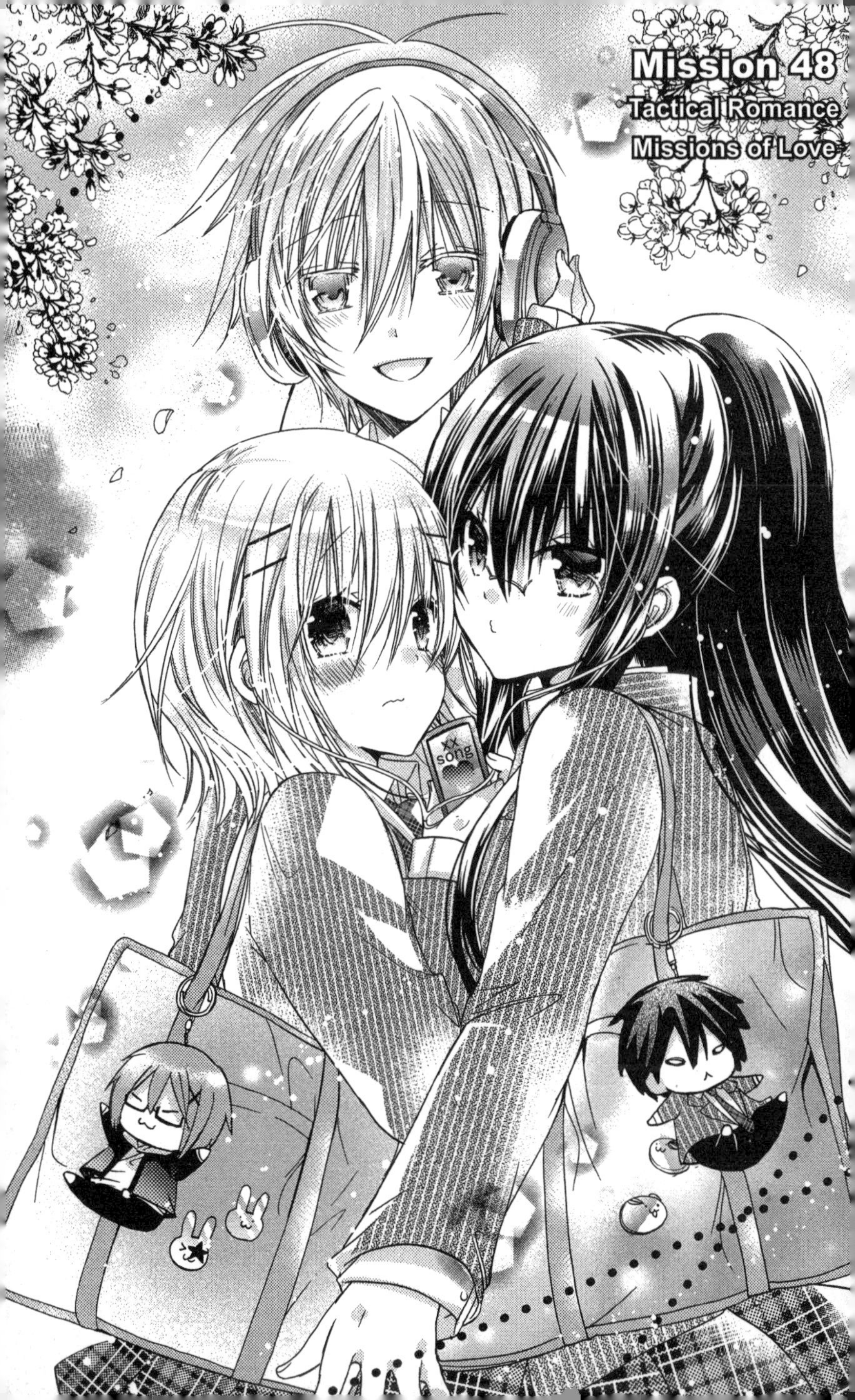
xx song

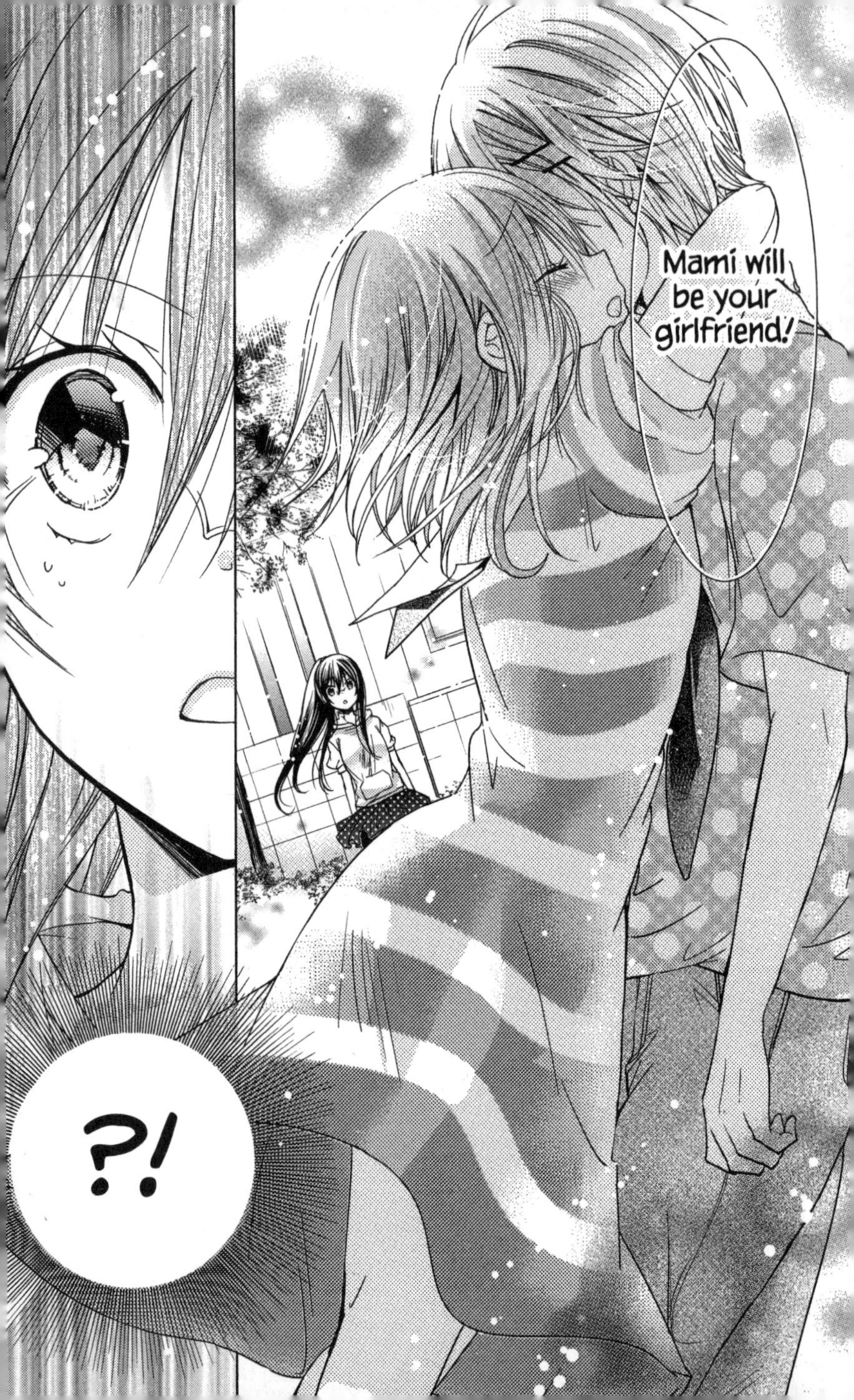
Mami will be your girlfriend!
?!

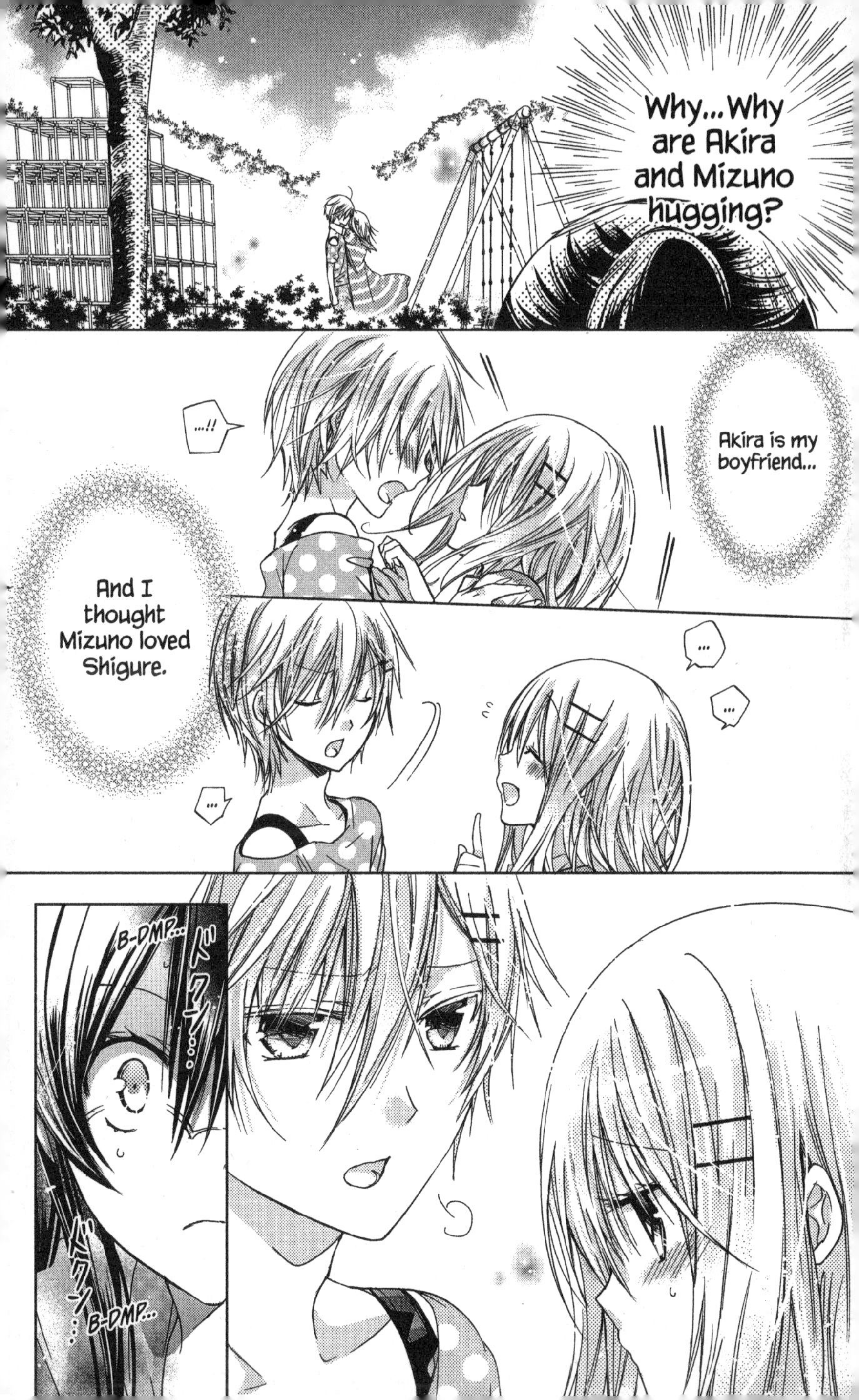
Why...Why are Akira and Mizuno hugging?
Akira is my boyfriend...
...!!
And I thought Mizuno loved Shigure.
...
...
...
B-DMP...
ドクン…
ドクン…
B-DMP...

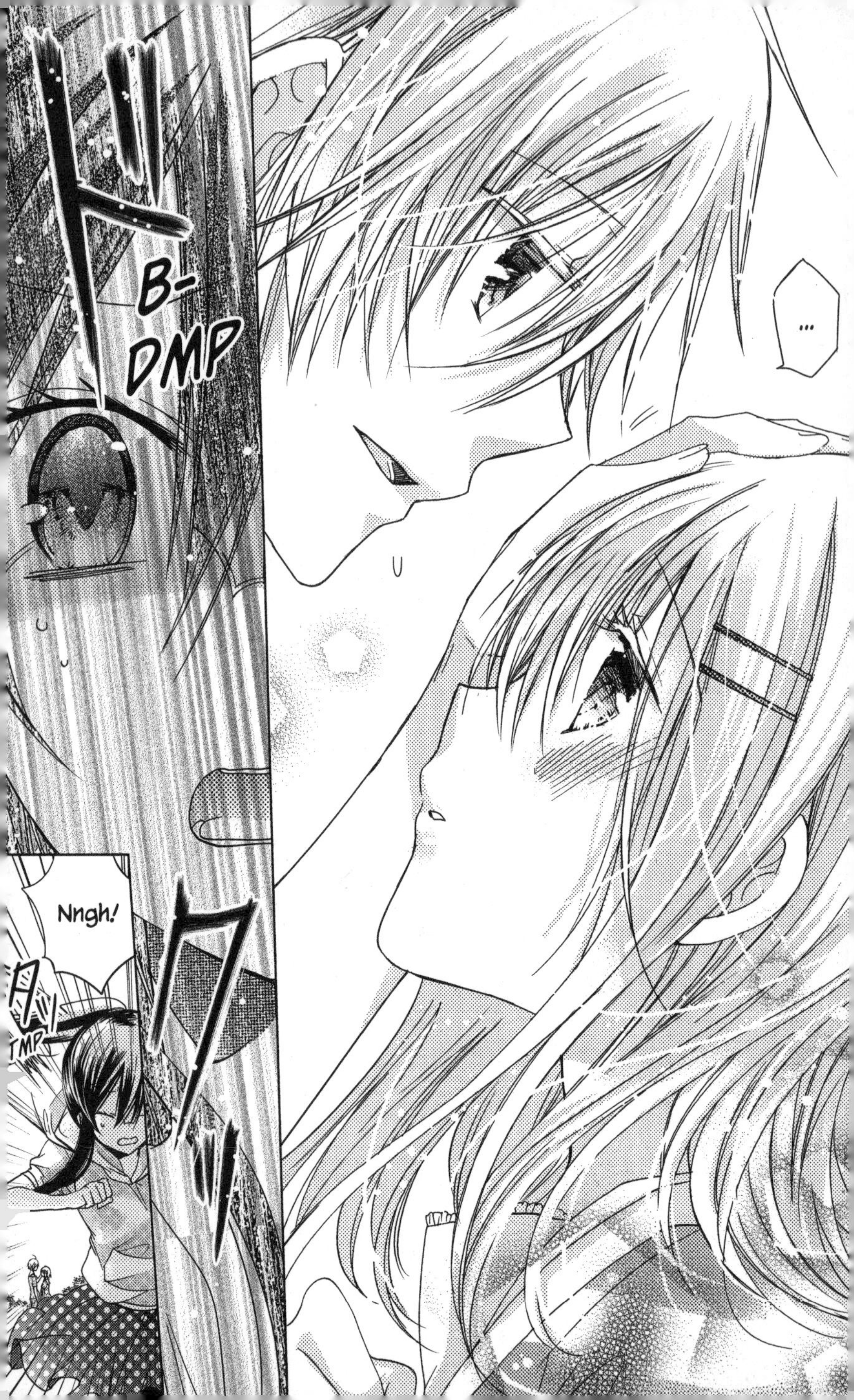
...
B-DMP
Nngh!
TMP

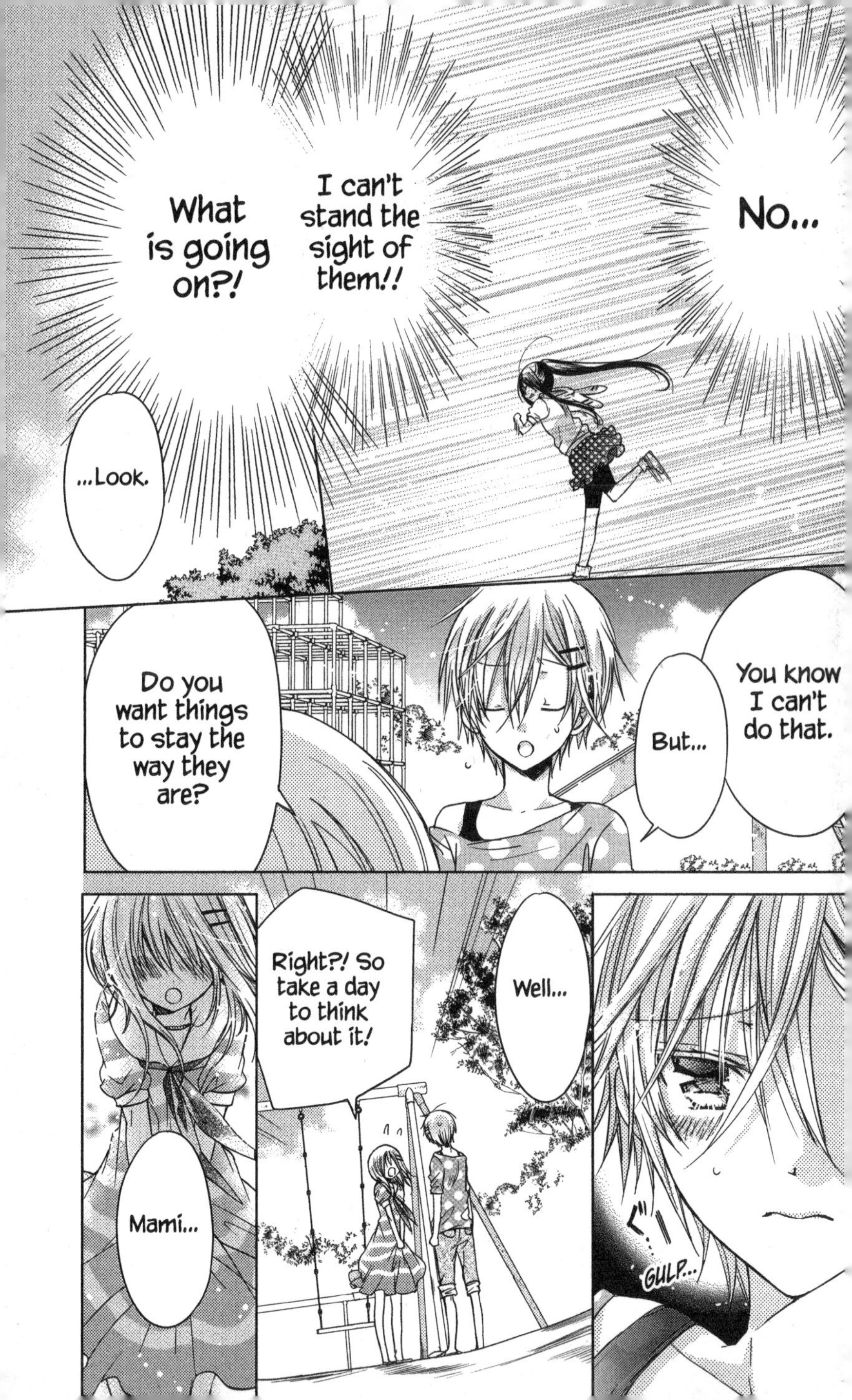
No...
I can't stand the sight of them!!
What is going on?!
...Look.
You know I can't do that.
But...
Do you want things to stay the way they are?
GULP...
Well...
Right?! So take a day to think about it!
Mami...

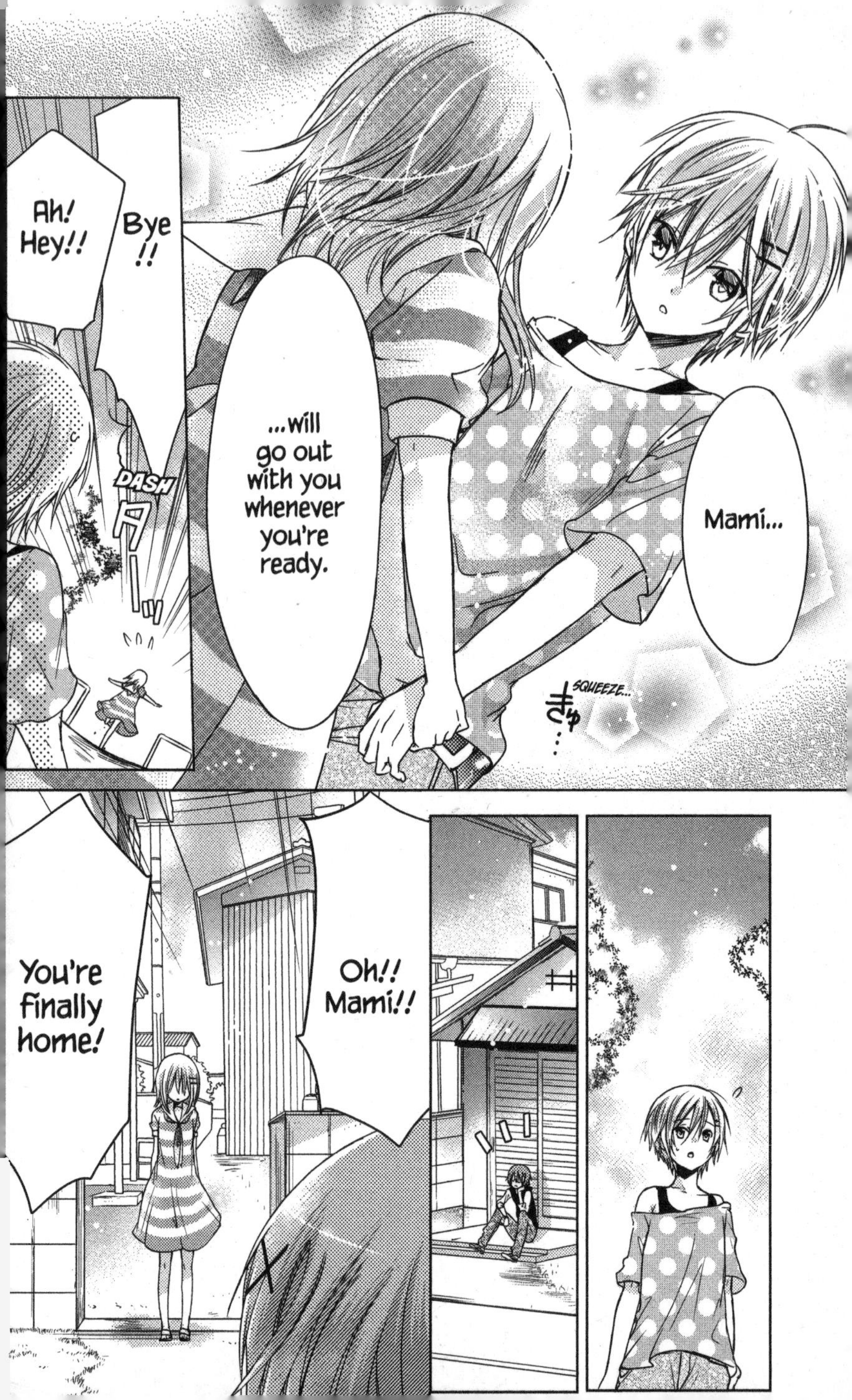
Mami...
...will go out with you whenever you're ready.
SQUEEZE...
Bye!!
Ah! Hey!!
DASH
Oh!! Mami!!
You're finally home!

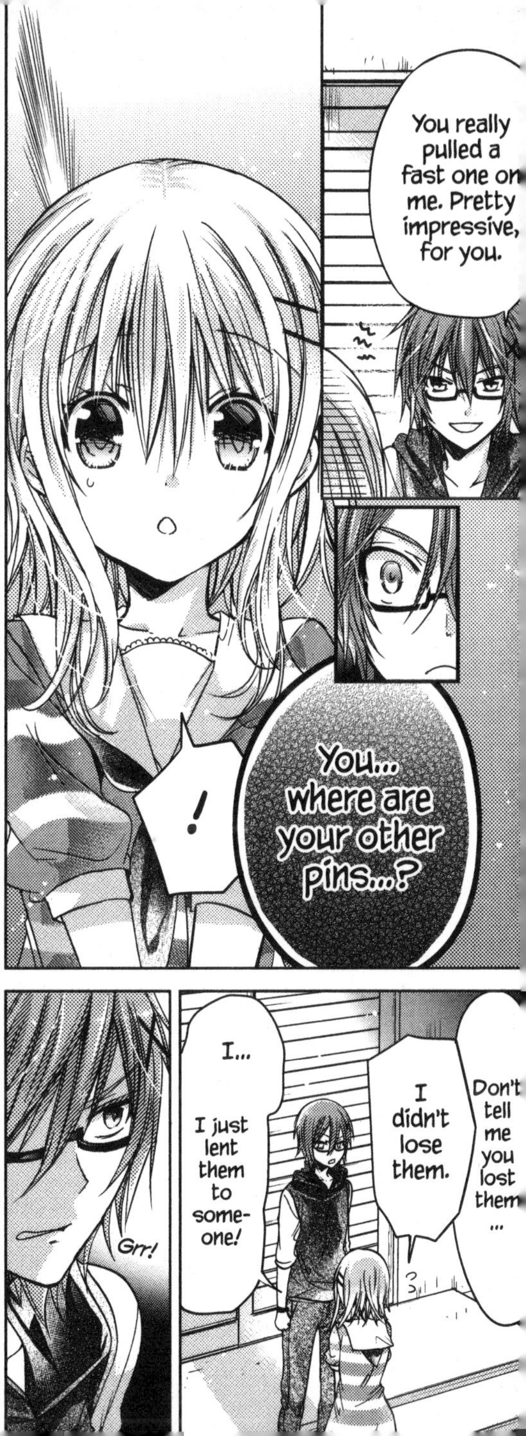
You really pulled a fast one on me. Pretty impressive, for you.
You... where are your other pins...?
!
Don't tell me you lost them...
I didn't lose them.
?
I...
I just lent them to someone!
Grr!

Alone at Last...

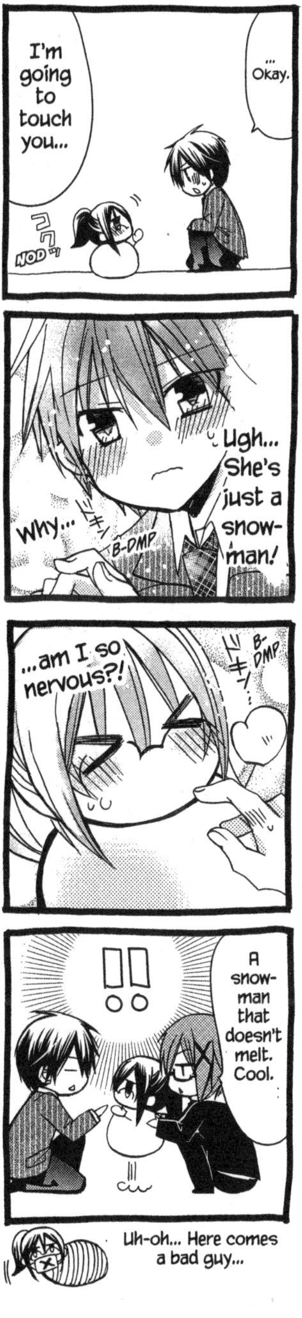
... Okay.
I'm going to touch you...
NOD
Ugh... She's just a snowman!
Why...
B-DMP
B-DMP
...am I so nervous?!
A snowman that doesn't melt. Cool.
!!
Uh-oh... Here comes a bad guy...

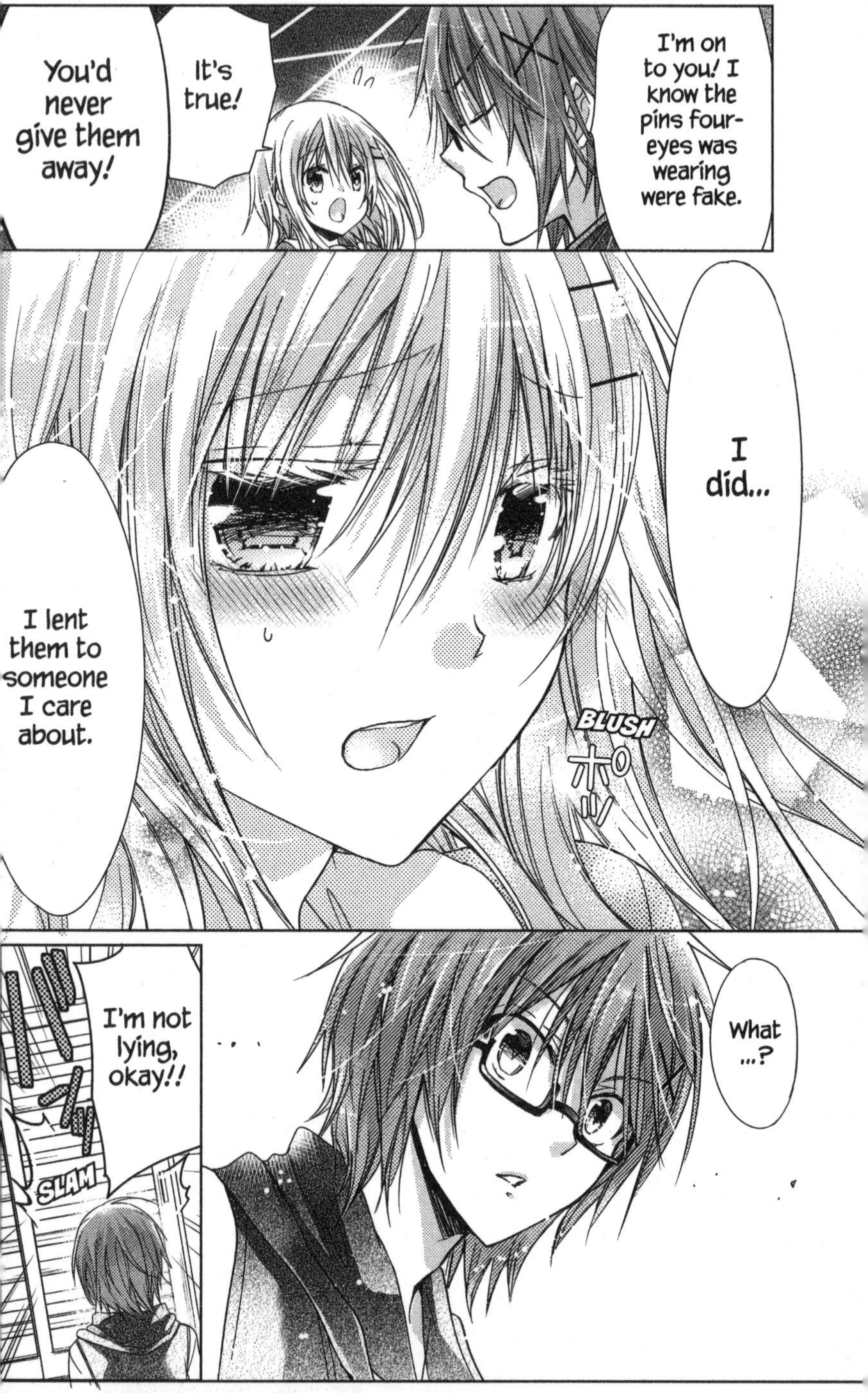
I'm on to you! I know the pins four-eyes was wearing were fake.
It's true!
You'd never give them away!
I did...
I lent them to someone I care about.
BLUSH
What ...?
I'm not lying, okay!!
SLAM

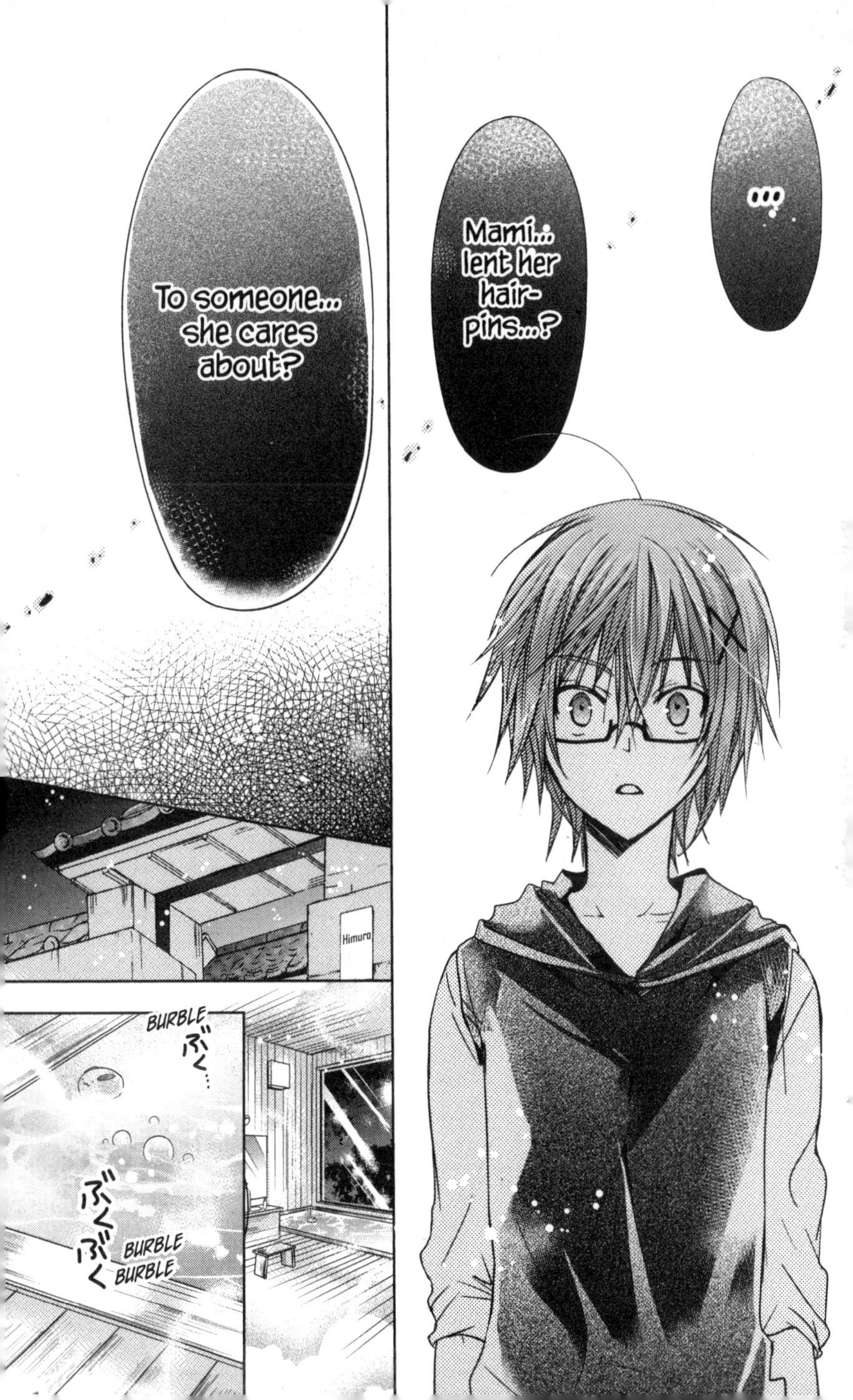
...
Mami... lent her hair-pins...?
To someone... she cares about?
Himuro
BURBLE
ぶく...
ぶくぶく
BURBLE BURBLE

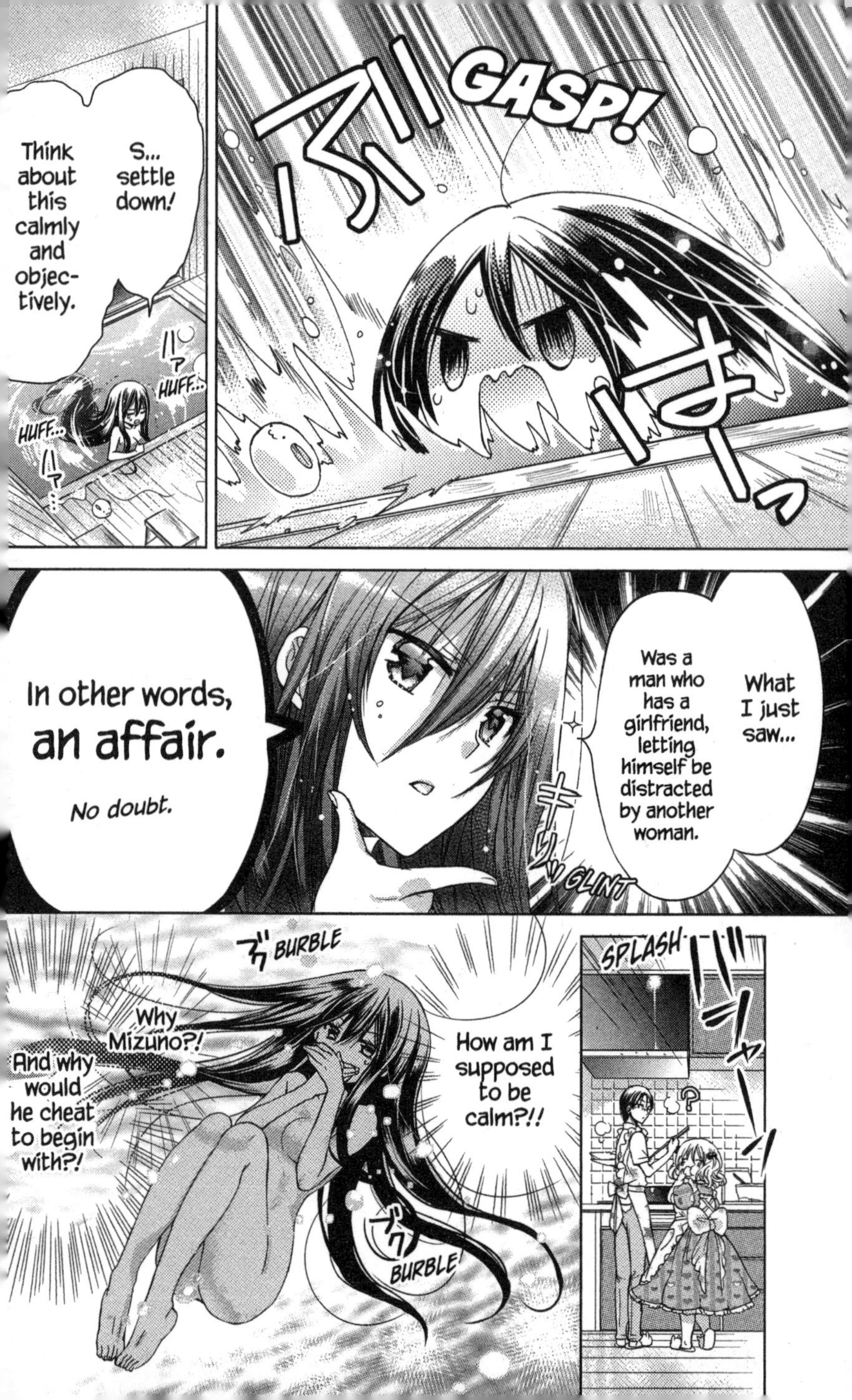
GASP!
S... settle down!
Think about this calmly and objectively.
HUFF...
HUFF...
What I just saw...
Was a man who has a girlfriend, letting himself be distracted by another woman.
GLINT
In other words, an affair.
No doubt.
SPLASH
BURBLE
How am I supposed to be calm?!!
Why Mizuno?!
And why would he cheat to begin with?!
BURBLE

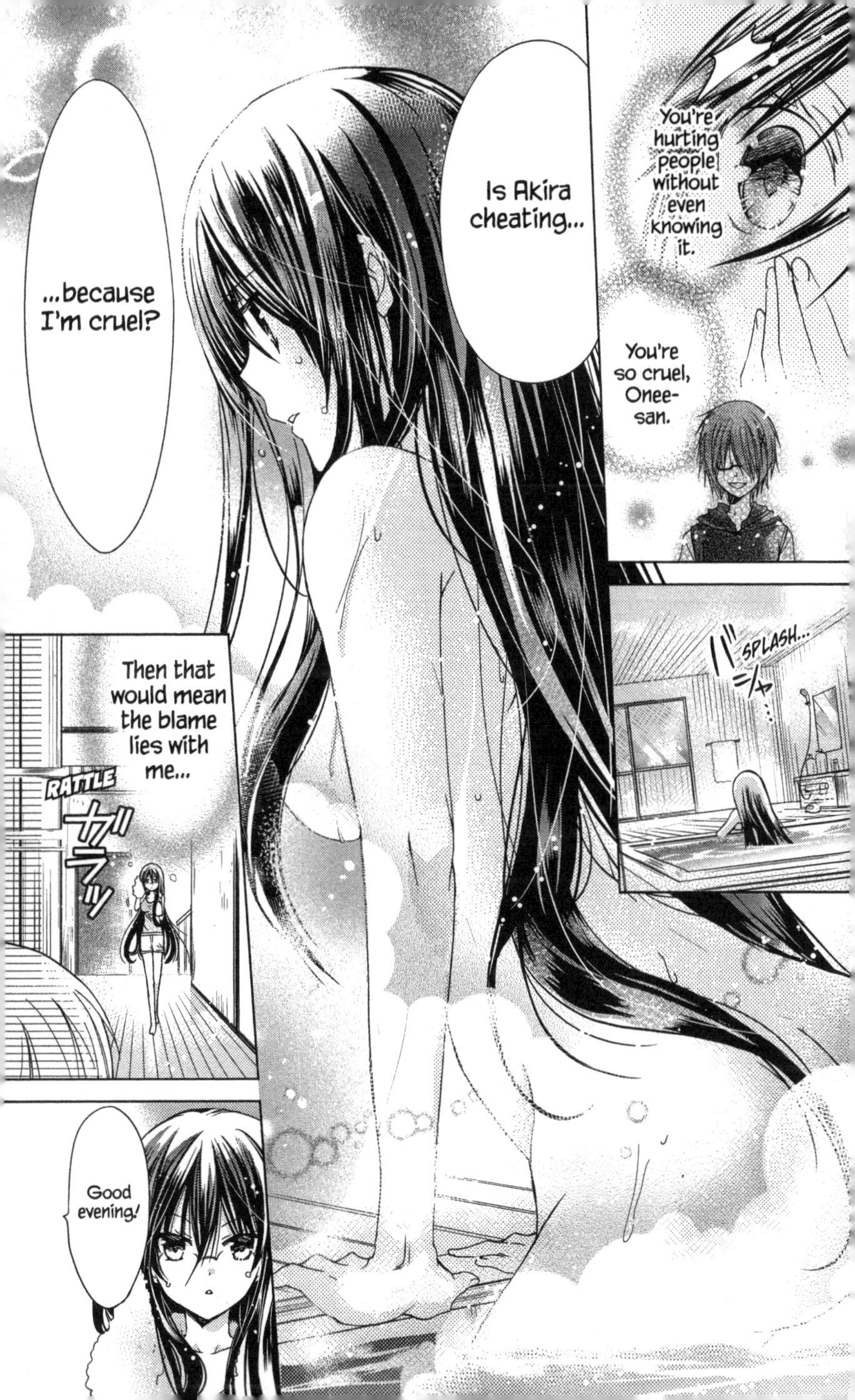
You're hurting people without even knowing it.
You're so cruel, Onee-san.
Is Akira cheating...
...because I'm cruel?
バシャ…
SPLASH...
Then that would mean the blame lies with me...
ガラッ
RATTLE
Good evening!

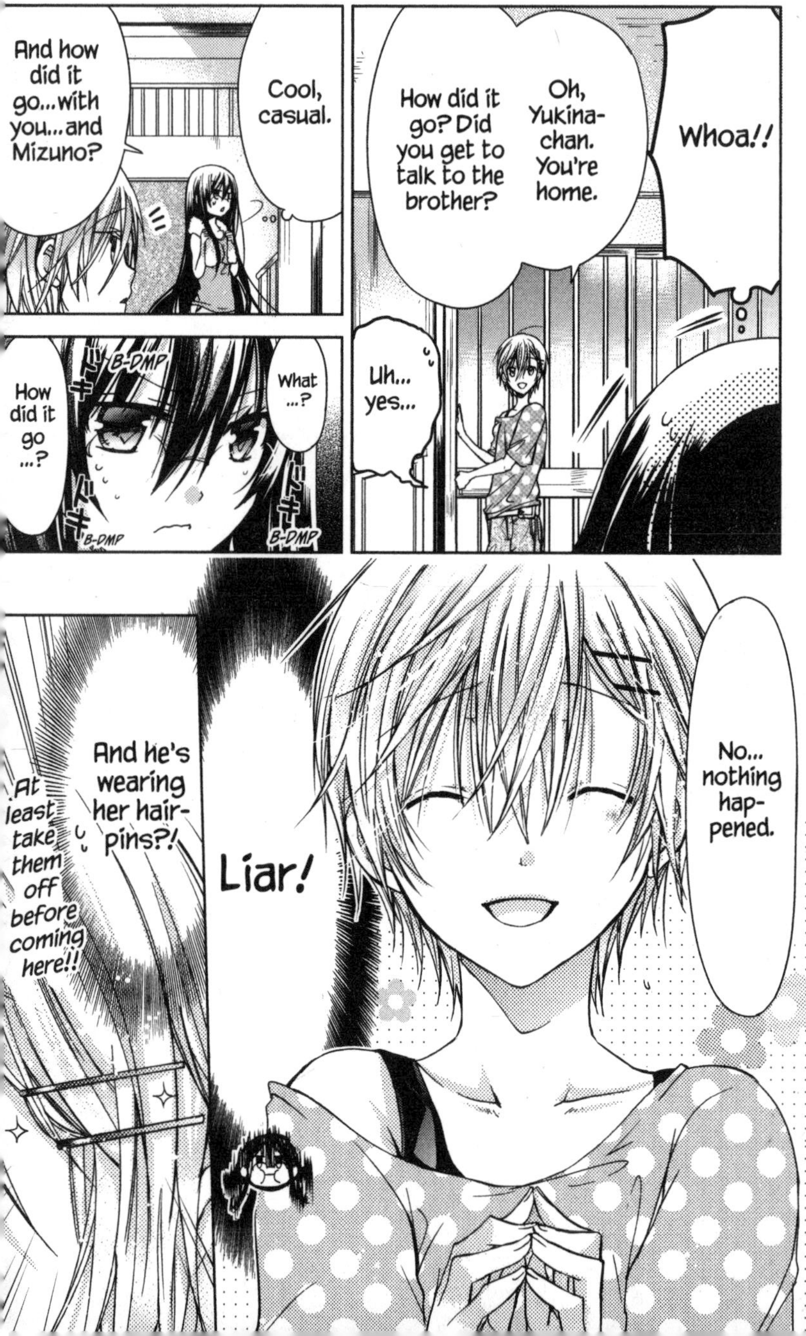
Whoa!!
Oh, Yukina-chan. You're home.
How did it go? Did you get to talk to the brother?
Uh... yes...
Cool, casual.
And how did it go...with you...and Mizuno?
What ...?
B-DMP
B-DMP
How did it go ...?
B-DMP
No... nothing hap-pened.
Liar!
And he's wearing her hair-pins?!
At least take them off before coming here!!

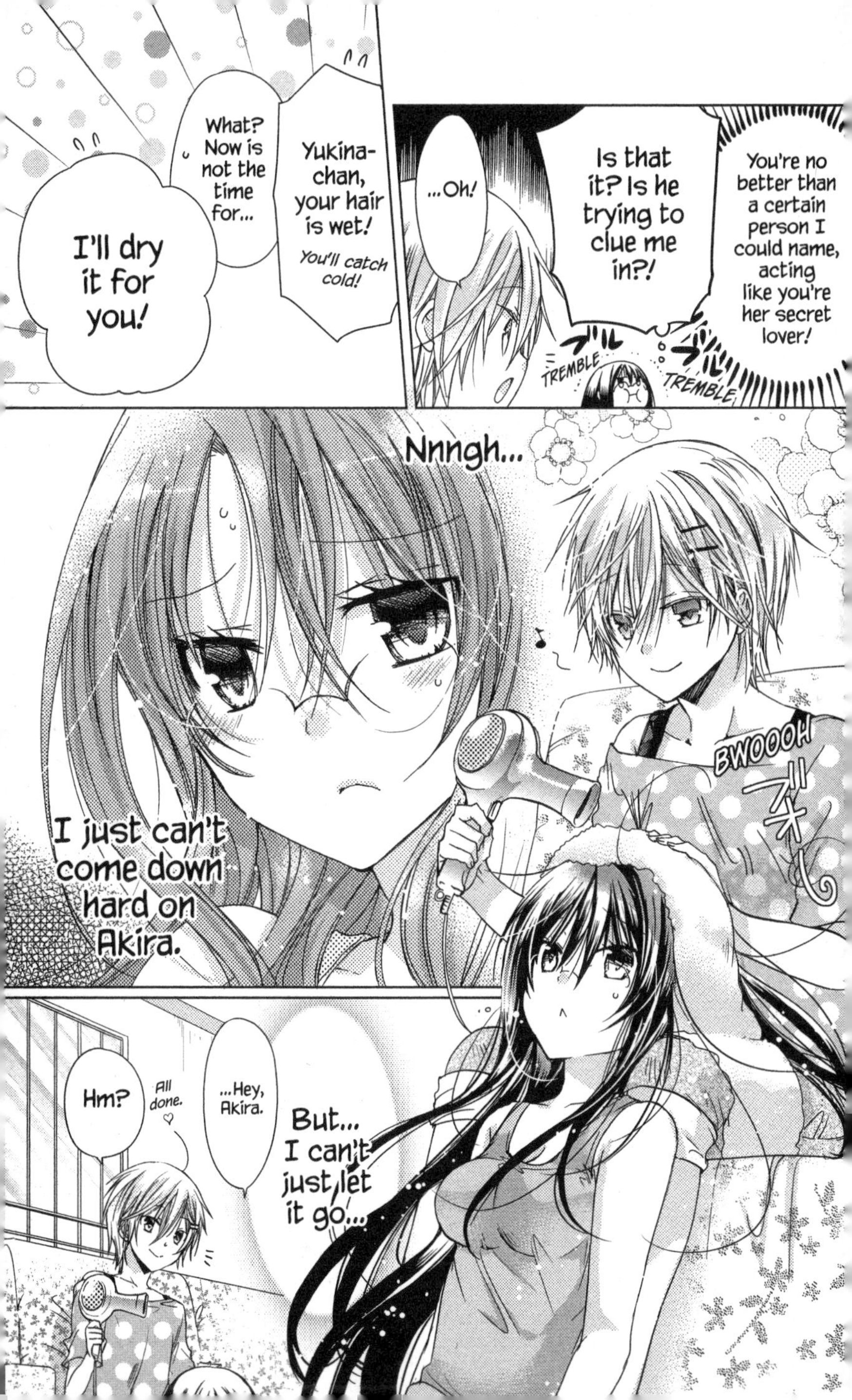
You're no better than a certain person I could name, acting like you're her secret lover!
Is that it? Is he trying to clue me in?!
...Oh!
TREMBLE
TREMBLE
Yukina-chan, your hair is wet!
You'll catch cold!
What? Now is not the time for...
I'll dry it for you!
Nnngh...
BWOOOH
I just can't come down hard on Akira.
But... I can't just let it go...
...Hey, Akira.
All done.
Hm?

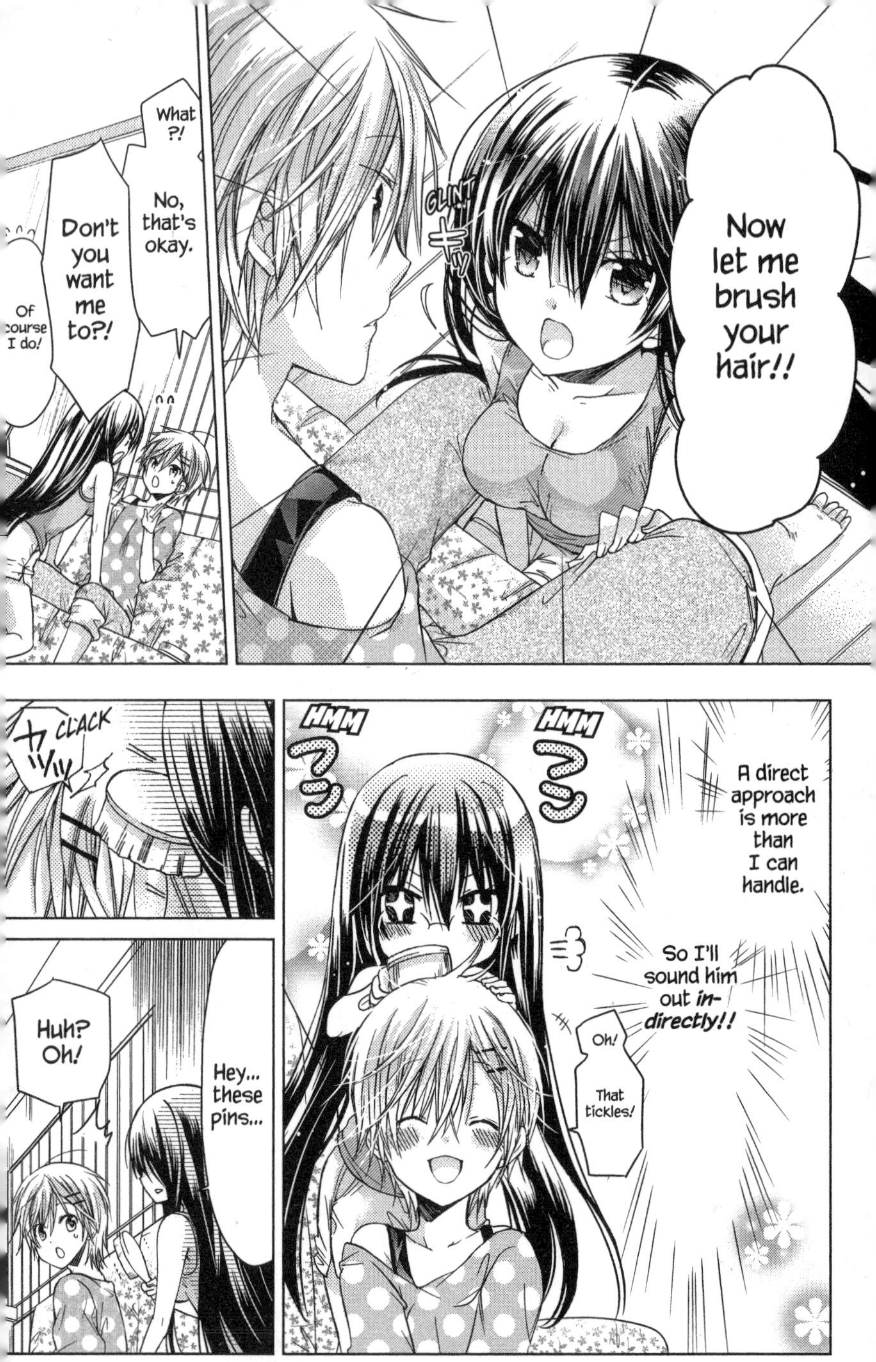
GLINT
Now let me brush your hair!!
What?!
No, that's okay.
Don't you want me to?!
Of course I do!
HMM HMM
A direct approach is more than I can handle.
So I'll sound him out *in-directly!!*
Oh!
That tickles!
CLACK
Hey... these pins...
Huh? Oh!

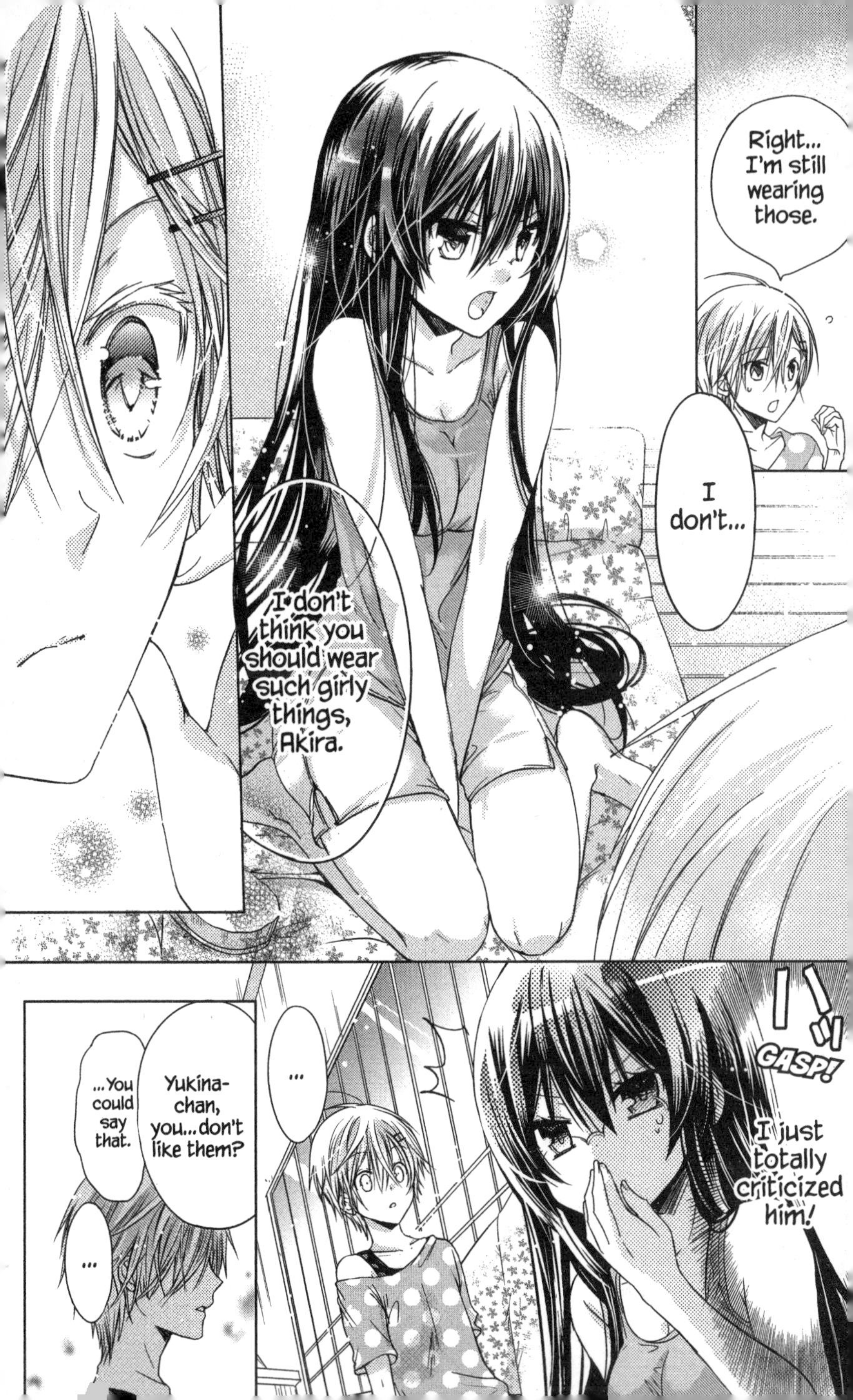
Right... I'm still wearing those.
I don't...
I don't think you should wear such girly things, Akira.
GASP!
I just totally criticized him!
...
Yukina-chan, you...don't like them?
...You could say that.
...

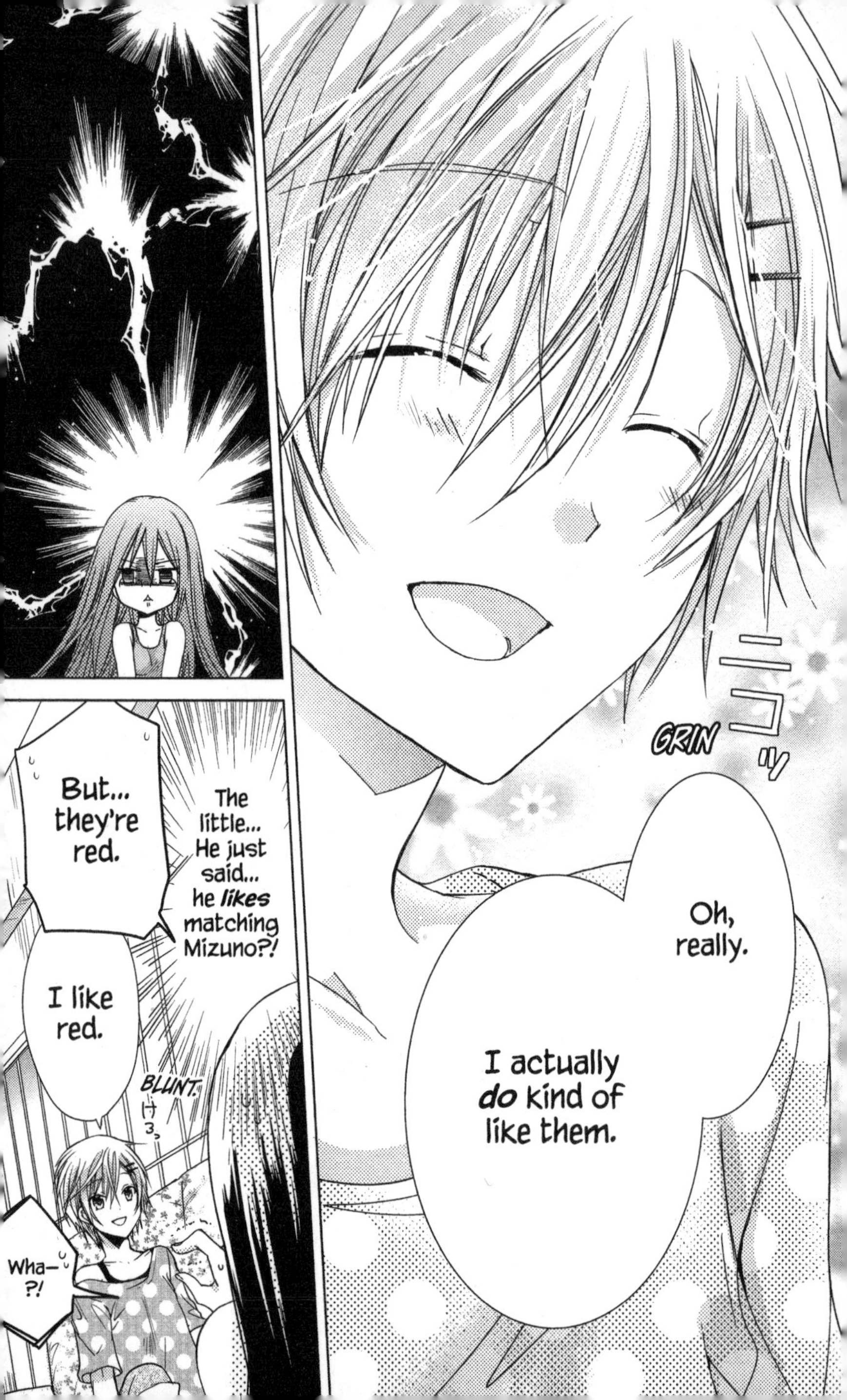

GRIN
Oh, really.
I actually *do* kind of like them.
But... they're red.
The little... He just said... he *likes* matching Mizuno?!
I like red.
BLUNT.
Wha— ?!

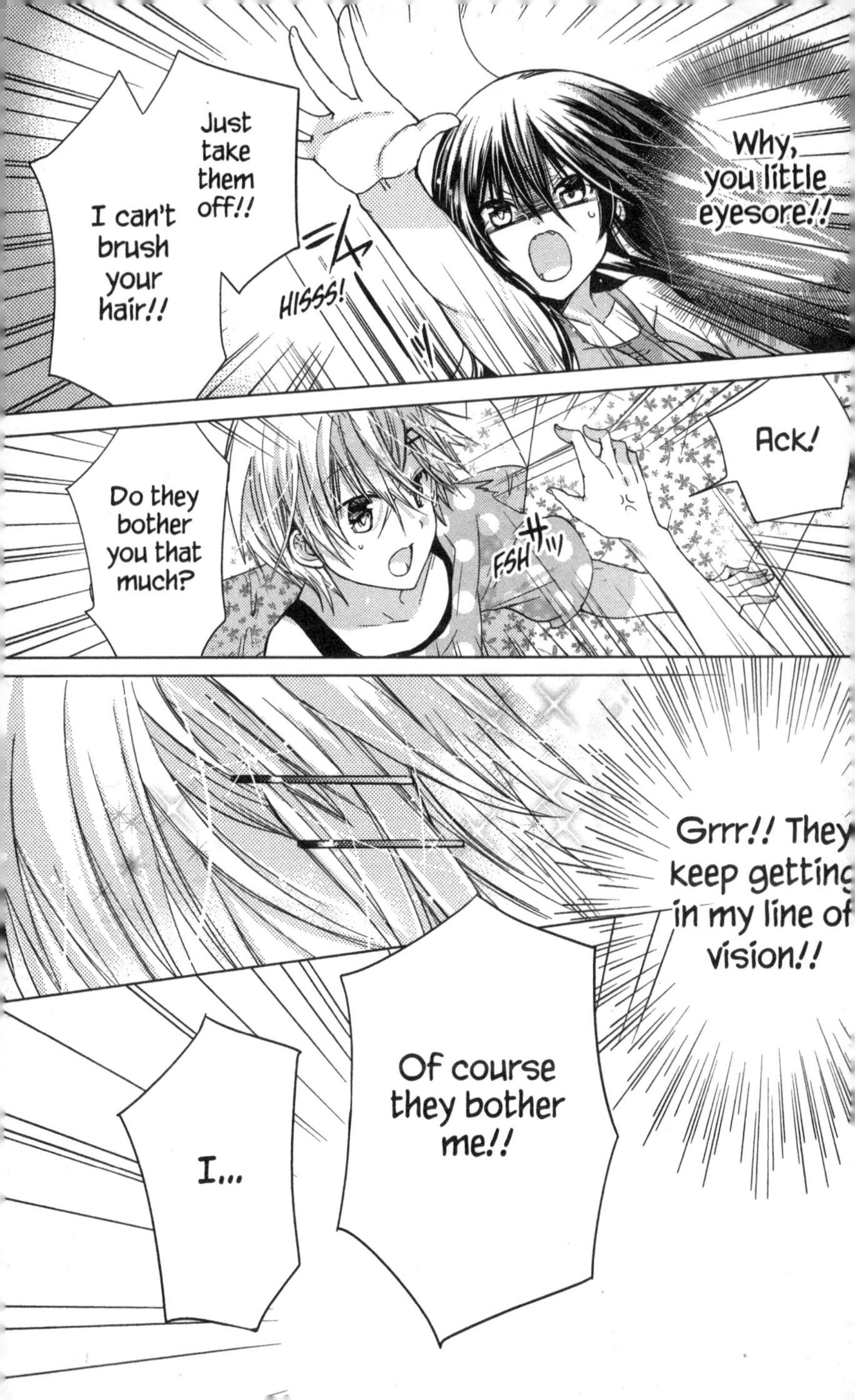

Why, you little eyesore!!
Just take them off!!
I can't brush your hair!!
HISSS!
Ack!
FSH
Do they bother you that much?
Grrr!! They keep getting in my line of vision!!
Of course they bother me!!
I...

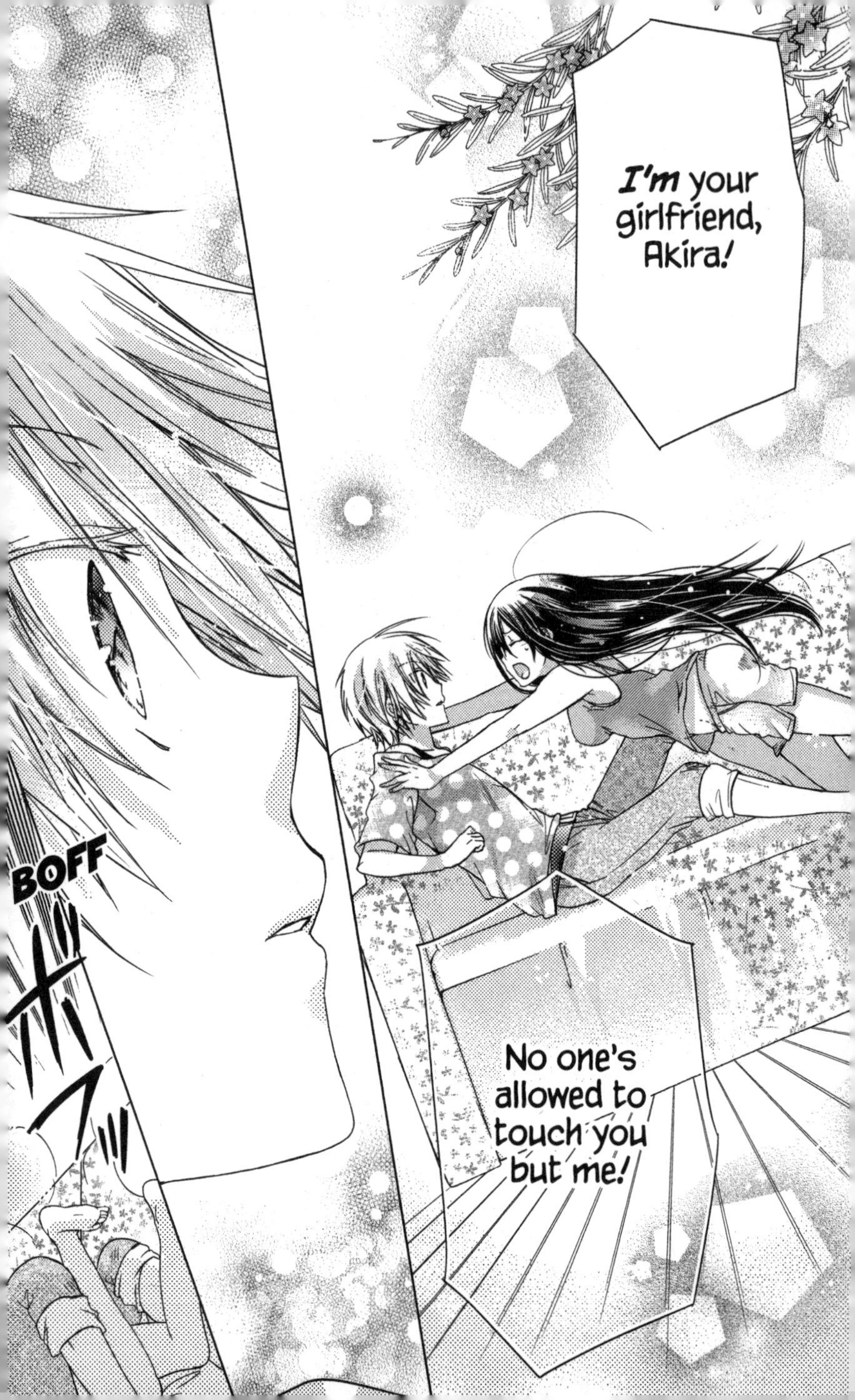
I'm your girlfriend, Akira!
No one's allowed to touch you but me!
BOFF

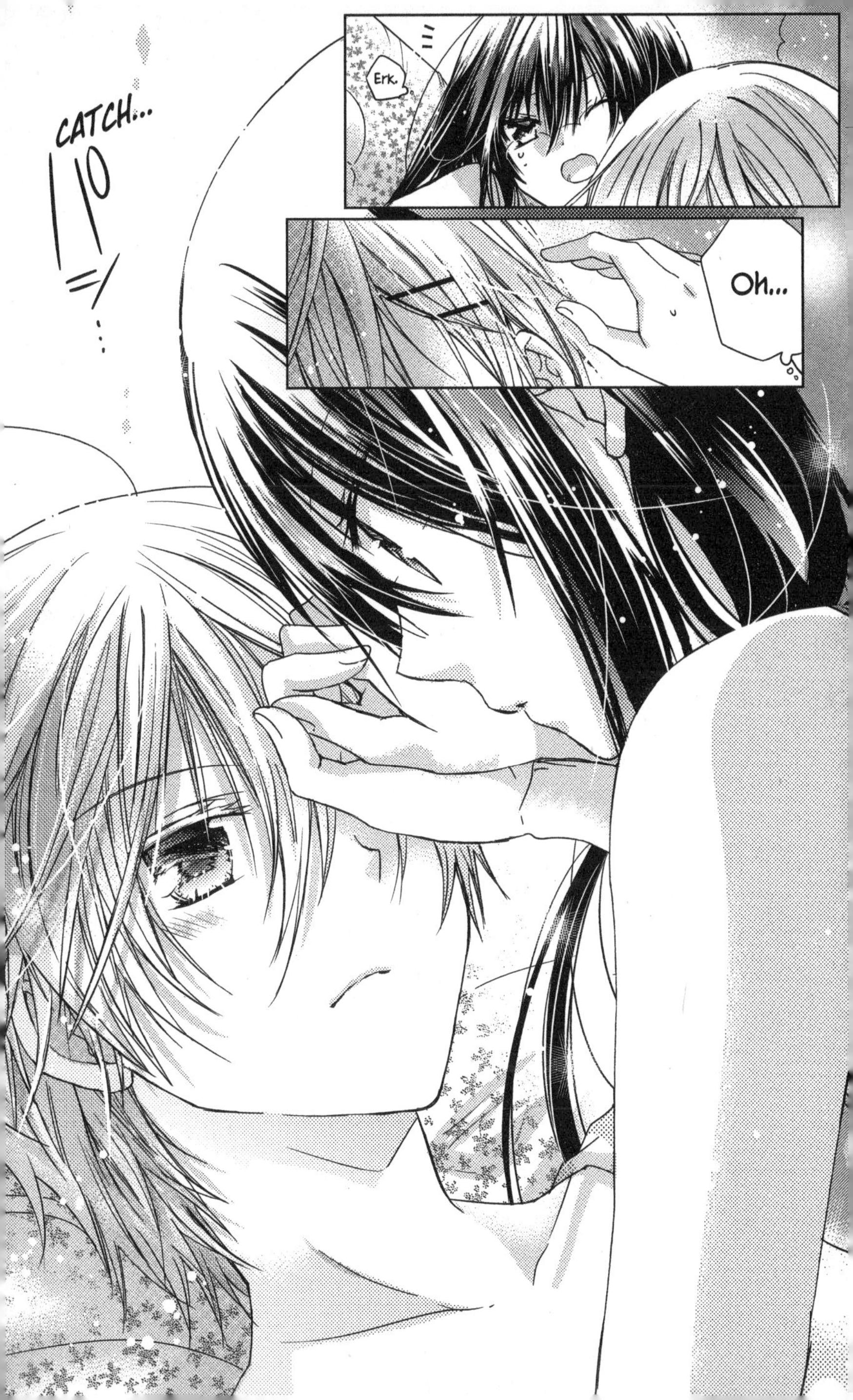
Erk.
Oh...
CATCH...

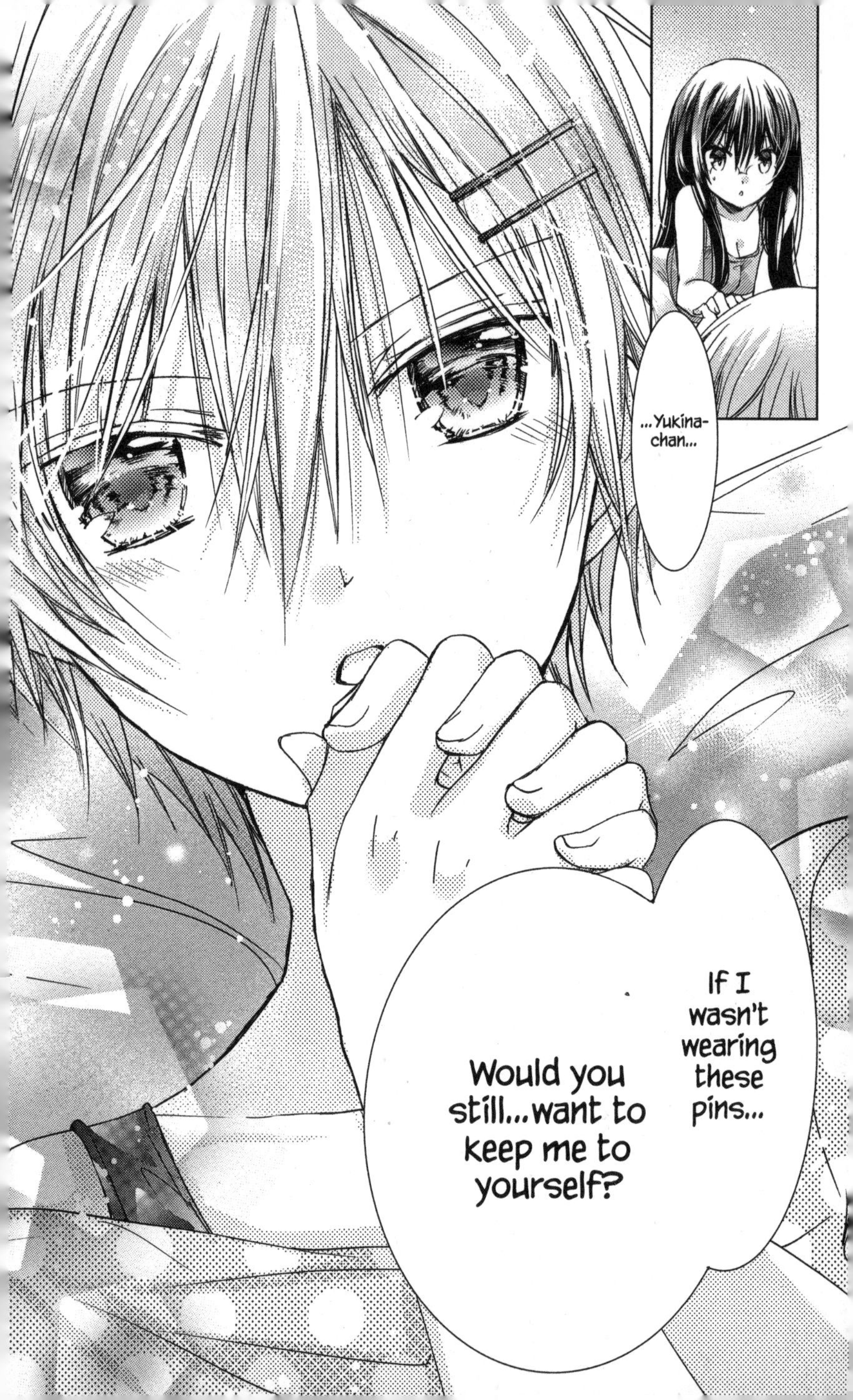
...Yukina-chan...
If I wasn't wearing these pins...
Would you still...want to keep me to yourself?

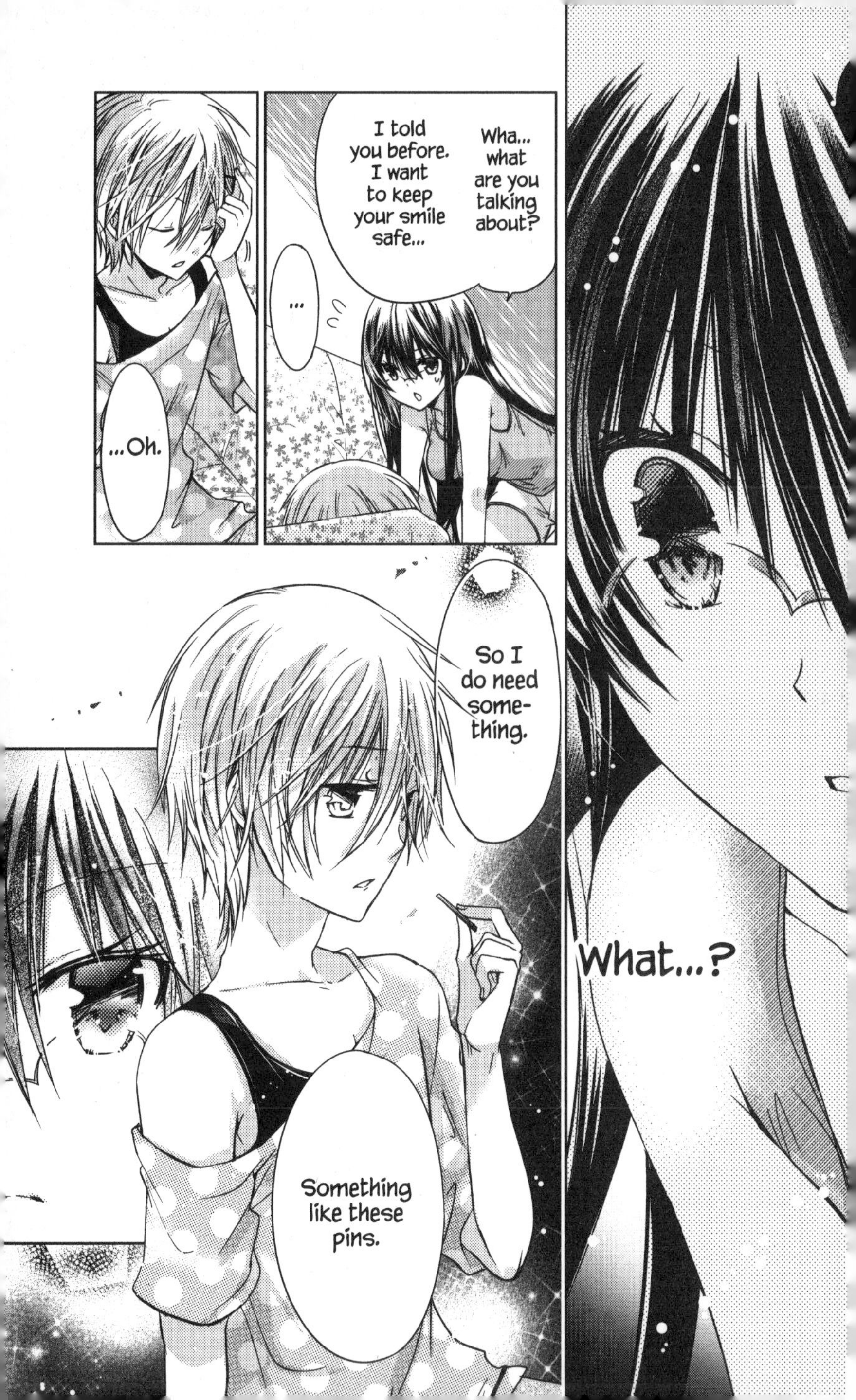
What...?
Wha... what are you talking about?
I told you before. I want to keep your smile safe...
...
...Oh.
So I do need something.
Something like these pins.

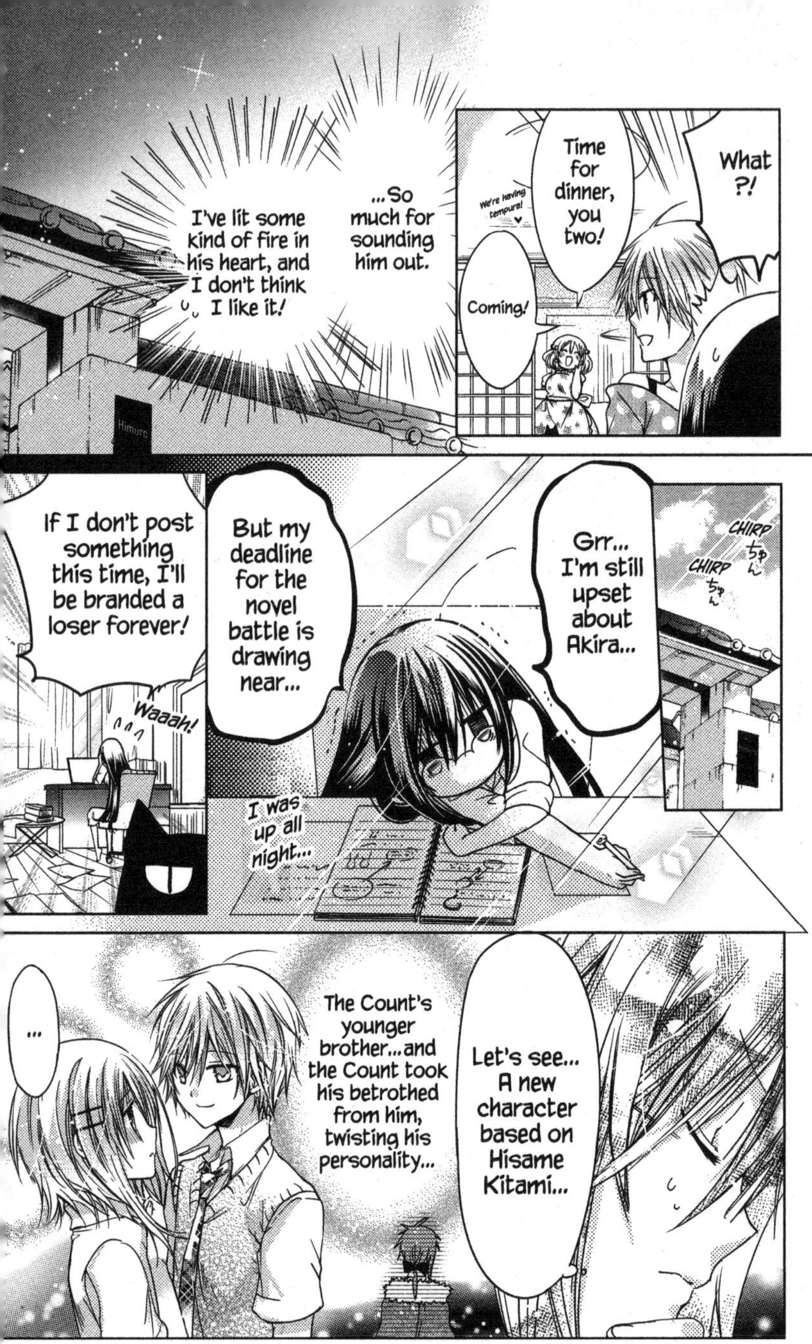
What?!
Time for dinner, you two!
We're having tempura!
Coming!
...So much for sounding him out.
I've lit some kind of fire in his heart, and I don't think I like it!
Himuro
CHIRP
CHIRP
Grr... I'm still upset about Akira...
But my deadline for the novel battle is drawing near...
I was up all night...
If I don't post something this time, I'll be branded a loser forever!
Waaah!
Let's see... A new character based on Hisame Kitami...
The Count's younger brother...and the Count took his betrothed from him, twisting his personality...
...

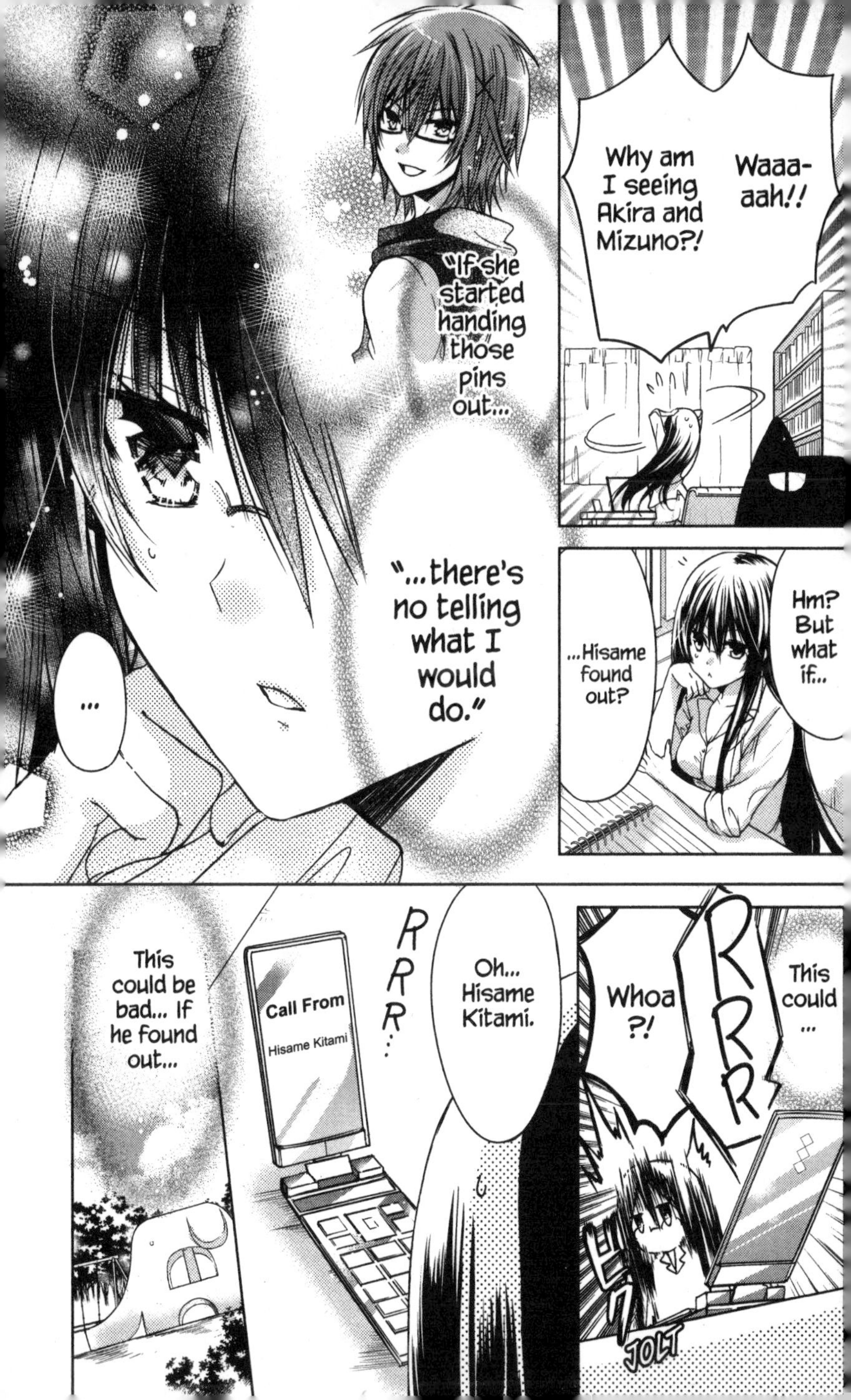
Waaa-aah!!
Why am I seeing Akira and Mizuno?!
Hm? But what if...
...Hisame found out?
"If she started handing those pins out...
"...there's no telling what I would do."
...
This could...
Whoa?!
RRR
JOLT
RRR...
Oh... Hisame Kitami.
Call From
Hisame Kitami
This could be bad... If he found out...

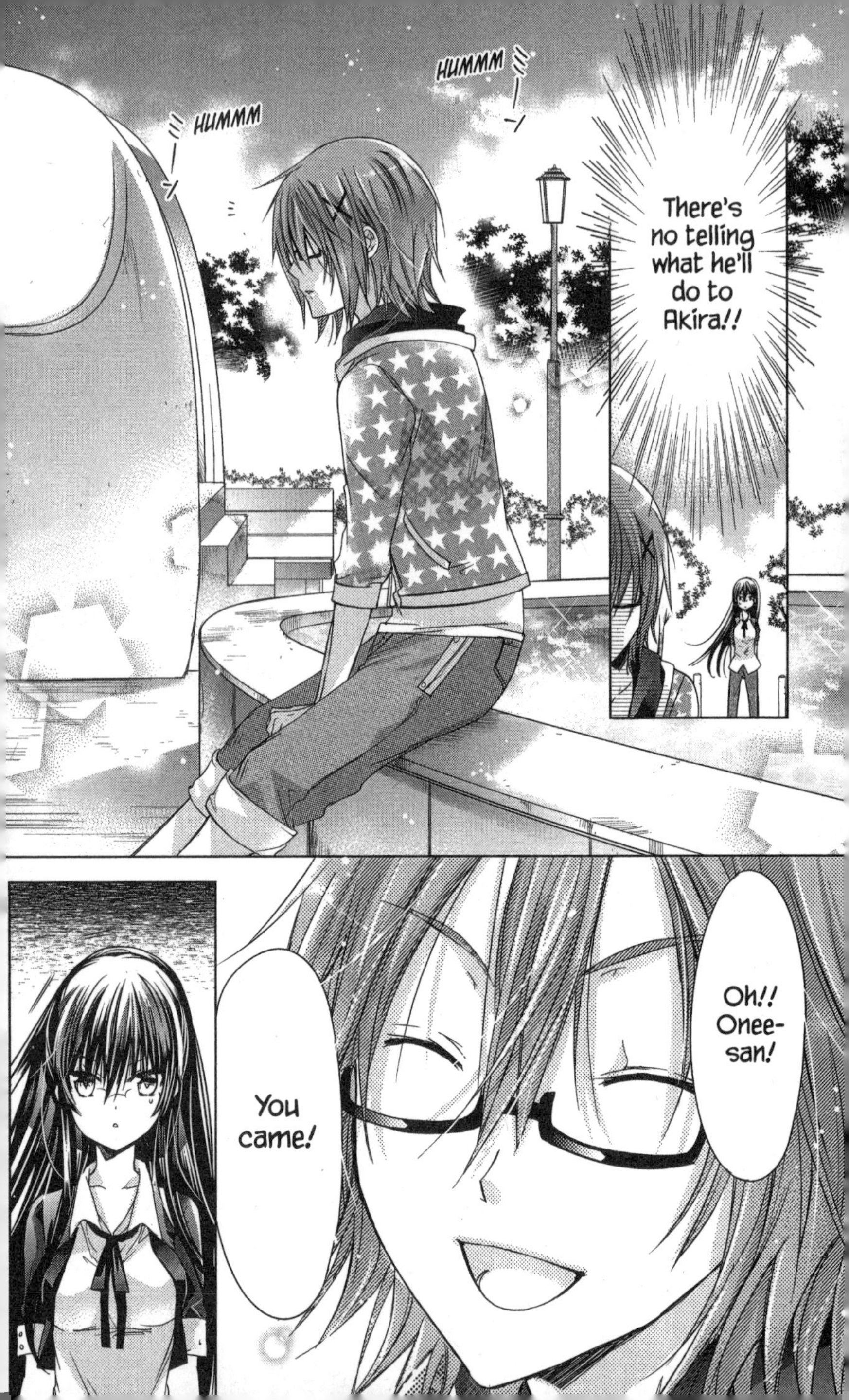
There's no telling what he'll do to Akira!!
HUMMM
HUMMM
Oh!! Onee-san!
You came!

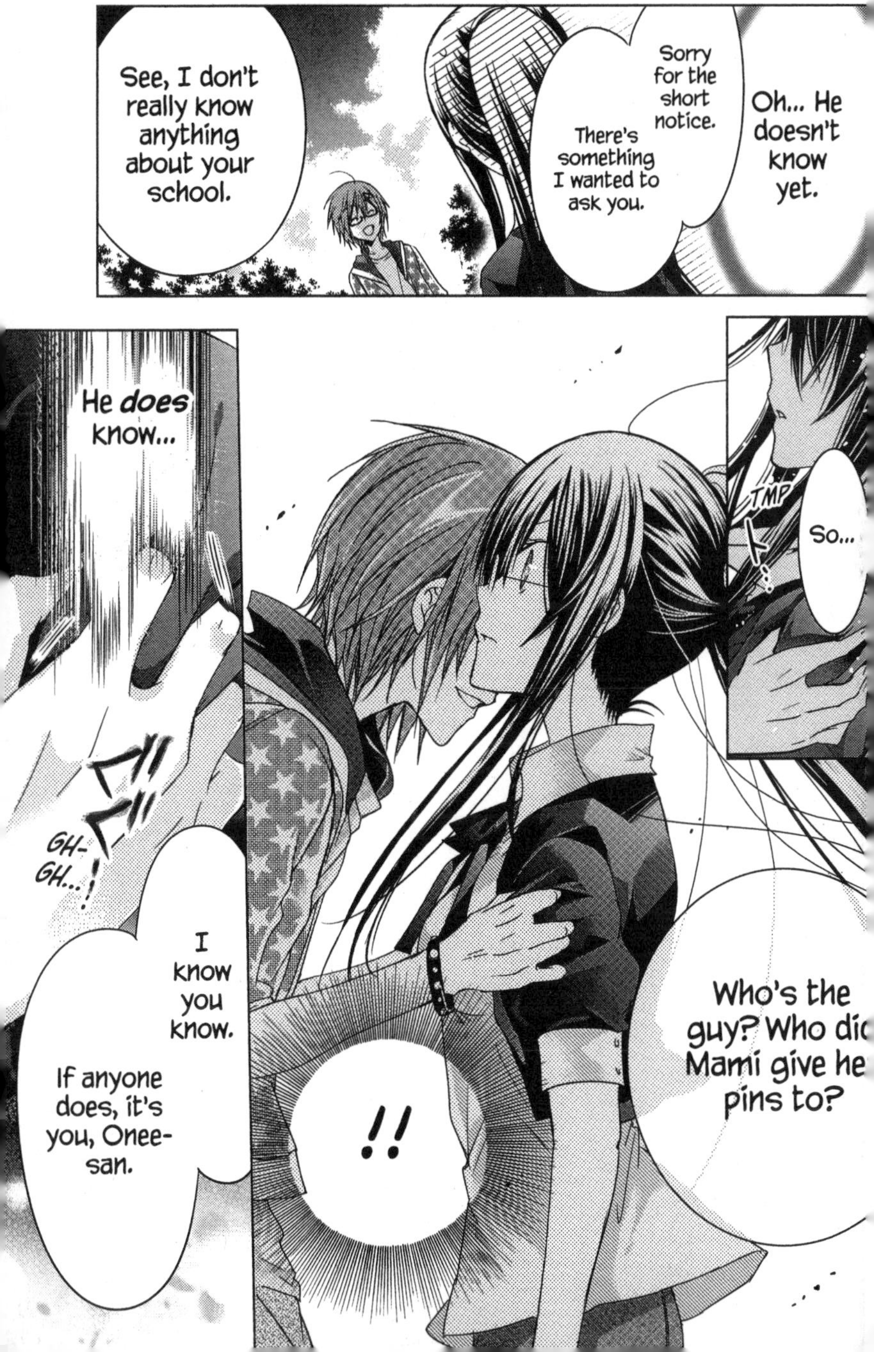

Oh... He doesn't know yet.
Sorry for the short notice.
There's something I wanted to ask you.
See, I don't really know anything about your school.
TMP
So...
Who's the guy? Who dic Mami give he pins to?
!!
He *does* know...
GH-GH...!
I know you know.
If anyone does, it's you, Onee-san.

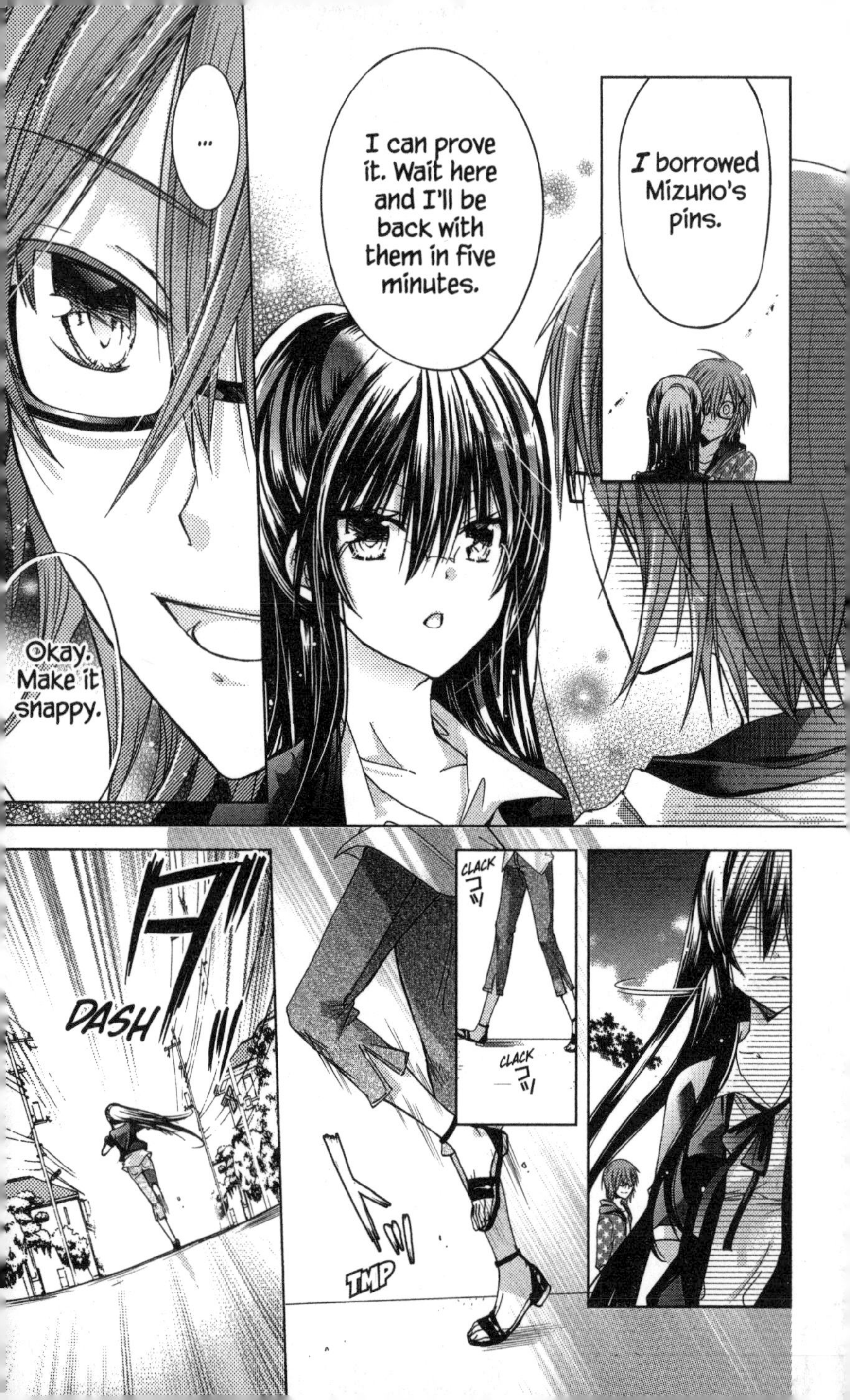
I borrowed Mizuno's pins.
I can prove it. Wait here and I'll be back with them in five minutes.
...
Okay. Make it snappy.
CLACK
CLACK
TMP
DASH

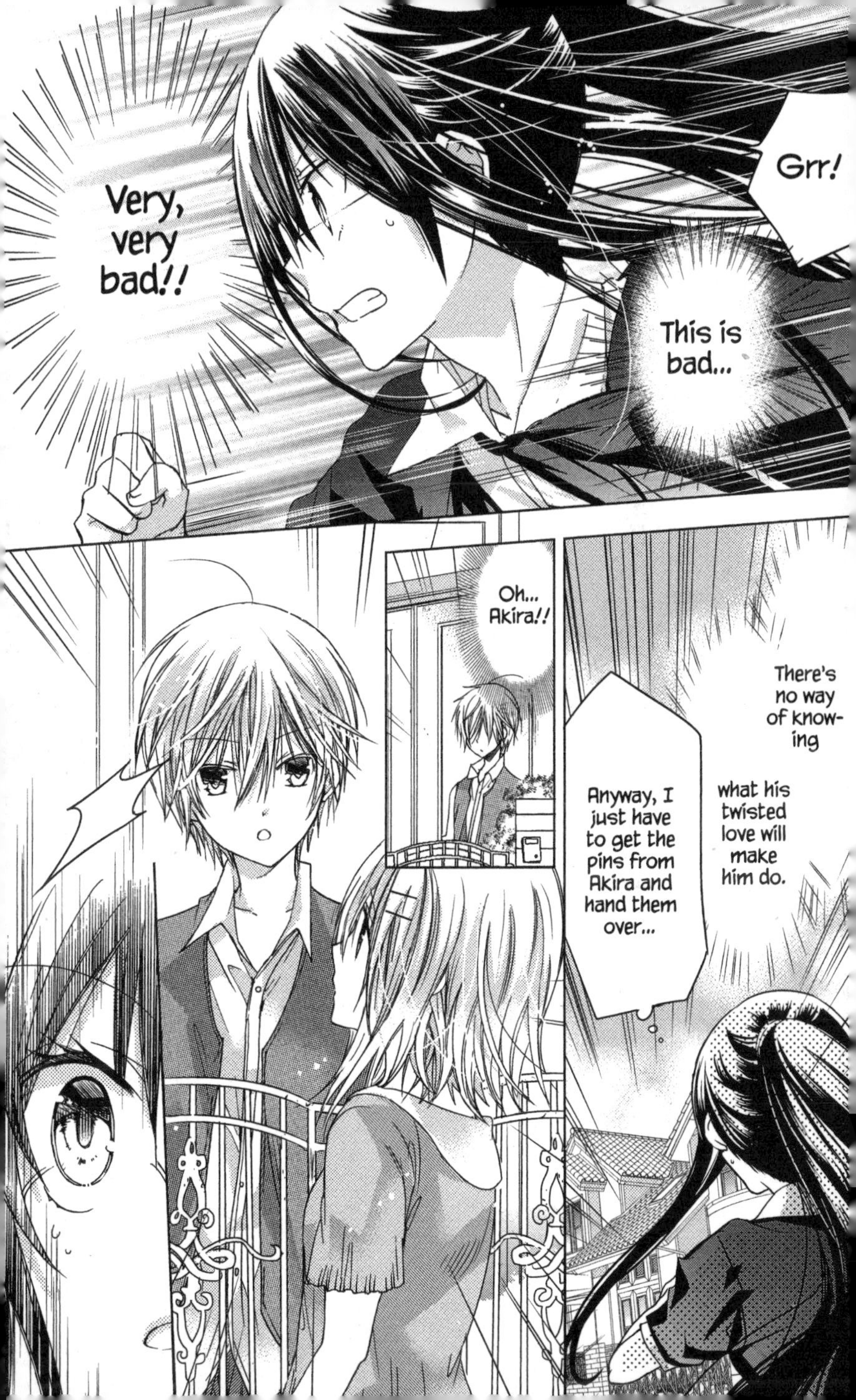
Grr!
This is bad...
Very, very bad!!
There's no way of know-ing
what his twisted love will make him do.
Anyway, I just have to get the pins from Akira and hand them over...
Oh... Akira!!

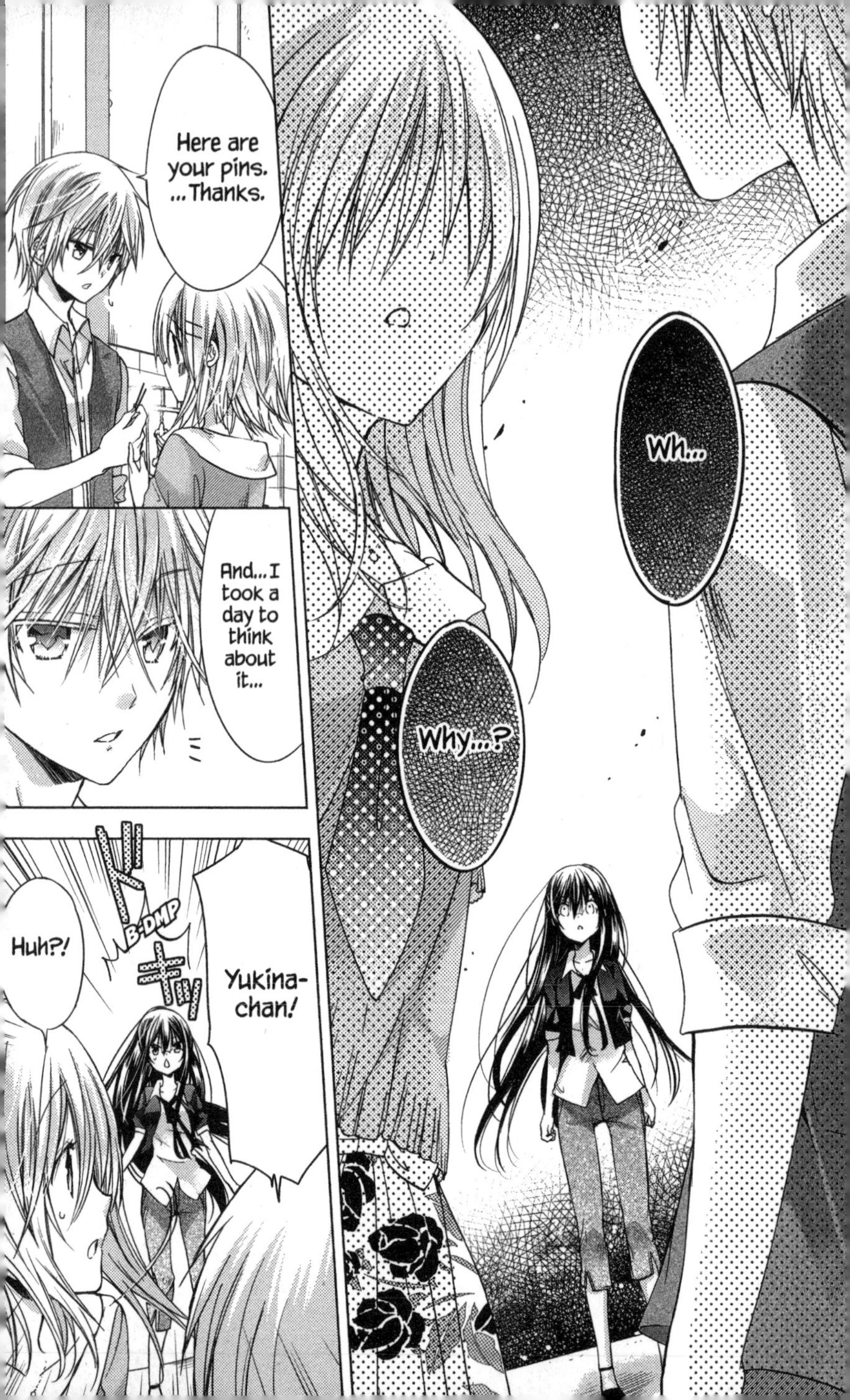
Wh...
Why...?
Here are your pins. ...Thanks.
And...I took a day to think about it...
Yukina-chan!
B-DMP
Huh?!

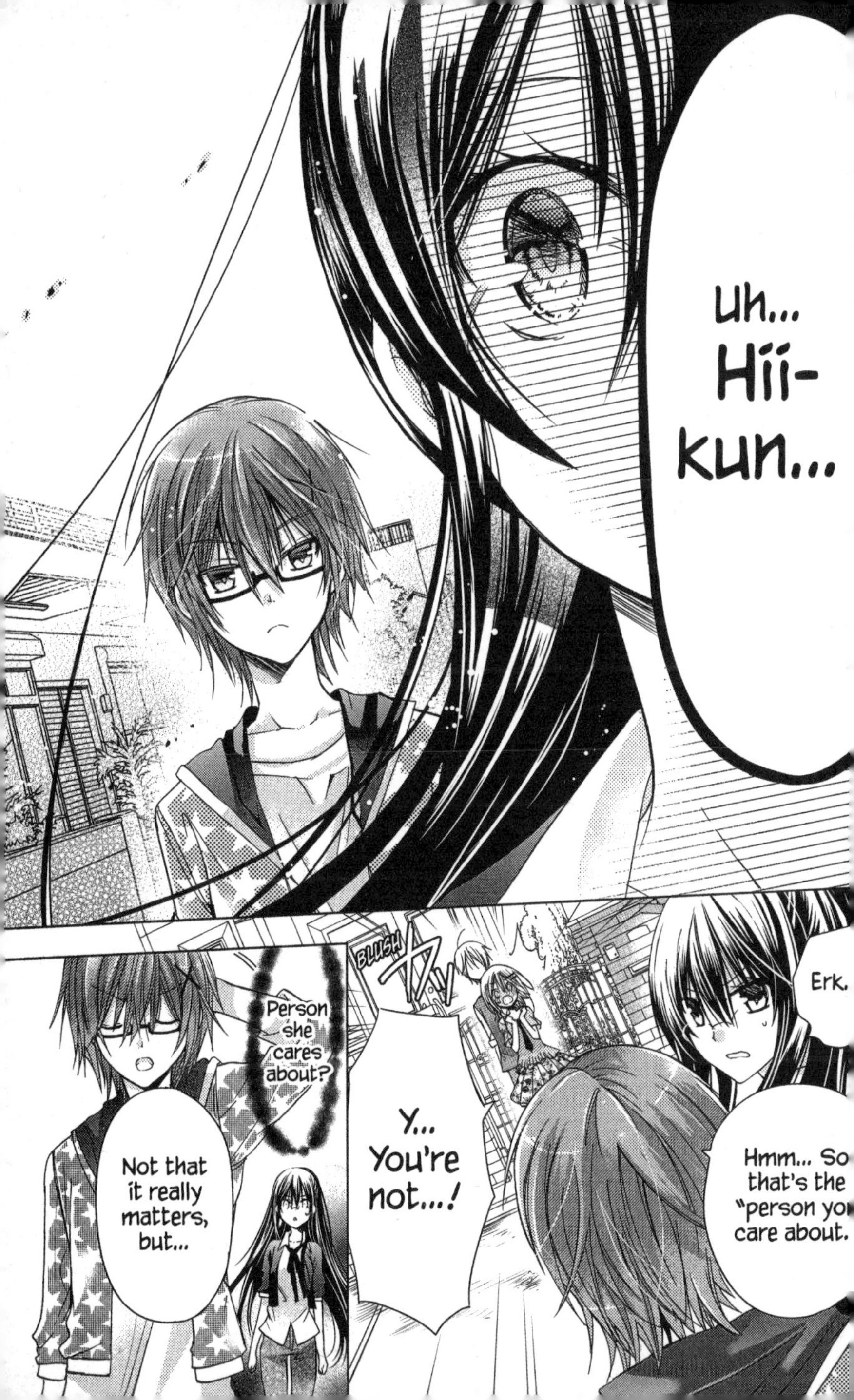
Uh... Hii-kun...
Erk.
Hmm... So that's the "person yo care about.
BLUSH
Y... You're not...!
Person she cares about?
Not that it really matters, but...

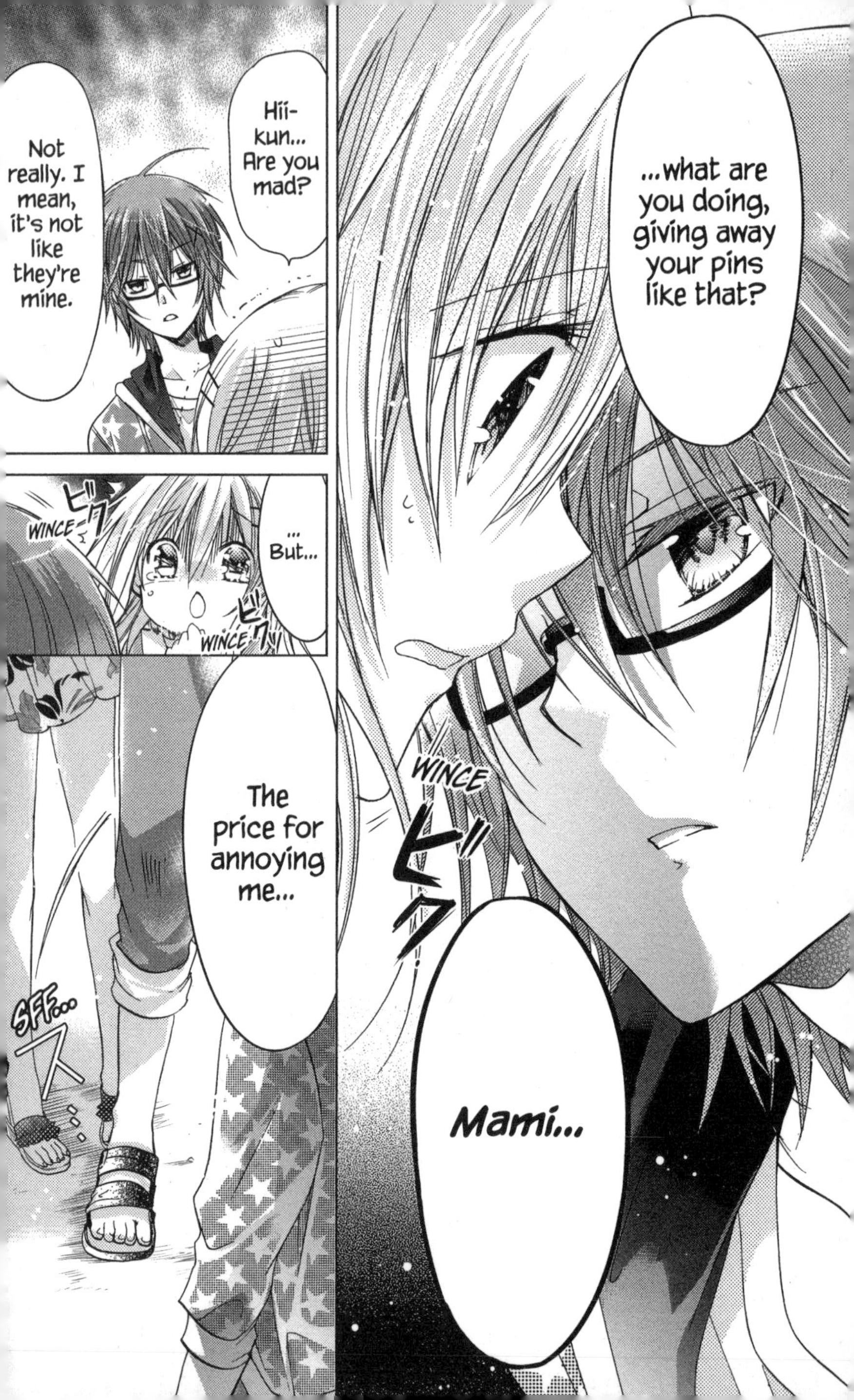
...what are you doing, giving away your pins like that?
WINCE
ビクッ
Mami...
Hii-kun... Are you mad?
Not really. I mean, it's not like they're mine.
... But...
ビクッ WINCE
ビクッ WINCE
The price for annoying me...
SFF...
ス...

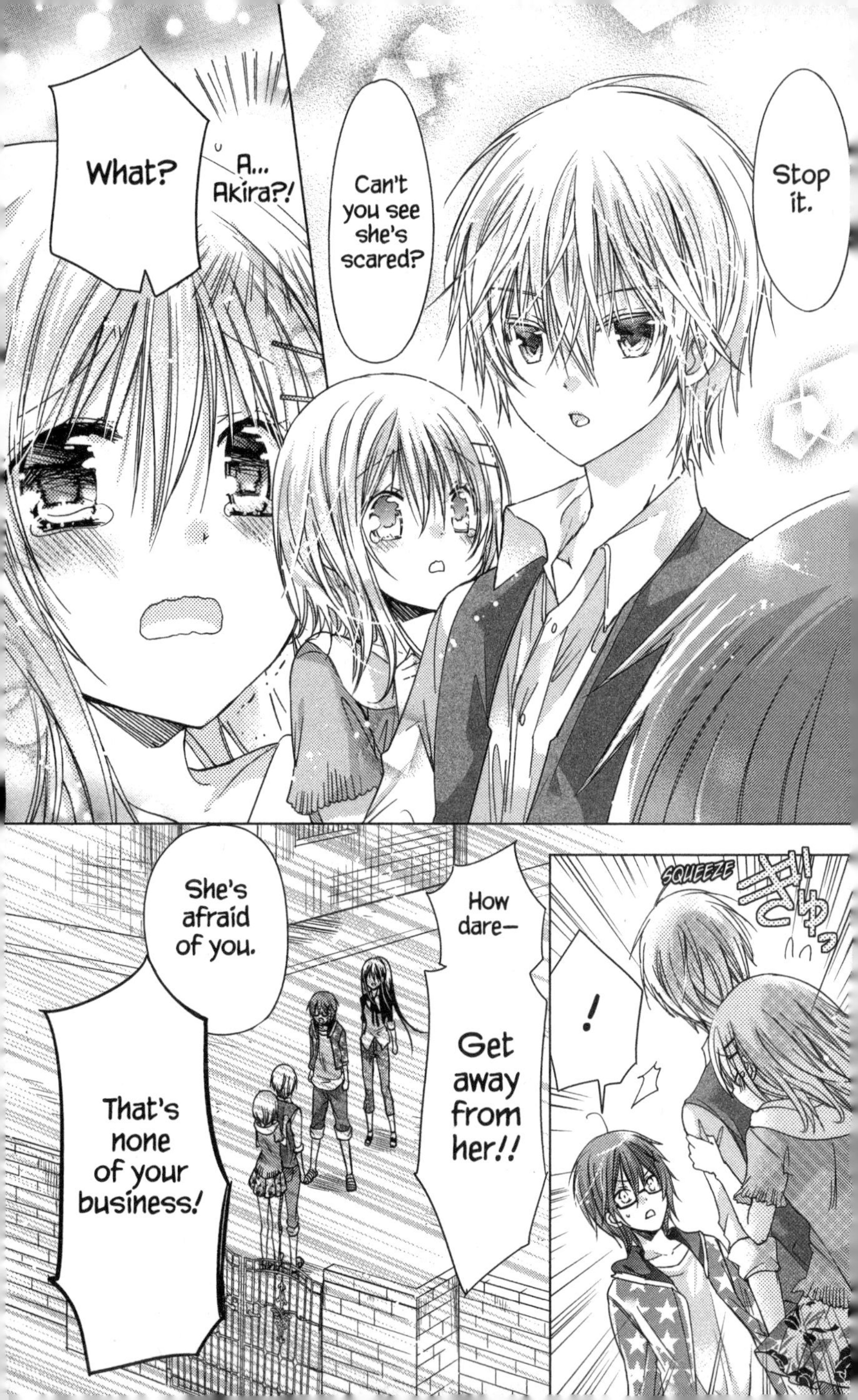
Stop it.
Can't you see she's scared?
A... Akira?!
What?
SQUEEZE
ぎゅっ
!
How dare—
Get away from her!!
She's afraid of you.
That's none of your business!

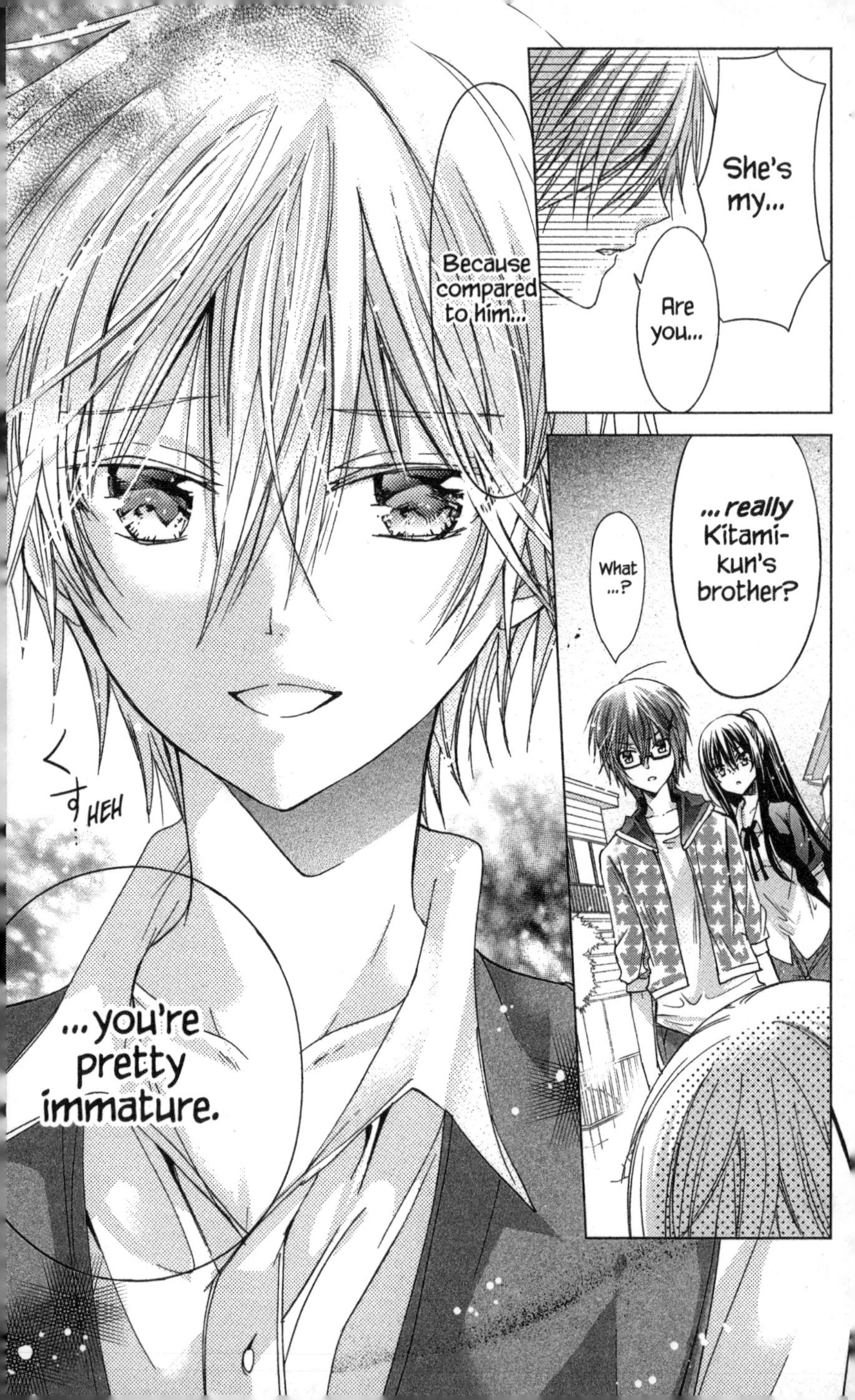
She's my...
Are you...
...really Kitami-kun's brother?
What ...?
Because compared to him...
くす HEH
...you're pretty immature.

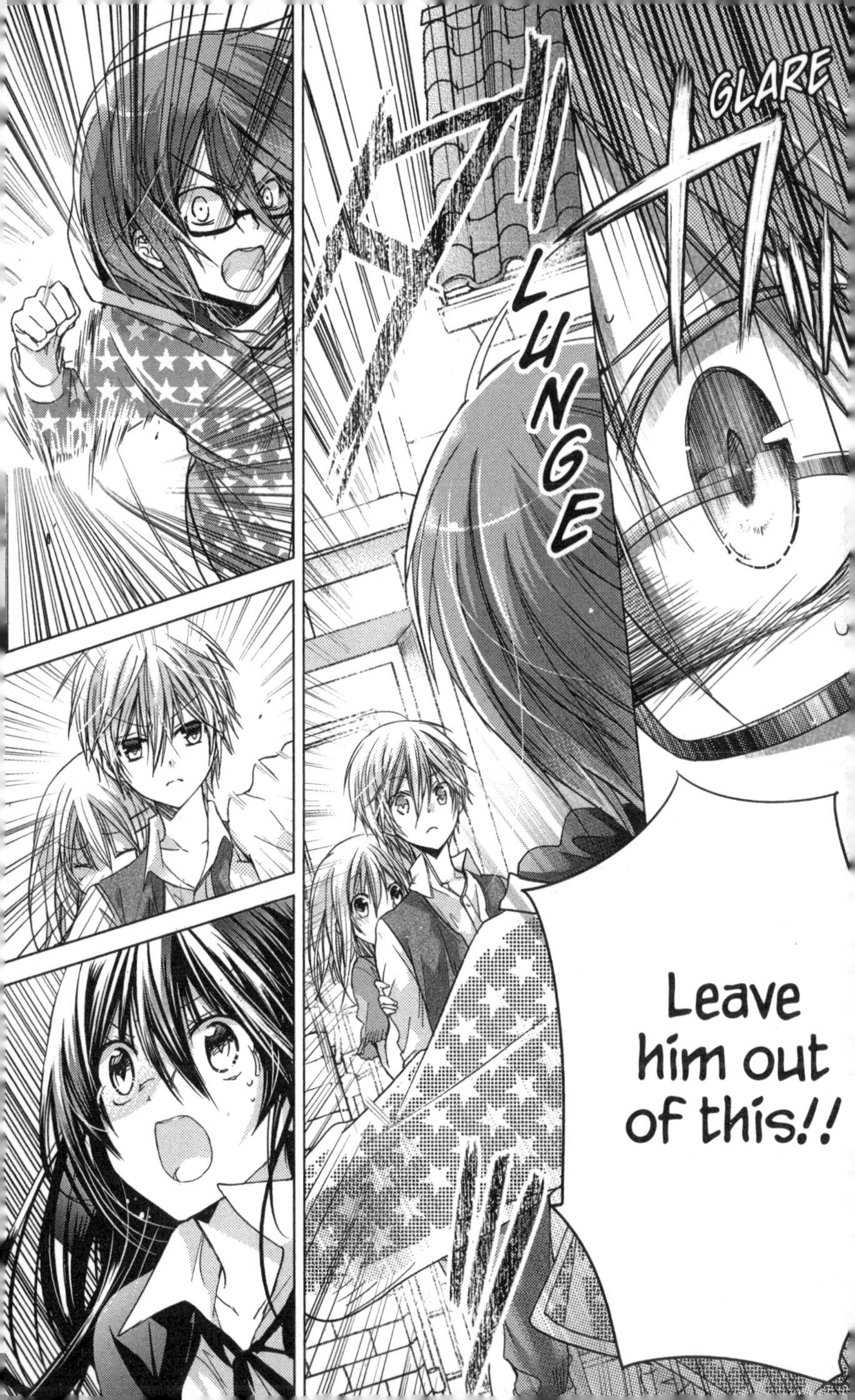
GLARE
LUNGE
Leave him out of this!!

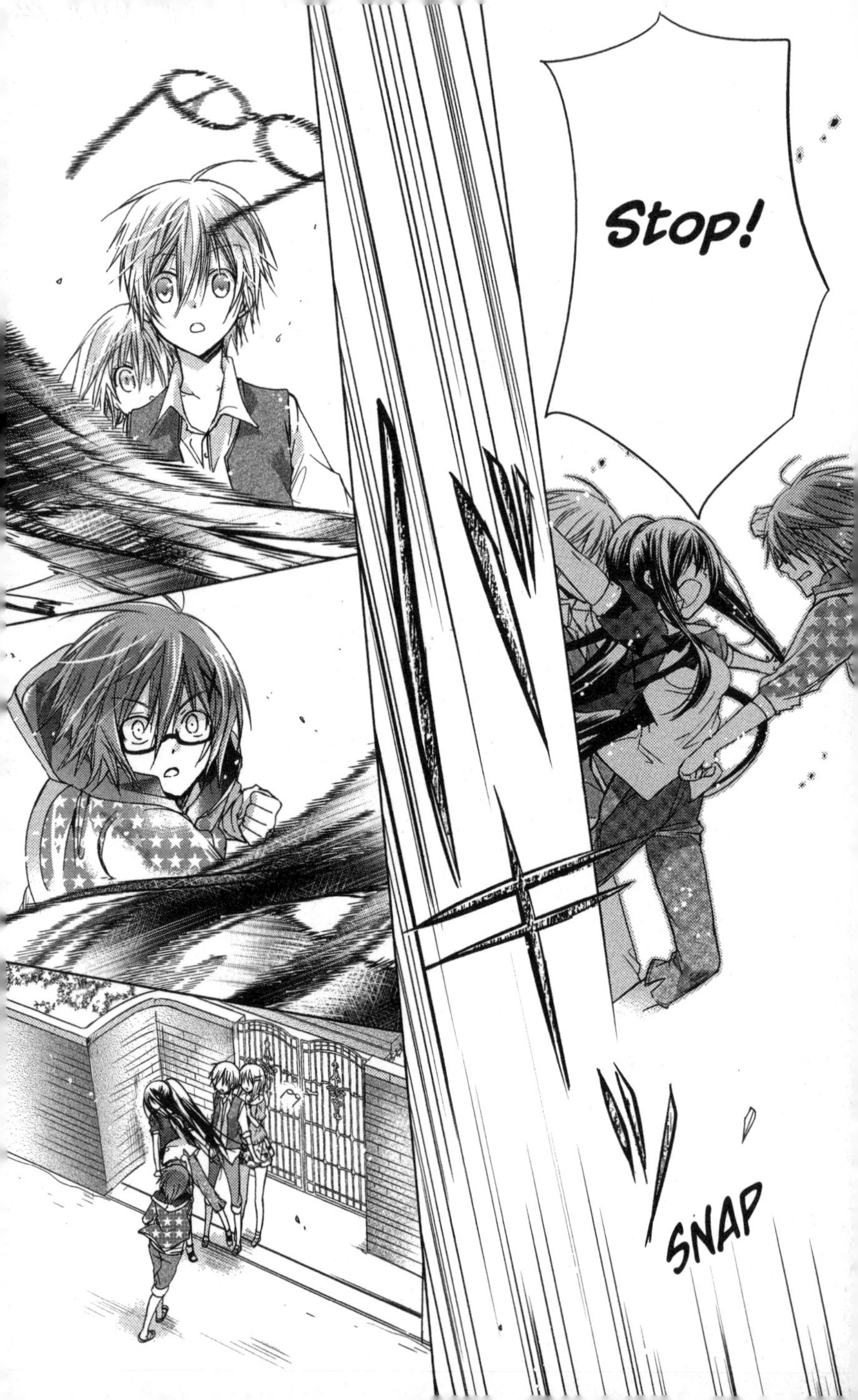
Stop!
SNAP

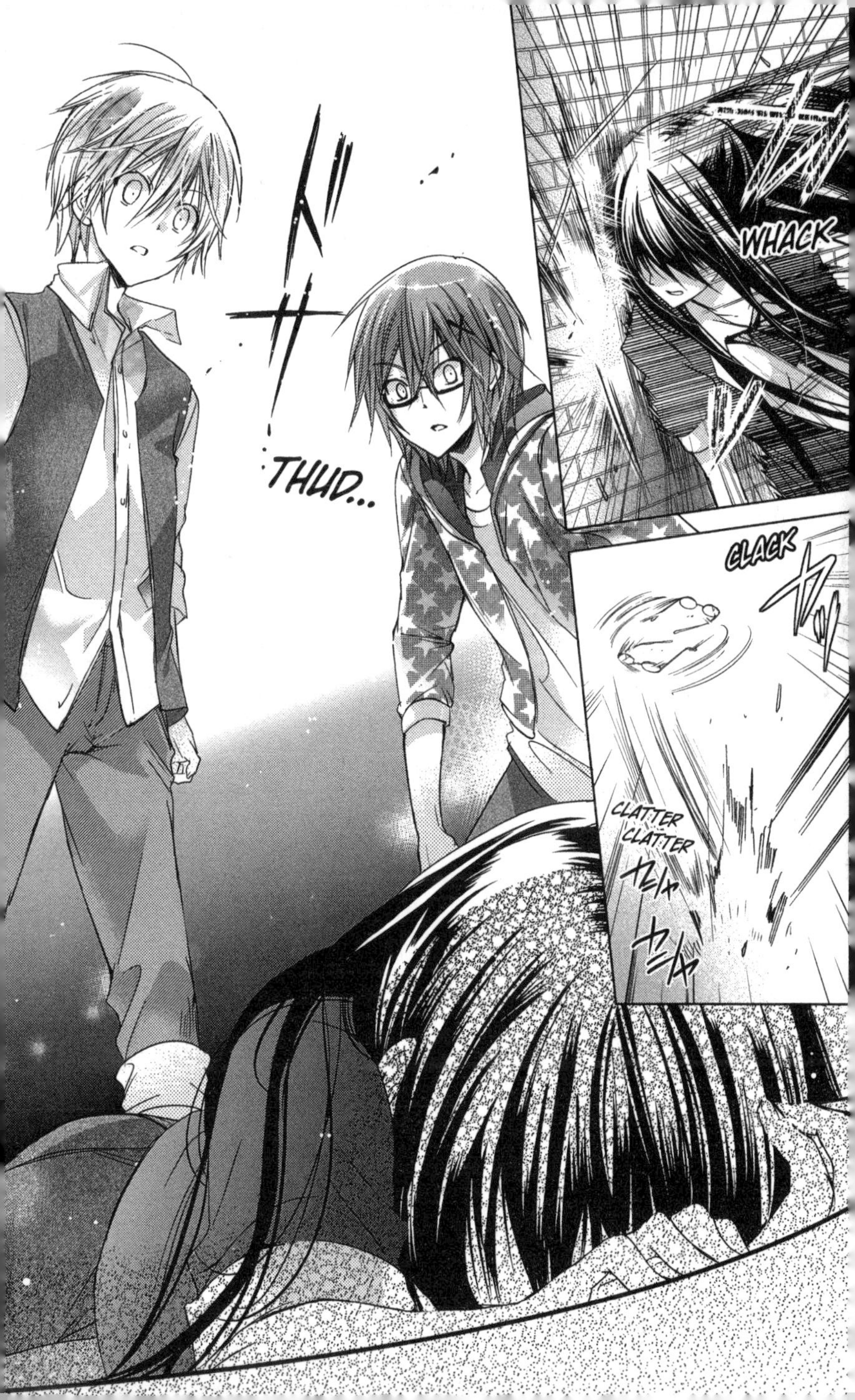
WHACK
CLACK
CLATTER
CLATTER
THUD...

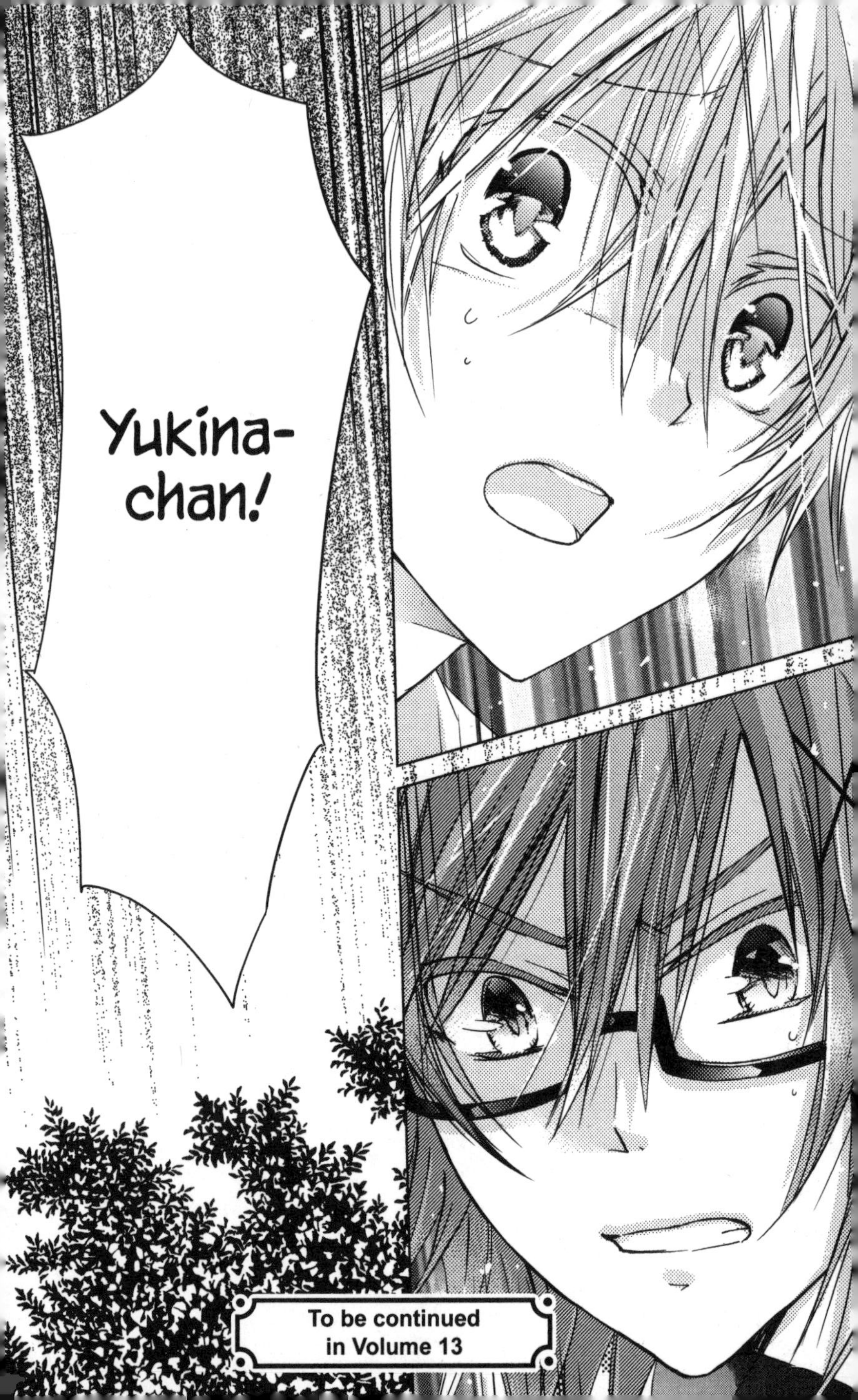
Yukina-chan!
To be continued in Volume 13

BONUS MISSIONS (BACKSTAGE) THEATRE

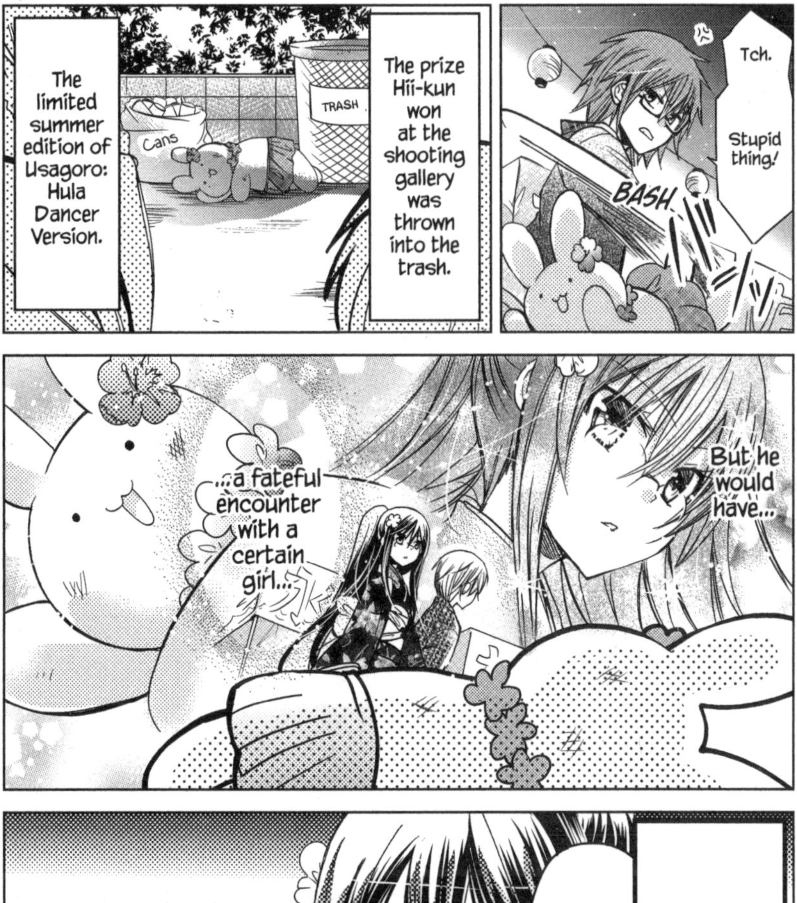
Tch.
Stupid thing!
BASH
The prize Hii-kun won at the shooting gallery was thrown into the trash.
TRASH
Cans
The limited summer edition of Usagoro: Hula Dancer Version.
But he would have...
...a fateful encounter with a certain girl...
...or not.
Oh. It's Usagoro.
?

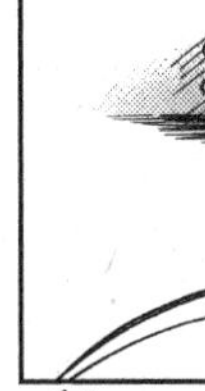
Caw.

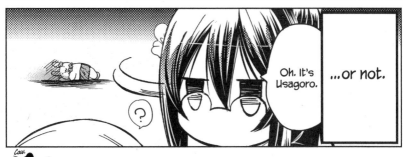

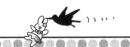

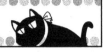

AFTERNOON IN THE PARK

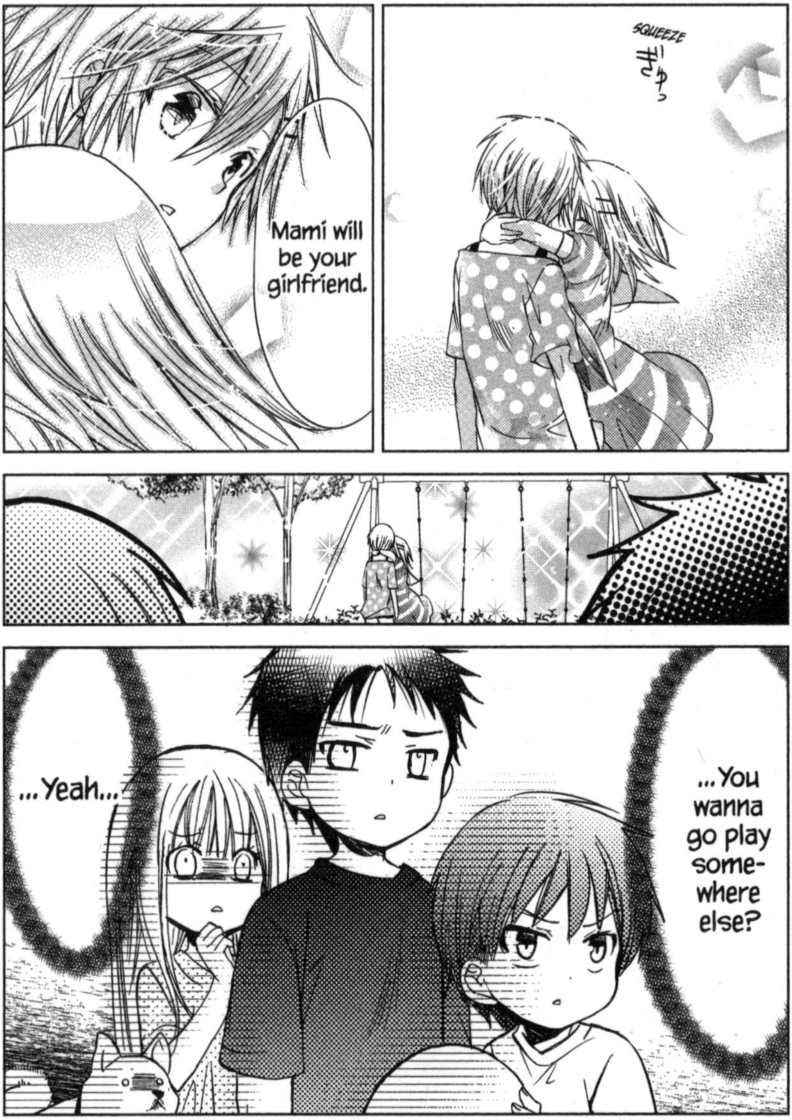
SQUEEZE
ぎゅっ
Mami will be your girlfriend.
...You wanna go play some-where else?
...Yeah...

SHIGURE'S ★ VACATION

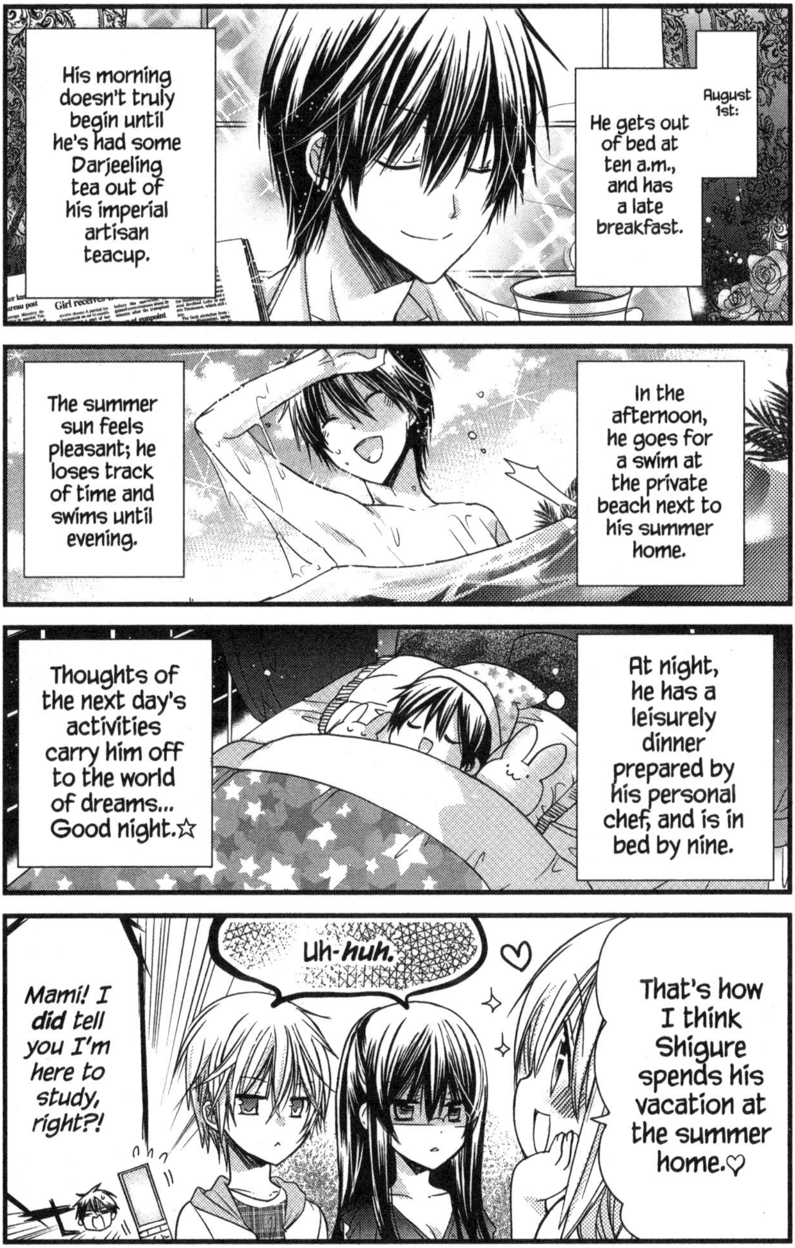
August 1st:
He gets out of bed at ten a.m., and has a late breakfast.
His morning doesn't truly begin until he's had some Darjeeling tea out of his imperial artisan teacup.
In the afternoon, he goes for a swim at the private beach next to his summer home.
The summer sun feels pleasant; he loses track of time and swims until evening.
At night, he has a leisurely dinner prepared by his personal chef, and is in bed by nine.
Thoughts of the next day's activities carry him off to the world of dreams... Good night.☆
That's how I think Shigure spends his vacation at the summer home.♡
Uh-*huh.*
Mami! I ***did*** *tell you I'm here to study, right?!*

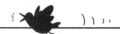

HE'S BACK. DUN DUN DUN.

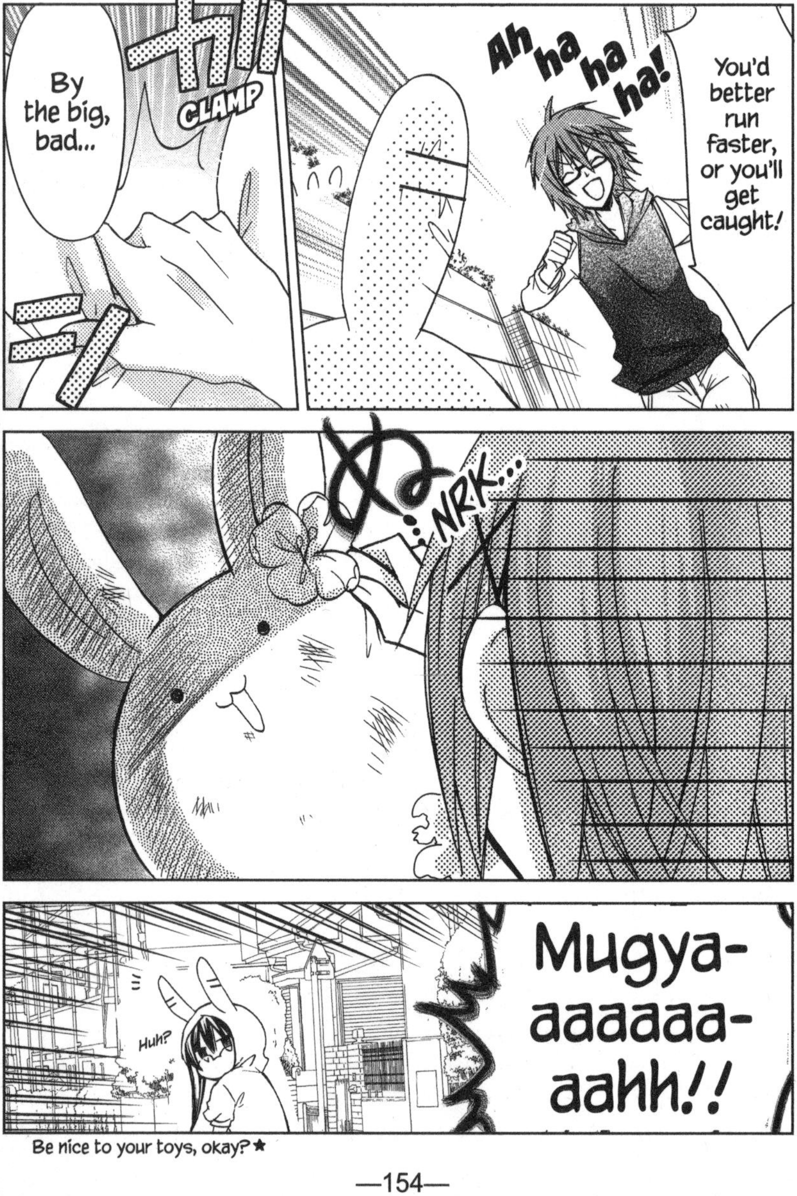

Ah ha ha ha!
You'd better run faster, or you'll get caught!
By the big, bad...
CLAMP
ぬ
NRK...
Mugya-aaaaaaa-aahh!!
Huh?

Be nice to your toys, okay?★

MAMI-MAMI THEATER 1

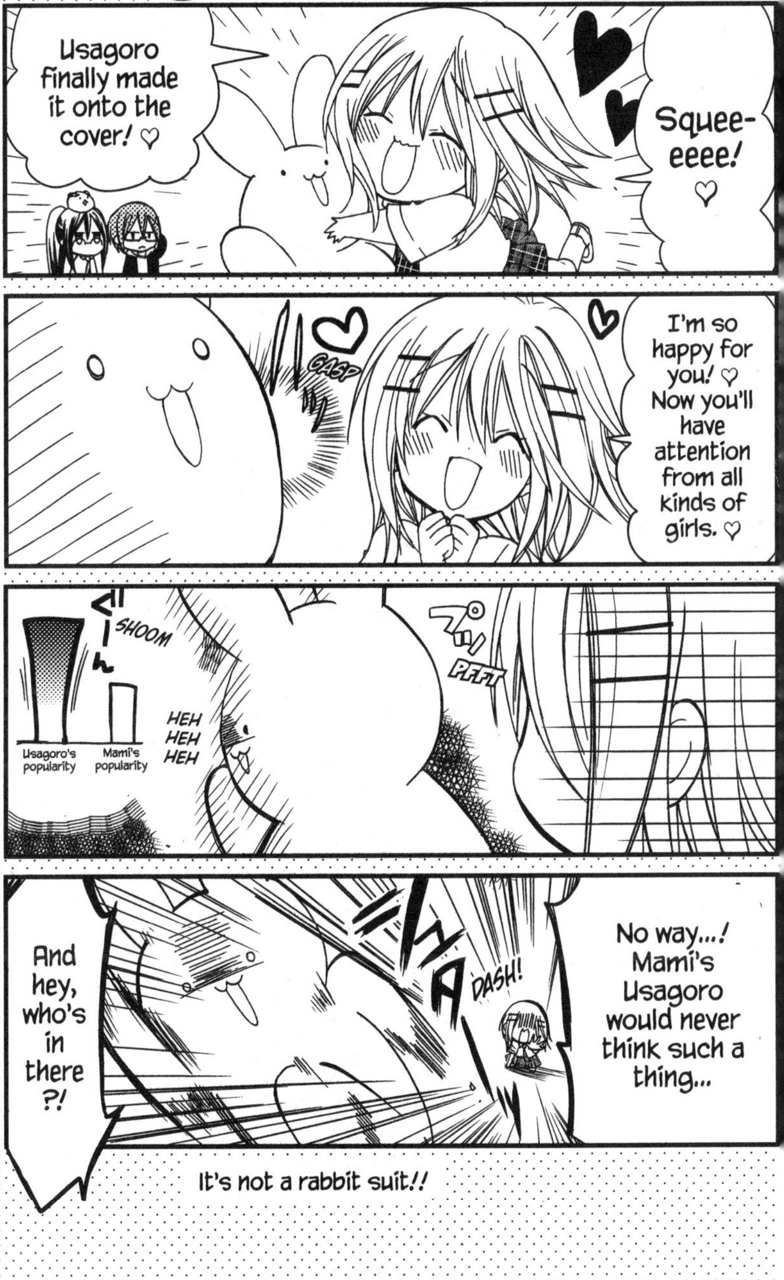
Squee-eeee! ♡
Usagoro finally made it onto the cover! ♡
I'm so happy for you! ♡ Now you'll have attention from all kinds of girls. ♡
GASP
PFFT
SHOOM
HEH HEH HEH
Usagoro's popularity
Mami's popularity
No way...! Mami's Usagoro would never think such a thing...
DASH!
And hey, who's in there?!

It's not a rabbit suit!!

MAMI-MAMI THEATRE 2

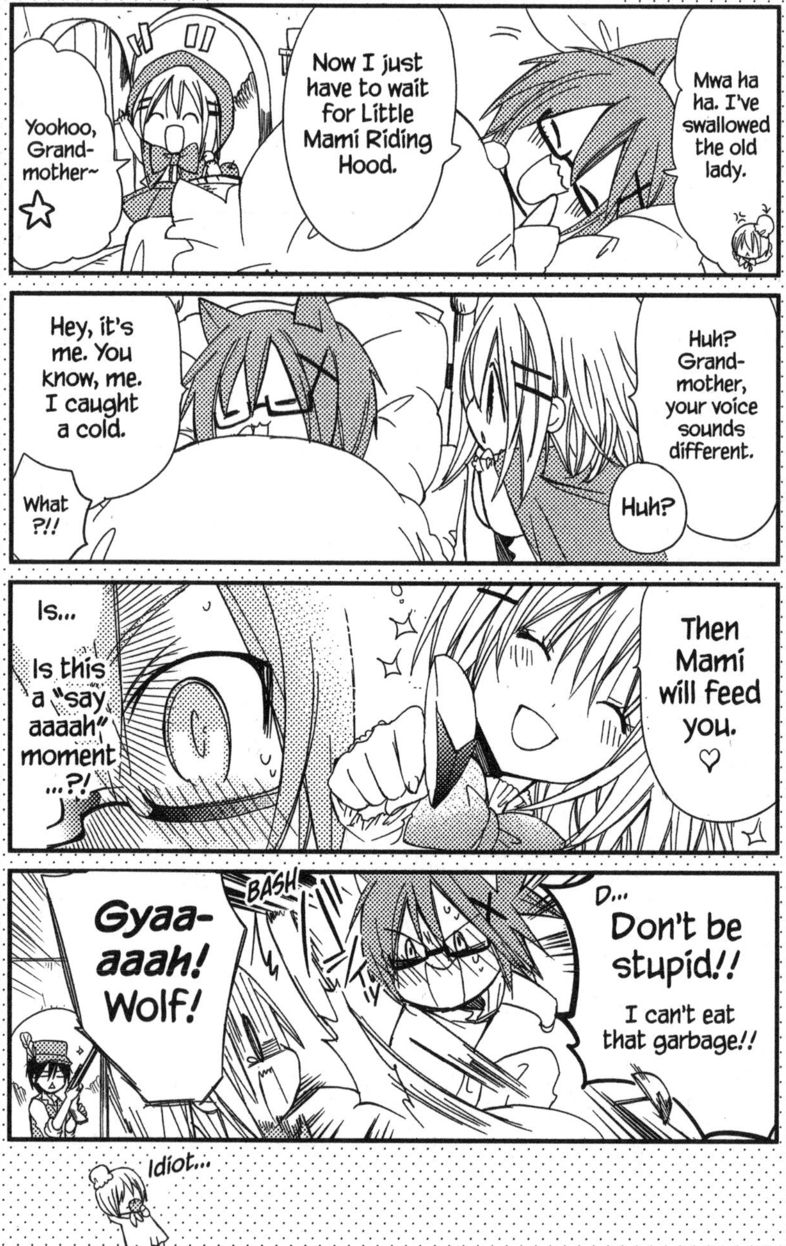
Mwa ha ha. I've swallowed the old lady.
Now I just have to wait for Little Mami Riding Hood.
Yoohoo, Grand-mother~ ☆
Huh? Grand-mother, your voice sounds different.
Huh?
Hey, it's me. You know, me. I caught a cold.
What ?!!
Then Mami will feed you. ♡
Is...
Is this a "say aaaah" moment ...?!
D...
Don't be stupid!!
I can't eat that garbage!!
BASH!
Gyaa-aaah! Wolf!
Idiot...

AFTERWORD

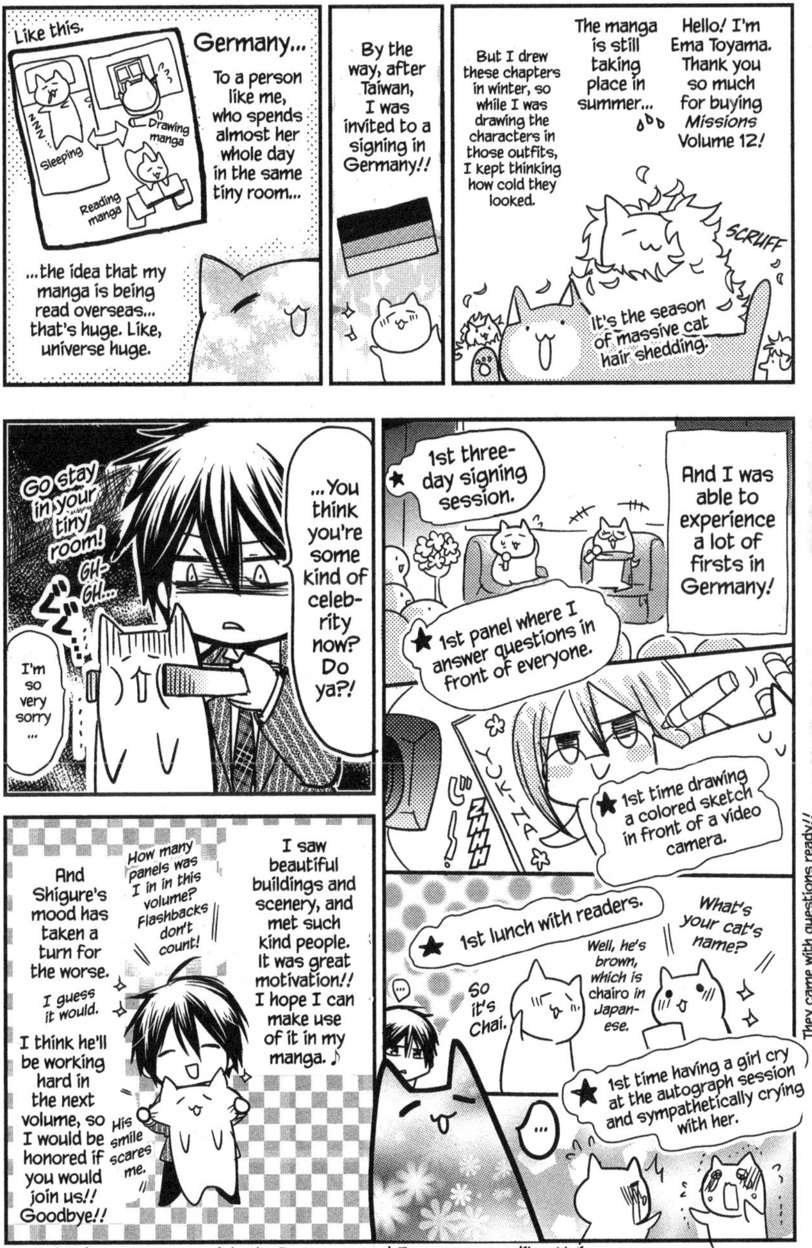

Hello! I'm Ema Toyama. Thank you so much for buying *Missions* Volume 12!
The manga is still taking place in summer...
But I drew these chapters in winter, so while I was drawing the characters in those outfits, I kept thinking how cold they looked.
SCRUFF
It's the season of massive cat hair shedding.
By the way, after Taiwan, I was invited to a signing in Germany!!
Germany...
To a person like me, who spends almost her whole day in the same tiny room...
Like this.
Sleeping
Drawing manga
Reading manga
...the idea that my manga is being read overseas... that's huge. Like, universe huge.
And I was able to experience a lot of firsts in Germany!
1st three-day signing session.
1st panel where I answer questions in front of everyone.
They came with questions ready!!
1st time drawing a colored sketch in front of a video camera.
YUKI-ZA
1st lunch with readers.
What's your cat's name?
Well, he's brown, which is chairo in Japanese.
So it's Chai.
1st time having a girl cry at the autograph session and sympathetically crying with her.
...
...You think you're some kind of celebrity now? Do ya?!
Go stay in your tiny room!
GH-GH...
I'm so very sorry...
I saw beautiful buildings and scenery, and met such kind people. It was great motivation!! I hope I can make use of it in my manga.♪
How many panels was I in in this volume? Flashbacks don't count!
And Shigure's mood has taken a turn for the worse.
I guess it would.
I think he'll be working hard in the next volume, so I would be honored if you would join us!! Goodbye!!
His smile scares me.

Special Thanks ❤ My assistants Ryo-sama and Zo-sama, my editor N-jima-sama

Translation notes

apanese is a tricky language for most Westerners, and translation is often more art than science. or your edification and reading pleasure, here are notes on some of the places where we could ave gone in a different direction in our translation of the work, or where a Japanese cultural eference is used.

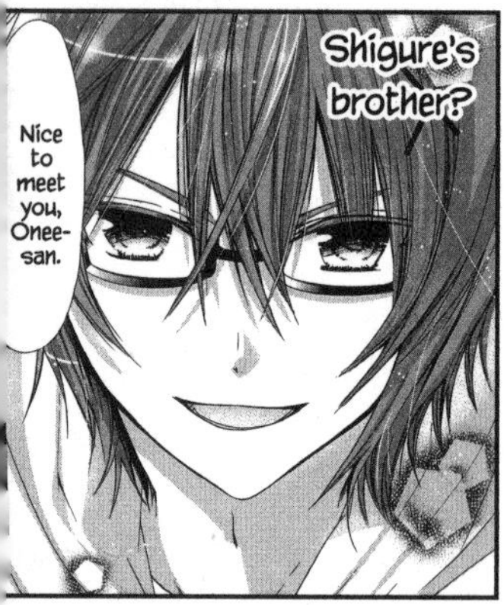
Shigure's brother?
Nice to meet you, Onee-san.

Onee-san, page 6

Onee-san literally means "older sister," and is often used as a polite way to address young women the speaker doesn't know. Hisame also seems to use it as a way of showing mock respect for his brother's female friends.

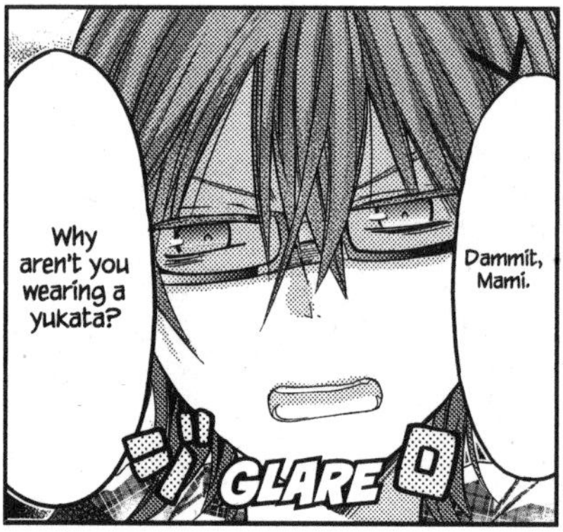
Dammit, Mami.
Why aren't you wearing a yukata?
GLARE

***ukata*, page 23**

 yukata is basically a summer kimono—it's nade out of lighter material, making it more comfortable to wear in hot summer months. t's common to wear them at traditional vents like summer festivals, and, at least in nanga, people often look forward to seeing heir significant other or crush all dressed up n one. Like kimono, they are fastened with a elt called an *obi*.

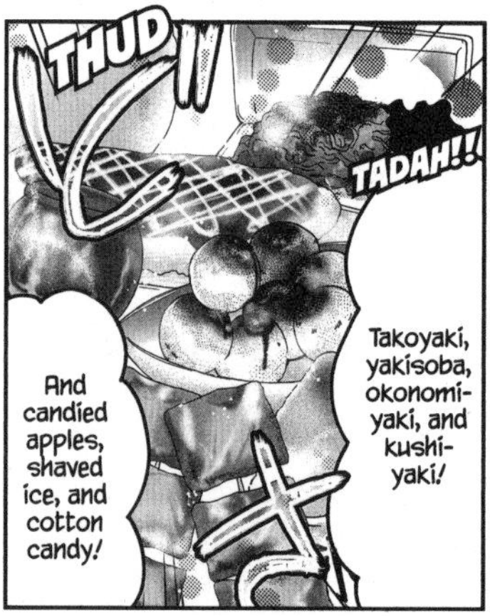
THUD
TADAH!!
Takoyaki, yakisoba, okonomi-yaki, and kushi-yaki!
And candied apples, shaved ice, and cotton candy!

Festival food, page 27

Just as America has carnival food, Japan has festival food, and Akira has procured many of the staples. *Takoyaki*, or "cooked octopus," is a kind of dumpling made from batter filled with minced octopus and other ingredients. *Yakisoba* is a noodle dish similar to chow mein. *Okonomiyaki*, meaning roughly "cooked as you like it," is often compared to a pizza—it's a kind of pancake with various savory toppings. *Kushiyaki* is skewered, grilled meat. On the sweet side, Akira bought some candied apples, shaved ice, and cotton candy, which are basically the same as what you might find in the United States.

Imperial artisan teacup, page 153
Specifically, Shigure's teacup came from the Purveyors to the Japanese Imperial Household Agency, meaning that the company that crafted the teacup has a royal warrant, giving them legal permission to advertise as someone who does work good enough for the emperor.

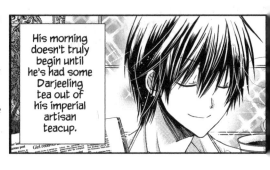

His morning doesn't truly begin until he's had some Darjeeling tea out of his imperial artisan teacup.

Hey, it's me, page 156
The wording Hisame uses here is very similar to that used in a type of phone fraud, sometimes called a "hey-it's-me" scam. A stranger will call on the phone and say, "Hey, it's me!", pretending to be a friend or relative, and then deliver a sob story in the hopes that the person picking up the phone will believe them and give them money. It usually doesn't work in person, because the victim would certainly realize that he or she doesn't recognize the scammer's face.

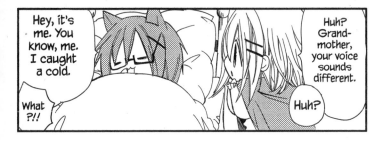

Huh? Grand-mother, your voice sounds different.
Huh?
Hey, it's me. You know, me. I caught a cold.
What?!!

Germany...
To a person like me, who spends almost her whole day in the same tiny room...
Like this.
Drawing manga
ZZZ...
Sleeping
Reading manga
...the idea that my manga is being read overseas... that's huge. Like, universe huge.

Toyama-sensei's tiny room, page 157
Specifically, the room is six *jō*, which means it would fit six *tatami* mats on the floor. In Japan, room sizes are often measured by *tatami* mats. A six-mat room would be roughly 108 square feet.

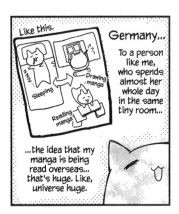

Missions of Love volume 12 is a work of fiction. Names, characters, places, and incidents are the products of the author's imagination or are used fictitiously. Any resemblance to actual events, locales, or persons, living or dead, is entirely coincidental.

A Kodansha Comics Trade Paperback Original.

Missions of Love volume 12 copyright © 2013 Ema Toyama
English translation copyright © 2016 Ema Toyama

All rights reserved.

Published in the United States by Kodansha Comics, an imprint of Kodansha USA Publishing, LLC, New York.

Publication rights for this English edition arranged through Kodansha Ltd., Tokyo.

First published in Japan in 2013 by Kodansha Ltd., Tokyo as *Watashi ni xx shinasai!*, volume 12.

ISBN 978-1-61262-990-2

Printed in the United States of America.

www.kodanshacomics.com

9 8 7 6 5 4 3 2 1

Translation: Alethea Nibley & Athena Nibley
Lettering: Paige Pumphrey
Editing: Lauren Scanlan
Kodansha Comics edition cover design: Phil Balsman